T0341927

HISTORY AND CHRONOLOGY OF THE EIGHTEENTH DYNASTY OF EGYPT

NEAR AND MIDDLE EAST SERIES

1. The Mosaic Tradition. By F. V. Winnett
2. Safaitic Inscriptions from Jordan. By F. V. Winnett
3. History and Chronology of the Eighteenth Dynasty of Egypt: Seven Studies. By Donald B. Redford

History and Chronology of the Eighteenth Dynasty of Egypt

SEVEN STUDIES

DONALD B. REDFORD

University of Toronto Press

Printed in U.S.A.
Reprinted in 2018
ISBN 978-1-4875-8541-9 (paper)

Contents

TO MARGARET

Preface

THE PRESENT COLLECTION of historical studies is the product of the writer's research for his doctoral dissertation entitled "A Study of the Chronology of the Eighteenth Egyptian Dynasty" (University of Toronto, 1965). To my teachers and colleagues who were kind enough either to read the manuscript or to proffer their discussion on sundry problems goes my warmest appreciation. These include Professors R. J. Williams, F. V. Winnett, A. K. Grayson, R. F. G. Sweet, and R.A. Parker. To Professor Parker I am also indebted for a photograph of the hieratic docket attached to EA 27.

This work has been published with the help of grants from the Humanities Research Council, using funds provided by the Canada Council, and from the Publications Fund of the University of Toronto Press.

D.B.R.

Toronto

ABBREVIATIONS

AAAL: Annals of Archaeology and Anthropology, Liverpool.
ABAW: Abhandlungen der bayerischen Akademie der Wissenschaften.
Acta Or: Acta Orientalia.
AfO: Archiv für Orientforschung.
Äg. Forsch: Ägyptologische Forschungen.
AJSL: American Journal of Semitic Languages and Literatures.
AKL: The Assyrian King List.
A Mainz AW: Abhandlungen der Akademie der Wissenschaften und der Literatur zu Mainz.
An. Aeg.: Analecta Aegyptiaca.
*ANET*²: J. B. Pritchard (ed.), *Ancient Near Eastern Texts Relating to the Old Testament* (2nd ed., Princeton, 1955).
AO: Der alte Orient.
AOB: Altorientalische Bibliothek.
APAW: Abhandlungen der preussischen Akademie der Wissenschaften.
ARE: J. H. Breasted, *Ancient Records of Egypt* (5 vols., Chicago, 1906).
AS: Assyriological Studies.
ASAE: Annales du Service des antiquités de l'Egypte.
BA: Beiträge zur Assyriologie und semitischen Sprachwissenschaft.
BASOR: Bulletin of the American Schools of Oriental Research.
Bib. Or.: Biblioteca Orientalis.
BIE: Bulletin de l'Institut de l'Egypte.
BIFAO: Bulletin de l'Institut française d'archéologie orientale.
Bilabel, *Geschichte:* F. Bilabel, *Geschichte Vorderasiens und Ägyptens vom* 16. *Jahrhundert v. Christus bis auf der Neuzeit* (Heidelberg, 1927).
Borchardt, *Mittel:* L. Borchardt, *Die Mittel zur zeitlichen Festlegung von Punkten der ägyptischen Geschichte* (Cairo, 1935).
Breasted, *History:* J. H. Breasted, *A History of Egypt from the Earliest Times to the Persian Conquest* (Bantam, New York, 1964).
BSFE: Bulletin de la Société française d'Egyptologie.
CAD: Chicago Assyrian Dictionary (Chicago, 1956–).
CAH: Cambridge Ancient History (Cambridge, 1962–).
CCG: Cairo, Catalogue générale du musée.
CdE: Chronique d'Egypte.
CoA: T. E. Peet, *et al., The City of Akhenaten* (4 vols., London, 1923–51).
CRAIBL: Comptes rendus de l'Académie des inscriptions et belles lettres.

CT: The Coffin Texts.

Drioton-Vandier, *L'Egypte*[4] E. Drioton and J. Vandier, *Les Peuples de l'Orient méditerranéen.* II. *L'Egypte* (4th ed., Paris, 1962).

EA: The El-Amarna Tablets (numbered according to Knudtzon).

EAT: J. A. Knudtzon, *Die El-Amarna Tafeln* (Leipzig, 1915).

EEF: The Egypt Exploration Fund.

EES: The Egypt Exploration Society.

FIFAO: Fouilles de l'Institut français d'archéologie orientale.

Gardiner, *AEO:* Sir A. H. Gardiner, *Ancient Egyptian Onomastica* (3 vols., Oxford, 1947).

Gardiner, *Grammar:*[3] Sir A. H. Gardiner, *Egyptian Grammar* (3rd ed., Oxford, 1957).

Gardiner, *RAD:* Sir A. H. Gardiner, *Ramesside Administrative Documents* (Oxford, 1948).

Gauthier, *DG:* H. Gauthier, *Dictionnaire des noms géographiques contenus dans les textes hiéroglyphiques* (7 vols., Cairo, 1925–31).

Gauthier, *Livre:* H. Gauthier, *Le Livre des rois d'Egypte,* vols. II, III (Cairo, 1912).

Griffith, *The Kahun Papyri* or *The Gurob Papyri*: F. Ll. Griffith, *Hieratic Papyri from Kahun and Gurob* (2 vols., London, 1898).

Helck, *Verwaltung:* W. Helck, *Zur Verwaltung des mittleren und neuen Reichs* (Leiden, 1958).

Hist. Zeitschr.: Historische Zeitschrift.

HSE: W. C. Hayes, *The Scepter of Egypt* (2 vols., Cambridge, Mass., 1958).

IEJ: Israel Exploration Journal.

IFAO: Institut français d'archéologie orientale.

JA: Journal asiatique.

JAOS: Journal of the American Oriental Society.

JBL: Journal of Biblical Literature and Exegesis.

JCS: Journal of Cuneiform Studies.

JEA: Journal of Egyptian Archaeology.

JNES: Journal of Near Eastern Studies.

JPOS: Journal of the Palestine Oriental Society.

JRAS: Journal of the Royal Asiatic Society.

JS: Journal des savants.

JWH: Journal of World History.

KAH: Keilschrifttexte aus Assur, historischen Inhalts.

KAJ: Keilschrifttexte aus Assur, juristischen Inhalts.

KBo: Keilschrifttexte aus Boghazköi.

KlF: Kleinasiatische Forschungen.

KUB: Keilschrifturkunden aus Boghazköi.

LD: R. Lepsius, *Denkmaeler aus Aegypten und Aethiopien,* vols. I, II (Berlin, 1849–59).

MAIBL: Mémoires présentées par divers savants à l'Académie des inscriptions et belles lettres.

Maspero, *Histoire:* Sir G. C. C. Maspero, *Histoire ancienne des peuples de l'Orient classique. II. Les Premières mêlées* (Paris, 1897).
MDIAK: Mitteilungen des deutschen Instituts für ägyptische Altertumskunde in Kairo.
MDOG: Mitteilungen der deutschen Orient-Gesellschaft.
Meyer, *Geschichte:* E. Meyer, *Geschichte des Altertums*, vol. II, pt. 1 (Stuttgart and Berlin, 1928).
MIFAO: Mémoires publiées par les membres de l'Institut français d'archéologie orientale du Caire.
MIOF: Mitteilungen des Instituts für Orientforschung.
MVAG: Mitteilungen der vorderasiatische-ägyptischen Gesellschaft.
Nachr. Gött.: Nachrichten der königliche Gesellschaft der Wissenschaften zu Göttingen.
Naville, *Festival Hall:* E. Naville, *The Festival Hall of Osorkon II in the Great Temple of Bubastis* (London, 1892).
NF: Neue Folge.
OIC: Oriental Institute Communications.
OIP: Oriental Institute Publications.
OLZ: Orientalische Literaturzeitung.
PEFQ: Palestine Exploration Fund Quarterly.
Petrie, *History:* Sir W. M. F. Petrie, *A History of Egypt*, vols. II, III (7th ed., London, 1924).
PJB: Palästinajahrbuch des deutschen evangelischen Instituts für Altertumswissenschaft des Heiligen Landes in Jerusalem.
P-M: B. Porter and R. Moss, *Topographical Bibliography of Ancient Egyptian Hieroglyphic Texts, Reliefs and Paintings* (7 vols., Oxford, 1927–60).
PRU: Palais royal d'Ugarit, vols. III, IV (Paris, 1955–56).
PSBA: Proceedings of the Society of Biblical Archaeology.
PT: The Pyramid Texts.
RA: Revue d'assyriologie et d'archéologie orientale.
Ranke, *Personennamen:* H. Ranke, *Die ägyptischen Personennamen* (2 vols., Glückstadt, 1935–53).
RB: Revue biblique.
RdE: Revue d'Egyptologie.
REA: Revue des études anciennes.
RHA: Revue hittite et asianique.
RHR: Revue de l'histoire des religions.
RlA: Reallexikon der Assyriologie.
RSO: Rivista degli studi orientali.
RT: Recueil de travaux relatifs à la philologie et l'archéologie égyptiennes et assyriennes.
SAOC: Studies in Ancient Oriental Civilizations.
SAWWien: Sitzungsberichte der Akademie der Wissenschaften zu Wien.
SBAW: Sitzungsberichte der bayerischen Akademie der Wissenschaften.
Sethe, *Thronwirren:* K. Sethe, *Die Thronwirren unter den nachfolgern Königs Thutmosis I, ihr Verlauf und ihre Bedeutung* (Leipzig, 1896).
SPAW: Sitzungsberichte der preussischen Akademie der Wissenschaften.
TA: Sir W. M. F. Petrie, *Tell el-Amarna* (London, 1894).

UET: *Ur Excavation Texts.*

Urk.: K. Sethe, W. Helck, and others, *Urkunden des ägyptischen Altertums* (Leipzig, 1906–).

VAT: Tontafelsammlung (Berlin), Vorderasiatische Abteilung.

VT: *Vetus Testamentum.*

Wb.: A. Erman and H. Grapow, *Wörterbuch der ägyptischen Sprache* (5 vols. with reference vols., Leipzig and Berlin, 1926–55).

Wiedemann, *Geschichte*: K. A. Wiedemann, *Ägyptische Geschichte* (Gottha, 1884).

WZKM: *Wiener Zeitschrift für die Kunde des Morgenlandes.*

ZA: *Zeitschrift für Assyriologie und verwandte Gebiete.*

ZÄS: *Zeitschrift für ägyptische Sprache und Altertumskunde.*

ZDMG: *Zeitschrift der deutschen morgenländischen Gesellschaft.*

ZDPV: *Zeitschrift des deutschen Palästina-Vereins.*

ZIS: *Zeitschrift für indogermanistik und allgemeine Sprachwissenschaft.*

HISTORY AND CHRONOLOGY OF THE EIGHTEENTH DYNASTY OF EGYPT

I

Ḫʿy and Its Derivatives

In ancient Egypt the day of a king's accession (usually the day following the death of his predecessor) was called the day of "the king's appearance" or "arising" (*ḫʿy-nsw*).[1] But the same verb *ḫʿy* and its derivatives could apparently also be used for the king's coronation, at which time he "arose" or "appeared" as king upon the throne in his official regalia.[2] Since the festival of the coronation would presumably have taken a considerable time to prepare, it has been assumed that it could not possibly have taken place at the same time as the accession.[3] Months, in fact, must have intervened between the accession and coronation. But herein lies a difficulty for the modern scholar; for, when *ḫʿy* is used together with a royal name, how is he to know whether the reference is to the accession or to the coronation? When, moreover, a date occurs in the same context as *ḫʿy-nsw*, the chronologist may be misled. The confusion which could arise in such cases has not always been appreciated by scholars. In the older literature,[4] and to some extent even in recent works,[5] the term

[1] *Wb.* III, 241:15.

[2] Cf. Borchardt, *Mittel*, 69; H. Frankfort, *Kingship and the Gods* (Chicago, 1948), 102 f.

[3] Frankfort, *ibid.;* A. H. Gardiner, *JEA* 31 (1945), 24.

[4] E. Naville, *Festival Hall*, 10; Borchardt, *Mittel*, 69; J. Černý, *ZÄS* 72 (1936), 109, n. 2; but see K. Sethe, *Thronwirren*, §18.

[5] Cf. S. Morenz, *Ägyptische Religion* (Stuttgart, 1960), 39.

"Krönungstag" has been used where "Regierungsantritt" would have been more correct, apparently without the assumption that the coronation took place on the accession day having been made. We do not mean to presuppose at the outset that the coronation did *not* take place on the accession; but until the evidence is examined it may be wise to preserve a tentative distinction.

The present chapter is concerned with an investigation of the use of *ḫʿy* and its more important derivatives in relation to the king. The question to be answered is: Did the Egyptians themselves feel and express in their inscriptions a difference between *ḫʿy* as used of the accession and *ḫʿy* as used of the coronation? The examples of the uses of *ḫʿy* to be quoted fall into six categories: (1) appearances of the king (other than on his accession or at his coronation) at festivals, audiences, and so on; (2) appearances of the king "as king (*m nsw*)" or "as king of Upper and Lower Egypt (*m nsw-bit*)"; (3) appearances of the king upon the throne of god N; (4) appearances of types (2) and (3) with specific reference to crowns; (5) "appearance(s) of the king (*ḫʿy-nsw*)"; and (6) "festival(s) of the appearance (*ḥb n ḫʿw*)."

1. Appearances of the king (other than on his accession or at his coronation) at festivals, audiences, and so on.

The verb *ḫʿy* means basically "to shine forth in dazzling splendour, to appear in glory, to arise,"[6] and was used primarily of the sun[7]. It could also be used of any celestial body, e.g. a star,[8] that made a spectacular appearance in the sky. In the Pyramid Texts the king is spoken of as appearing "as a star,"[9] or "as a great god,"[10] and the literal meaning of *ḫʿy* here is graphically illustrated by the use in parallel texts of *qꜣ*, "be high,"[11] and *bꜣ*, "appear in the sky as a

[6] For translations and discussions of *ḫʿy*, see Borchardt, *Mittel*, 69; A. Badawi and H. Kees, *Handwörterbuch der ägyptischen Sprache* (Cairo, 1958), 175; Černý, *ZÄS* 72 (1936), 109, n. 2; R. O. Faulkner, *A Concise Dictionary of Middle Egyptian* (Oxford, 1962), 185f.; H. Frankfort, *Ancient Egyptian Religion* (New York, 1948), 53; W. Erichsen, *Demotisches Glossar* (Copenhagen, 1954), 350f.; *Wb.* III, 239ff.

[7] According to Gardiner the hieroglyph *ḫʿ*, , represents "a hill over which are the rays of the rising sun": *Grammar*[3], 489 (N 28).

[8] *Wb.* III. 239:9; used with *ḥtp* to denote the rising and setting of a star: F. Lexa, *Papyrus Insinger* (Paris, 1926), I, 102. [9] PT 263b. [10] PT 467a.

[11] K. Sethe, *Übersetzung und Kommentar zu den altägyptischen Pyramidentexte* (Glückstadt and Hamburg, no date), II, 92.

bai."[12] By a slight semantic extension a cult image that put in an appearance at a festival could be said to have "arisen in glory";[13] and this rather frequent use gave rise to the noun *ḫ'y*, "festival,"[14] which survived in the Coptic ϣⲁⲓ .[15] Those who conducted the festival could be said to have "caused the god to appear (*sḫ'y nčr*),"[16] and the same verb could even be used of so insignificant an act as carrying the cult image in one's arm.[17]

Since the king was also a god, closely related mythologically to the sun, he too could "appear in glory" on certain festive occasions; and a "window of appearances"[18] was provided for such times. The following are examples of the use of *ḫ'y* to denote the appearance of the king at ceremonies and festivals (other than the coronation).

(*a*) At the reception of prisoners or tribute

(1) *sč ḥm.f ḫ'w ḥr čnčȝt ḫft sčȝ sqrw-'nḫ in.n mš' pn n ḥm.f*, "lo, his majesty appeared on the dais when the living captives which this army of his majesty had brought were dragged in": *Urk.* IV, 140.

(2) *ḫ't nsw m st wrt m 'ḥ n 'Iwnw Šm' ib.f ȝw r 'ȝt wrt m qnt m mḫt m-ḫt nn in.tw inw n bȝw ḥm.f m ḫȝswt Rčnw ḫst*, "his majesty appeared on the great throne in the palace of southern Heliopolis, his heart very happy in might and in victory; afterwards the tribute was brought to the might of his majesty from the lands of vile Retenu": *Urk.* IV, 951.

(3) *ḫ'yt ḥm.f m-ẖnw Wȝst ḥr čnčȝyt 'ȝt r [šsp] biȝt n mš' [pn]*, "his majesty appeared in the midst of Thebes on the great dais to [receive] the marvels of [this] army": *Urk.* IV, 1345.

(4) *ist ḥm.f* [ ] *ḫ'w ḥr ispt nt ms inw*, "lo, his majesty [ ] appeared upon the throne (designated) for the presentation of tribute": *Urk.* IV, 2087.

[12] *Ibid.*, II, 145.

[13] *Wb.* III, 240:4ff.; as with a celestial body, *ḥtp* was used to mark the end of the *ḫ'y*, i.e. in this case the festival; cf. Naville, *Festival Hall*, 18.

[14] *Wb.* III, 241:4ff. In late bilingual and trilingual inscriptions the noun *ḫ'y* is rendered by πανήγυρις, "solemn feast," or occasionally by ἐπιτολή "rising"; see F. Daumas, *Moyens d'expressions du Grec et de l'Egyptien comparés dans les décrets de Canope et de Memphis* (*ASAE Supp.* 16 [Cairo, 1952], 176ff. and 225.

[15] W. E. Crum, *A Coptic Dictionary* (London, 1939), 542f.

[16] *Wb.* IV, 236f.

[17] P. Derchain, *CdE* 26(1951), 278.

[18] R. A. Caminos, *Late Egyptian Miscellanies* (London, 1954), 64f.

(*b*) Upon a chariot at a hunt or ceremony

(5) *ḫ't ḥm.f ḥr ḥtr mš'.f tm m-ḫt.f*, "his majesty appeared in a chariot, his entire army behind him (for the hunt)": *Urk.* IV, 1739.

(6) *ḫ'yt ḥm.f '. w. s. ḥr ḥt(r)i ḥr wrryt '3t n(t) ḏ'm*, "his majesty appeared, mounted upon a great chariot of electrum (to renew his oath concerning the boundaries)": *Urk.* IV, 1982.

(*c*) At the presentation of rewards

(7) *ist ḥm.f ḫ'w mi R' m 'ḥ.f n 'nḫ w3s m-ḫt irt 'qw n it.f 'Imn*, "lo, his majesty appeared like Re in his palace of life and prosperity, after making food offerings to his father Amun" (there follows the presentation of a reward to a faithful servant): *Urk.* IV, 2177.

(*d*) On the battlefield

(8) *ḫ't nsw tp-dw3yt . . . wḏ3 ḥm.f ḥr wrryt nt ḏ'm*, "the king appeared early in the morning . . . his majesty rode in a chariot of electrum": *Urk.* IV, 657.

(*e*) At an audience

(9) *ḫ't nsw ḥr st wrt*, "the king appeared on the great seat": *Urk.* IV, 1022; cf. *Urk.* IV, 1210.

(10) *ist ḥm.f ḥms ḥr bḥdw n ḏ'm ḫ'w m sšd šwty*, "lo, his majesty was sitting upon a throne of electrum, appearing in the fillet of two feathers": C. E. Sander-Hansen, *Historische Inschriften der 19. Dynastie* (Bibliotheca Aegyptiaca, IV [Brussels, 1933]), 30.

2. Appearances of the king "as king (*m nsw*)" or "as king of Upper and Lower Egypt (*m nsw-bit*)"

(*a*) In religious texts and formal reliefs

(11) *ḏd-mdw Wsir N ḫ'.n.k m nsw-bit*, "recitation: O Osiris N, you have appeared as king of Upper and Lower Egypt": PT 776a.

(12) *ḥbss n.f t3 sqrw n.f wdnt ḫ' N m nsw s'ḫi n.f nst.f*, "the earth is hacked for him, an offering is made for him, N appears as king, his throne is worthy of him (?)": PT 1138a.

(13) *sm3w pn ḫ' m nsw ḫ' m bit*, "this uniter had appeared as king of Upper Egypt, he has appeared as king of Lower Egypt": Memphite Theology, 4.

(14) (Khnum to Hatshepsut) *di.n.(i) n.č wnn ḫnt k3w 'nḫw nb ḫ'.ti m nsw-bit*, "I grant you the leadership of all living *ku's*, you having appeared as king of Upper and Lower Egypt": *Urk.* IV, 223.

(15) (Meskhont to Hatshepsut) *wḏ.n.(i) čn n ʿnḫ n wḏ3 n snb n mnḫ(t) n špss n 3wt-ib n ḥw n ḥtpt n ḏf3 n ḫt nb nfrt ḫʿ.ti m nsw-bit*, "I commend you to life, well-being, health, excellence, richness, happiness, sustenance, offerings, provisions, and every good thing, you having appeared as king of Upper and Lower Egypt": *Urk.* IV, 227.

(16) *tw.i ḫʿ.kwi mi Rʿ m nsw ḥr Kmt*, " I have arisen like Re as king over Egypt": E. Naville, *The Temple of Deir el Bahari*, II (EEF Memoir 14 [London, 1895]), Pl. 46.

(17) (Thoth to king) "we come to see you" *m ḥb.k ḫʿ.k m nsw*, "in your festival when you appear as king": *Wb.* Belegstellen III, 74.

(18) (A god to king) "I give you . . . (certain gifts)," *ḫʿ.ti m nsw-bit*, "you having appeared as king of Upper and Lower Egypt": *ibid.*

(19) *iw.f ḫʿy m nsw-bit*, "he (Horus) has appeared as king of Upper and Lower Egypt": *ibid.*

(20) *ḫʿ.k psd.k ḥr psd mwt.k ḫʿ.ti m nsw nčrw*, "you appear, you shine on the back of your mother, you having appeared as king of the gods": *Urk.* IV, 1603.

(21) *wnn nsw Sn-wsrt ḫʿw m nsw t3wy mi 'Itm m 'Ipt-swt*, "King Senwosret is arisen (?) as king of the Two Lands like Atum in Karnak": *LD* III, 48b.

(*b*) In historical texts

(22) *ist grt ḫʿ.n ḥm.f m nsw m ḥwn nfr ip.n.f ḏt.f qm.n.f rnpt* 18, "now his majesty appeared as king as a fine youth, having matured (lit. "counted his body")[19] and having completed eighteen years": *Urk.* IV, 1279.

(23) *ist rf ḫʿ.n ḥm.f m nsw*, "lo, his majesty appeared as king" (there follows a description of the anarchy which prevailed at the time): *Urk.* IV, 2026.

(24) *tw.n ḥr ptr qnw m bi3t.k ḏr ḫʿ.k m nsw t3wy*, "we have been witnessing a host of your miracles since you appeared as king of the Two Lands": Sander-Hansen, *Historische Inschriften der* 19. *Dynastie*, 31.

[19] Perhaps "having reached full growth", or "having come of age"; cf. A. De Buck, *Analecta Orientalia*, 17 (1937) 55, n. 26; for *ḏt* used with *rḫ* or *ḫm* to indicate physical maturity or immaturity, see *Wb.* V, 504:11ff. "To grow up" (see E. E. Knudsen, *Acta Or.* 23 [1958–59], 114) is perhaps a little too loose a translation.

It must be admitted that there examples are ambiguous. Those from religious texts and reliefs could almost without exception refer to a specific ceremony of coronation. Number 17 seems to allude to such a ceremony, and the motif of the throne (no. 12) and gifts (nos. 15 and 18) seems applicable to a formal festival of coronation. But the three examples from historical texts seem to refer to the inception of the reign, i.e. presumably the accession, and do not concern themselves with the coronation per se. Even so, the language is everywhere so flowery that *ḫʿy* could, in a given example, conceivably refer either to accession or to coronation.

3. Appearances of the king upon the throne of god N

(*a*) Upon the throne of Horus

(25) *msy.(i) m [ḥꜣt]-sp* 27 *ḫr ḥm n nsw-bit Nb-kꜣw-rʿ mꜣʿ-ḫrw ḫʿ ḥm n nsw-bit Ḫʿ-kꜣw-rʿ mꜣʿ-ḫrw m nsw-bit ḥr st Ḥr nt ʿnḫw,* "I was born in [year] 27 under the majesty of the king of Upper and Lower Egypt Nebkaure, deceased; then appeared the majesty of the king of Upper and Lower Egypt Khakaure, deceased, as king of Upper and Lower Egypt upon the throne of Horus of the living": K. Sethe, *Aegyptische Lesestücke* (Leipzig, 1924), 83.

(26) *di.n.(i) n.k ʿnḫ ğd nb ḫʿ.ti ḥr st Ḥr,* "I give you all life and stability, you having appeared on the throne of Horus": Sir W. M. F. Petrie, *Koptos* (London, 1896), Pl. 7.

(27) *mk in.tw n.k wğ pn n nsw r rdit rḫ.k ntt ḥm.i ʿ. w. s. ḫʿw m nsw-bit ḥr st Ḥr nt ʿnḫw,* "behold, this command of the king is brought to you in order to inform you that my majesty, l.p.h., has arisen as king of Upper and Lower Egypt upon the throne of Horus of the living": *Urk*. IV, 80.

(28) *sꜣ Rʿ n ẖt.f mry.f Ğḥwty-ms ḫʿ mi Rʿ mry Wsir . . . di ʿnḫ ğd wꜣs snb ḫʿ m nsw-bit ḥr st Ḥr nt ʿnḫw,* "bodily son of Re, his beloved Thutmose, risen like Re, beloved of Osiris . . . given life, stability, prosperity, health, having appeared as king of Upper and Lower Egypt upon the throne of Horus of the living": *Urk*. IV, 103.

(29) *ḥꜣt-sp 1 ꜣbd 2 ꜣḫt sw 8 ḫʿt ḥr ḥm n* (full titulary of Thutmose II) *ḥr st Ḥr nt ʿnḫw,* "regnal year 1, second month of *akhet,* day 8. Appearance under the majesty of (Thutmose II) upon the throne of Horus of the living": *Urk*. IV,137.

(30) (Khnum to Hatshepsut) *di.n.(i) n.č ḫ't ḥr st Ḥr mi R'*, "I grant you an appearance upon the throne of Horus like Re": *Urk.* IV, 223.

(31) *twt nsw itt ḫ' ḥr st Ḥr n 'nḫw ǧt,* "you are a king who shall seize an appearance upon the throne of Horus of the living for ever":[20] *Urk.* IV, 229.

(32) *di.n n.č it.č ['Imn] ḫ't ḥr st Ḥr,* "your father [Amun] grants you an appearance upon the throne of Horus": *Urk.* IV, 229.

(33) (Coronation of Hatshepsut; words by the *iwn-mwt.f*) (Hatshepsut) . . . *ḫ'.ti ḥr st Ḥr sšmt 'nḫw nbw,* "having appeared upon the throne of Horus, the leader of all the living": *Urk.* IV, 252.

(34) *di.n.(i) n.č wḥm ḫ' ḥr st Ḥr mi R'*, "I grant you further appearances (?)[21] upon the throne of Horus like Re": *Urk.* IV, 279.

(35) *di.n.(i) n.č rnpwt n nḥḥ m nsw tꜣwy ḫ'.ti ḥr [st] Ḥr nt 'nḫw mi R'*, "I grant you years of eternity as king of the Two Lands, you having appeared upon the throne of Horus of the living like Re": Naville, *The Temple of Deir el Bahari,* II, Pl. 45.

(36) *wḥm.n.(i) n.č irt ḥḥ m sdw 'šꜣ wrt ḫ'.ti m nsw-bit ḥr st Ḥr n 'nḫw nbw mi R' ǧt,* "I repeat for you the performance of millions of *sd*-festivals, very many indeed, you having appeared as king of Upper and Lower Egypt, upon the throne of Horus of all the living like Re for ever": *Urk.* IV, 300.

(37) *tit ꜣḫt nt 'Imn sḫ't.n.f m nsw ḥr st Ḥr,* "effective image of Amun, whom he has caused to appear as king upon the throne of Horus": *Urk:* IV, 357; cf. *Urk.* IV, 389.

(38) *di.n.(i) n.k 'nḫ wꜣs nb snb nb ḫr.i ꜣwt-ib nb ḫ'.ti m nsw-bit ḥr st Ḥr mi R'*, "I give you all life and prosperity and all health which I have, and all happiness, you having appeared as king of Upper and Lower Egypt upon the throne of Horus like Re": Naville, *The Temple of Deir el Bahari,* I, Pl. 23.

(39) *di.n.(i) st.i nst.i iw't.i ḫrt.i n nb tꜣwy* (Thutmose III) *ḫ' ḥr nst R' ḥr st Ḥr nt 'nḫw,* "I give my throne, my seat, my inheritance, and what is in my charge, to the lord of the Two Lands (Thutmose III),

20 *Ḫ'* here could perhaps be taken as "crown"; it could also, however, be the abstract noun "appearance"; cf. H. Gauthier, *Kêmi,* 2 (1929), 43f.

21 Is this an allusion to the *sd*-festival, and therefore tantamount to "I grant you length of reign"? This passage is scarcely a "Beziehung auf die Thronwirren" as Sethe suggests: *Urk.* IV, 279, n. *c.*

who has appeared upon the seat of Re, upon the throne of Horus of the living": *Urk.* IV, 563.

(40) *wnn.(i) wnn.k tp tꜣ ḫʿ.ti m nsw-bit ḥr st Ḥr nt ʿnḫw,* "as long as I shall exist you shall exist upon earth, you having appeared as king of Upper and Lower Egypt upon the throne of Horus of the living": *Urk.* IV, 570.

(41) *di.n.(i) n.k ʿnḫ wꜣs Mn-ḫpr-rʿ n ẖt.i* [*rn*]*n.ti r nsw tꜣwy ḫʿ.ti ḥr st Ḥr nt ʿnḫw,* "I grant you life and prosperity, O Menkheperre of my body, you having been reared to be king of the Two Lands, and having appeared upon the throne of Horus of the living": *Urk.* IV, 570.

(42) *wnn.f ḫnt kꜣw ʿnḫw nb ḫʿw* ⟨*m*⟩ *nsw-bit ḥr st Ḥr,* "he shall take the lead of the living *ku's*, having appeared as king of Upper and Lower Egypt upon the Throne of Horus"; *Urk.* IV, 1348; cf. also *ASAE* 23 (1923), Pl. 4.

(43) (Titulary of Ay followed by) *ḫʿ ḥr st Ḥr nt ʿnḫw mi it.f* [*Rʿ*] *m pt rʿ nb,* "appearing upon the throne of Horus of the living like his father [Re] in heaven every day": *Urk.* IV, 2129.

(44) *ḫʿʿ Ḥr nsw-bit Wsr-mꜣʿt-rʿ Stp-n-rʿ nb tꜣwy ḥr st Ḥr,* "Horus appears, king of Upper and Lower Egypt, Usermare Setepenre, the lord of the Two Lands, upon the throne of Horus": *JEA* 20 (1934), Pl. 3:3.

(*b*) Upon the throne of Amun

(45) *sḫʿt.n ʾImn ḏs.f ḥr nst.f m ʾIwnw Šmʿ,* "whom Amun himself caused to appear upon his throne in southern Heliopolis": *Urk.* IV, 361.

(46) *nḏty mr nčrw di ʿnḫ mi Rʿ ḏt wnn nsw ʿꜣ-ḫprw-rʿ ḫʿ ḥr nst it.f ʾImn ꜣw ib.f sšm.f ʿnḫw nb ḫꜣswt nbt ẖr st-ḥr.f mi Rʿ ḏt,* "the avenger beloved of the gods, given life like Re for ever; King Okheprure appears upon the throne of his father Amun, his heart happy; he leads all the living, all foreign lands being under his control like Re for ever": *Urk.* IV, 1348.

(47) *ir.n.f m mnw.f n it.f ʾImn-rʿ . . . swꜣḏ.n.f n.f tꜣw nbw mi Rʿ ḫʿw* (text: *ḫʿ.ti*) *ḥr nst.f,* "he made it (a temple) as his monument to his father Amunre . . ., when he had bequeathed all lands to him like Re, he (Amenhotpe III) having appeared upon his seat": *Urk.* IV, 1702.

(*c*) Upon the throne of a solar deity

(48) *it.t ḫ'w m nsw-bit m ḥrt-tp nst 'Itm mi wḏt.n nb nṯrw*, "you shall achieve an appearance as king of Upper and Lower Egypt upon the seat of Atum, as the lord of the gods has ordained": *Urk.* IV, 231.

(49) (Akhenaten) . . . *ḫ'w ḥr st R' n 'nḫ* [*w*] *mi it.f 'Itn r' nb*, "appearing on the throne of Re of the living like his father Aten, every day": *Urk.* IV, 1965.

(50) *wn.in ḥm.*[*i*] *ḥr nhp ḥr T3-mry r w3ḏ 'nḫ n imyw.s ḫft ḫ''.f ḥr nst R'*, "[my] majesty arose early over Egypt to prosper the lives of those who are in it, when he appeared upon the seat of Re": *Urk.* IV, 2157.

(51) *ḫ' m nsw m wi3 n ḥḥ m ḥry-tp nst 'Itm mi R'*, "who has appeared as king in the 'barque of millions' upon the seat of Atum like Re": *Urk.* IV, 291 (epithet of Thutmose III).

(52) (Amenhotpe II) *snb ḫ ḥr nst 'Itm*, "healthy, having appeared upon the seat of Atum": *Urk.* IV, 1358.

(53) (Amenhotpe III) *mr.n.k ḫ''*[22] *ḥr nst.k Nb-m3't-r' pw p3 mr.n.k*, "whom you (Atum?) wish to appear upon your seat; it is Nebmare whom you love": *Urk.* IV, 1679.

(54) (Akhenaten and Nefertity) *ḫ'.wy*[23] *ḥr st it.sny*[23] *p3 'Itn 'nḫ* [*m*] *m3't*, "appearing upon the throne of their father, the Aten, living on truth": N. de G. Davies, *The Rock Tombs of El-Amarna* (EEF Arch. Surv. Mem. 14 [Cairo, 1904]), II, Pl. 29.

(*d*) Upon the throne of Geb

(55) *di.n.*(*i*) *ḫ' Mn-ḫprw-r' ḥr nst Gb*, "I cause Menkheprure to appear on the throne of Geb": *Urk.* IV, 1539.

(56) *ḥ3t-sp 2 nt ḫ'.f iw ḥm.f ḥr nst Gb*, "regnal year 2 after he appeared, his majesty being upon the seat of Geb": *Urk.* III, 111.

(*e*) Upon the throne of "his father"

(57) (Various localities are in festive mood) *m33.sn* (the king) *ḫ'w ḥr st it.f*, "when they see (the king) appearing upon the throne of his father": *Urk.* IV, 1363.

(58) (The passage follows the description of the anarchy which preceded Tutankhamun's reign) *ḥr m-ḫt hrw sw3 ḥr-s3 nn ḫ'y* [*ḥm.f*] *ḥr st it.f* (text: *it.i*) *ḥq3.n.f idbw Ḥr*, "now when (some) days had passed

[22] Presumably the geminating *sḏm.f* with omitted resumptive: Gardiner, *Grammar*,[3] § 385.

[23] Dual.

after this [his majesty] appeared upon the throne of his father and ruled the regions of Horus": *Urk.* IV, 2028.

Again it is difficult to tell in any of these examples whether *ḫ'y* refers to the act of accession or to the coronation. Examples 26, 33, and 44 are taken from relief scenes showing the coronation rite itself, and it would seem reasonable to conclude that *ḫ'y* in these examples has some connexion with that rite. The same may be true of no. 39, for a parallel passage[24] adds *wrrt.i*, "my crown," after *nst.i*, which would be appropriate in a coronation context. Yet these examples do not appear to differ formally from others that clearly refer to the accession. Number 27 is from a letter informing a provincial official that a new king has come to the throne, and no. 25 is tantamount to a statement that Senwosret III came to the throne, not merely that he was crowned. Number 29 is a trifle more difficult to interpret, but in the present writer's opinion there is no doubt that the specific date refers to the accession rather than the coronation.[25] In no. 50 Haremhab seems to mean that he has been working tirelessly for Egypt all the time that he has been king, i.e. since his accession. It seems likely that the Sphinx's utterance (no. 55) is a promise that Thutmose IV shall succeed his father, rather than that he shall merely be crowned. Number 56 must refer to the accession, since, as will appear shortly, Egyptian kings began dating their regnal years with their accession, not their coronation. Again, in no. 58 the anarchic conditions that prevailed before Tutankhamun's reign are contrasted with the reforms begun on that king's accession. If these examples seem to overbalance the scale in favour of the accession as opposed to the coronation, there are those examples like nos. 34, 36, and 52 which appear in contexts which have to do with *sd*-festivals;[26] and the latter, it will be remembered, were primarily re-enactments of the rite of crowning the king and equipping him with the symbols of kingship.[27] The gods' promises to baby Hatshepsut (nos. 30 to 32) are couched in vague language, but it would seem that their predictions concern her eventual accession, not

[24] *Urk.* IV, 571.

[25] Gardiner, *JEA* 31 (1945), 25f.; *contra* W. Helck, *Studia Biblica et Orientalia*, III. *Oriens Antiquus* (Rome, 1959), 115f.

[26] Cf. also the relief of Thutmose II at Karnak: *ASAE* 30 (1930), Pl. 5.

[27] Frankfort, *Kingship and the Gods*, 79 ff.

merely her coronation. In many examples, far from denoting the coronation, an "appearance" seems to be used as a synonym for "reign": cf. nos. 30, 31, 32, 48, and 56; cf. also the illuminating Middle Kingdom text from Armant:[28] *ḥ3t-sp tpt* (!) *nt ḫ'w ḫr* [ ], "first regnal year of the appearance under [ ]."

Finally, it is not immediately obvious what the distinction, if any, is between the "thrones" of the various gods. The "throne of Horus" is the usual designation of the seat and office of the king as the incarnate Horus. But the "throne of Geb" is virtually the same thing, Horus in the myth assuming the kingly office formerly held by his grandfather Geb. Again, like the "throne of Horus," the "throne of Atum" seems to symbolize the rule over the Two Lands. Although in the original myth Amun found no place at all, the "throne of Amun" in the New Kingdom examples seems to be only a variant of the "throne of Horus." The "throne of Re," however, is used slightly differently. Here the allusion seems to be (cf. especially no. 51) to the divine seat of the god witihn his boat, which daily traversed the heavens.

4. Appearances of types 2 and 3 with specific reference to crowns

(*a*) In religious texts

(59) *iḫ'.k Tty m ḫt-ḥ3t* (?),[29] "you appear, Tety, in a . . .": PT 731a.

(60) *iḫ'y Ppy m nsw iq3y.f m Wp-w3wt šsp.n.f hǧt w3ǧt,* "Pepy has appeared as king, he is elevated as Wepwawet, he has received the crowns (of Upper and Lower Egypt)": PT 1374ab.

(61) *Wsir N d.n n.k Ḥr irt.f m ḥ3t.k m rn.s n Wrt-ḥk3w Wsir N ḫ'.ti m nsw-bit,* "O Osiris N, Horus has on your behalf placed his eye upon your brow in its name 'Great-of-Magic.' O Osiris N, you have appeared as king of Upper and Lower Egypt": PT 1795ab.

(62) *'ḥ' Ḥr tp t3 sw dmǧ t3 pn m3č m rn wr T3-čnn rsy-inb.f nb ǧt rwd.n Wrt-ḥk3w m tp.f sw Ḥr pw ḫ'w m nsw-bit,* "Horus stood over the land, he united this land named with the great name 'the Rising Land south of his wall, the lord of eternity.' The 'Great-of-Magic' sprouted

[28] Sir R. Mond and O. H. Myers, *The Temples of Armant* (London, 1940), Pl. 99:10 (*temp.* Amenemhet I).

[29] Apparently the expression for a kind of head-dress; cf. Sethe, *Übersetzung und Kommentar . . .*, III, 355.

on his head, he was Horus who appeared as king of Upper and Lower Egypt": Memphite Theology, 13c–14c.

(63) *hꜣ Wsir N pr irt Ḥr*[30] *ḥḏt m tp.k rdi.n n.k Ḥr irt.f pr irt Ḥr mḥt m tp.k ḫʿ.k m nsw-bit,* "Ho Osiris N, the eye of Horus has come forth, the white crown upon your head. Horus has given you his eye. The eye of Horus has come forth, the crown of Lower Egypt upon your head. (Now) you appear as king of Upper and Lower Egypt":[31] CT I, 178.

(64) *šsp n.č ꜣtfw Ḥr smn.t n.č ḥḏt ḥr čntꜣt mi iryt n Ḥr m ḫʿw.f in Rʿ,* "receive to yourself the *atef*-crowns of Horus, crown yourself with the white crown on the dais as was done for Horus at his appearance by Re": CT I, 257.

(65) *iꜣw n nb ꜣbḏw mi ḥʿʿ ꜣIst hrw ḫʿʿ Ḥr ḥr čntꜣyt ḫnm.n.f sḫmt m ʿnḫ wꜣs,* "adoration to the lord of Abydos, as Isis exulted on the day when Horus appeared on the dais after he had joined himself to *pschent* in life and prosperity": J. J. Clere, *ZÄS* 84 (1959), Pl. 5 (top).

(66) *ḫʿ Ḥr šsp.n.f šwty nsw,* "Horus has appeared, he had received the two regal feathers": Naville, *Festival Hall,* Pl. 14, 25 (VI).

(*b*) In coronation texts and reliefs

(67) *sḫm.č m tꜣwy ič.č ḫʿkw-ib ḫʿ.č m ʿḥ ḫkr ḥꜣt.č m sḫmt ḥtp.t m iwʿt Ḥr ms čn,* "you shall exert power over the Two Lands, you shall seize the recalcitrant ones, you shall appear in the palace, your brow shall be adorned with *pschent,* you shall be satisfied with the inheritance of Horus who begot you" (there follow further references to crowns, and then Thutmose I introduces Hatshepsut to the court): *Urk.* IV, 256.

(68) *wḏ ḥm.f in.tw ḫryw-ḥb r mꜣč rnw.s wr nw šsp sʿḥw.s*[32] *n nsw-bit . . . rḫ.f nfr n ḫʿw n wpt-rnpt,* "his majesty commanded the lector-priests to be brought in order to set her titulary, at the time of (?) the reception of her emblems of the kingship over Upper and Lower Egypt . . . (for) he knew the excellence of an appearance on New Year's day":[33] *Urk.* IV, 261.

30 Written with the road determinative, 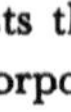 ; cf. P. Lacau, *ZÄS* 51 (1914), 58f.

31 The juxtaposition of these clauses suggests that the last is something more than a simple, unrelated statement, and incorporates a nuance of purpose or result.

32 Determined by  .

33 Cf. also the unpublished texts of the later coronation of Hatshepsut in the second regnal year of Thutmose III: S. Schott, *Nachr. Gött.* (1955), 212f.

(69) *sꜣt.i mrt H̱nmt-ʾImn Ḥꜣt-špswt šsp n.t ḫʿw.č m ibs ẖkr ḫʿ ḫsbdy imy tp n it.č Rʿ ḫʿ.č im.f,* "my beloved daughter Khnumet-Amun Hatshepsut, receive to yourself the *ibs*-diadem, the resplendent lapis lazuli ornament which was upon the head of your father Re, that you may appear in it": *ASAE* 26 (1926), Pl. 5 (C).

(70) [*smn.n.f*] *ḫʿw.i wd.*⟨*f*⟩ *n.i nẖbt ğs.f smn.n.f bik.i tp srḫ snḫt.n.f wi m kꜣ-nḫt di.n.f ḫʿ.i m ẖnw Wꜣst,* "[he established] my crowns, ⟨he⟩ himself set the titulary for me, he established my hawk on the *serekh,* he empowered me as 'Mighty-Bull,' he caused me to appear in the midst of Thebes": *Urk.* IV, 160.

(71) *šsp.k ḥğ grg ʿfnt m ḥꜣt.k wčs.k nb.ty ḫʿ.k im.sn,* "receive the white crown, implant the royal headpiece on your brow, elevate the Two Ladies that you may appear in them": *Urk.* IV, 292f.

(72) (At the coronation, after Haremhab's crown had been set in place, and his titulary established) *ḥpt.n.f nfrw.f ḫʿw m ḫprš,* "he (Amun) embraced his beauty, he (Haremhab) appearing in the blue crown": *JEA* 39 (1953), Pl. 2.

(73) *psğt nbw pr-nsr m ihhy n ḫʿʿ.f,* "the Ennead, the lords of the 'Fire House,' were rejoicing at his appearance":[34] *ibid.*

(*c*) In other formal texts of royal authorship

(74) *sn-nwt rnpt n bs.tw.f ḫʿt.f m ḥry-tp tꜣwy r ḥqꜣ šnt.n ʾItn . . . snğm.f ḥr nst Gb wčs.t*(*w*) *ḫʿw sḫmty,* "the second year after his being inducted, his appearance as overlord of the Two Lands, to rule that which Aten surrounds . . . when he had seated himself upon the seat of Geb and the crowns and *pschent* were elevated": *Urk.* IV, 82.

(75) *di.n.*(*i*) *it.*[*s*] *wrrt ḫʿw m nsw n nḥḥ m nḥḥ n ğt* ⌜*ist*⌝ [*sy*] *m nsw ʿnḫw* [ ] *nsw-bit m tꜣ pn ḫʿ.ti* [*ḥr*] *nst.i,* "I cause [her] to seize the great crown, appearing as king for ever and ever eternally. ⌜Lo,⌝ [she] is king of the living [ ] king of Upper and Lower Egypt in this land, having appeared upon my seat": *Urk.* IV, 283.

(76) *di.n.*(*i*) *n.*[*č*] *wꜣğty ḥr-tp.*[*č*] *ḫʿ.sn r-imy inḥ.*[*č*] *mnt ḥr*[*č*] *irt sꜣw.*[*č*] *ḫʿ.č ḥr nst Ḥr,* "I place for [you] the 'Two Flourishing Ones' upon [your] head, that they may appear between [your] eyebrows; the *mnit*-necklace is with [you] providing [your] protection, you appear upon the seat of Horus": *Urk.* IV, 287.

34 It is not clear whether this refers to Haremhab's "coronation," or merely to his appearance again outdoors after his introduction to Amun's daughter.

(77) *smn.(ỉ) gnwt nt sꜣt.(ỉ) [Mꜣꜥt-kꜣ-]Rꜥ m tpt ḥḥ m sd ꜥšꜣ wrt ḫꜥ.tỉ m nsw-bỉt Šmꜥ Mḥw m Ḥr ḥms* (*sic*) *ẖnm.n.* [*č*] *Wrt-ḥkꜣw m tp.č,* "I establish the annals for my daughter [Maka]re as the first of millions of very many *sd*-festivals, you having appeared as king of Upper and Lower Egypt, of the Southland and of the Northland, as Horus who sits after (?) [you] had joined 'Great-of-Magic' to your head": *Urk.* IV, 288.

(78) *wčs.ỉ hǧt ḫꜥ.ỉ m dšrt,* ". . . as surely as I elevate the white crown and appear in the red crown": *Urk.* IV, 366 (a royal oath).

(79) *dỉ.n.(ỉ) n sꜣ.(ỉ) n ẖt.(ỉ)* (Thutmose III) *st.ỉ nst.ỉ wrrt.ỉ ḫꜥ m nsw-bỉt ḥr st Ḥr mỉ Rꜥ ǧt,* "I give my throne, my seat, my crown to my bodily son (Thutmose III), he having appeared as king of Upper and Lower Egypt upon the throne of Horus like Re for ever": *Urk.* IV, 571.

(80) (Amenhotpe II) . . . *ḫꜥw m nsw ḥr st wrt ẖnm.n.f Wrt-ḥkꜣw snsn.n sḫmty tp.f ꜣtfw Rꜥ m wpt.f ḥr.f ẖkr m Šmꜥ-s Mḥ-s ỉt.n.f sšd ḫprš ỉbs šwty wrty m tp.f ḥpt.n nms rmny.f(y) sḫwy n ḫꜥw ꜥItm,* "having appeared as king upon the great throne, he joined himself[35] to 'Great-of-Magic,' *pschent* kissed his head, the *atef-crown* of Re being upon his brow, his face adorned with the Upper Egyptian and Lower Egyptian crowns, he seized the fillet and the blue crown, the *ỉbs*-head-dress and the two feathers being on his head, the royal headcloth embraced his shoulders—the assemblage of the crowns of Atum": *Urk.* IV, 1277.

(81) *m.ḫt nn sḫꜥw ḥm.f m nsw Wrt ḥtp.s st.s m wpt.f,* "after these things (i.e. Amenhotpe II's boyhood) his majesty was caused to appear as king and the 'Great One'[36] took her place on his brow": *Urk.* IV, 1283.

(82) *ỉw.f ḥtp m ꜣḫty.f mỉ psǧt ỉrw n.f ỉ.ỉrt nt Rꜥ ẖnyt m pꜣy.f wỉꜣ-nsw ḥr-tp ỉtrw ḥtp m ḥwt.f nḥḥ ỉmntt Wꜣst ỉw ỉt.ỉ ꜥImn nb nčrw Rꜥ-ꜥItm Ptḥ-nfr-ḥr sḫꜥw.ỉ m nb tꜣwy r st wtt.ỉ . . . ḫꜥ.kwỉ m ꜣtf ḥr ỉꜥrꜥrt ẖnm.ỉ ḫꜥ.ỉ šwty.ỉ mỉ Tꜣ-tnn snǧm.k(wỉ) m tnčꜣyt Ḥr-ꜣḫty ǧbꜣ.k(wỉ) m ẖkrw mỉ ꜥItm,* "he (Sethnakhte) rested in his horizon like the Ennead. There was done for him that which is done for Re, he was rowed[37] in his royal

[35] Or could the following *sǧm.n.f* forms be rendered as past temporal clauses depending on *ḫꜥw:* "appearing as king . . . after (or when) he had joined himself, etc."?

[36] Determined by  .

[37] For this absolute use of the infinitive, see A. Erman, *Neuägyptische Grammatik* (2nd ed., Leipzig, 1933), §415.

barque upon the river and laid to rest in his castle of eternity on the west of Thebes. My father Amun, lord of the gods, Re-Atum and Ptah-beautiful-of-face caused me to appear as lord of the Two Lands in the place of my begetter . . . I appeared in the *atef*-crown bearing the uraeus, I joined myself to my crown and two feathers like Tatenen, seated upon the dais of Horakhty adorned with ornaments like Atum": Papyrus Harris, 76:1ff.

(*d*) *Ḫʿy*, "to appear," used of the crowns themselves

(83) *ink Ḥr wčs irt.f ḫʿt b3t q3t*, "I am Horus who elevates his eye, risen, beatified, lofty": CT IV, 106.

(84) (The uraeus serpent) *mnt m tp Sbk . . . ḫʿt m ḥ3t.f*, "firm on the head of Sobk . . . who appears on his forehead": A. Erman, *APAW* (1911), 26.

(85) *ḫʿ Nt tp.k Sbk*, "the red crown appears upon you, O Sobk": *ibid.*, 46.

(86) *šsp.f hḏt čs.f dšrt mn. sn m tp.f ḫʿ.sn m wpt.f*, "he (Amenhotpe I) receives the white crown, he elevates the red crown that they may be firm on his head and appear upon his brow": Papyrus Chester Beatty, IX, ro. 12/9.

One would expect that a passage in which crowns are mentioned in the same context as the verb *ḫʿy* would undoubtedly be an allusion to a coronation per se. This seems eminently true of the examples from religious texts, in which (note especially examples 60 through 63) the description of the donning of the crowns is in close juxtaposition to a clause referring to the appearance as king. Strangely, however, in the half dozen passages cited from actual "coronation" inscriptions, the phrase *m nsw-bit* is notably absent. In its place are such adverbial complements as "in the palace" (67), "on New Year's day" (68), "in the midst of Thebes" (70), "in them (the crowns)" (71), and "in the blue crown" (72). *Ḫʿy* seems to be used in these examples with reference merely to the festal "appearance" of the royal figure at a ceremony, in the same way that it would be used of the central figure, god or king, at any festival.

In section (*c*) a number of the examples appear to allude definitely to a coronation ceremony. The high-flown, but vivid, description of the "crowns of Atum" in no. 80 seems to find its milieu in such a ceremony. Number 82 also describes a coronation, and interestingly enough in this case, if the order of events is significant, the coronation day cannot be identical with the day of accession, since the former took place after the embalming and burial of the king's predecessor, a process which probably occupied the usual seventy days beginning with the monarch's death. Example 77 contains a reference to the *sd*-festival, which was *inter alia* a re-enactment of the coronation.

In two cases at least, however, *ḫ'y* is used to describe the accession of a king. The Tombos stela (no. 74) is dated in Thutmose I's second regnal year, which is further qualified as "the second year after his induction, his appearance as overlord of the Two Lands." The verb *bs*, "to introduce, induct," is used frequently in the sense of installing a person in the kingly office;[38] but whether its use is confined to either accession or coronation, or whether it can be used of both, is not clear. In example 74, however, regnal year 2, a locution which reflects the normal dating beginning with a king's accession, is equated with the second year of the royal induction and "appearance." This fact would tend to suggest that the induction and "appearance" are to be identified with Thutmose I's accession. Example 81, taken from the Sphinx-stela of Amenhotpe II, alludes to the accession of the king on the death of Thutmose III. There is some evidence,[39] gleaned in part from this very stela, that strongly suggests that Amenhotpe II had already been made king while his father lived, and had enjoyed a short coregency with him. If so, he would undoubtedly have undergone a coronation before the time referred to in this passage.

Finally, it remains to be noted that the verb *ḫ'y* as used in section (d) has nothing to do with the notion of a coronation. The Egyptian expression meaning "to crown" is *smn ḫ'w*, lit. "to make firm the appearing one." Rather, the crowns themselves are regarded as the logical subject of the action denoted by the verb *ḫ'y:* they "sprout" or "appear" on the brow of the king in the metaphorical language of the texts. Hence a crown is par excellence the "appearing one" (*ḫ'w*).

The examples cited in sections 2 to 4 have been divided into three groups on the basis of a purely formal criterion, but they remain essentially a unity. We have been dealing throughout with a

[38] *Wb.* I, 473:8.

[39] E. Hornung, *Untersuchungen zur Chronologie und Geschichte des Neuen Reiches* (Ägyptologische Abhandlungen, 11 [Wiesbaden, 1964]), 33f.

single formula of three parts, which may be paraphrased as follows: (a) king N appears as king, (b) upon the throne of god N, and (c) wearing such and such a crown. Each part may be juggled or modified slightly—(c) appears to be treated most freely—or even left out altogether; but these seem to be merely stylistic variations. The formula is found frequently in formal texts, i.e. religious and royal inscriptions, reliefs, etc., but not in popular tales, letters, or business documents. This absence is understandable, as the formula belongs to the flowery style of the monuments rather than to the prosaic diction of daily speech.

Up to this point all the passages cited have been scrutinized carefully with a view to making them allude to either an accession or a coronation. But it may be premature to present a choice between these alternatives as inevitable. We have first to ask ourselves: What did the expression "to appear as king" mean to the Egyptians? Was it the equivalent of "to arise (*'ḥ'*)[40] as king," i.e. to accede to the throne immediately after the death of the previous ruler? Or did an heir apparent not really appear as king, i.e. not fully warrant the title *nsw-bit* and others, until he had undergone at a later date a coronation? When the question is put this way, the answer is obvious. If an heir apparent "appeared as king" solely by virtue of a formal coronation, the presence of a host of ephemeral monarchs in Egyptian history would be inexplicable. The Turin Canon teems with kings, all granted the titles of kingship, who reigned each but a few days or months. If, as many scholars believe, the coronation followed several months after the day of accession, such short-lived kings would have scarcely had a chance to celebrate a formal ceremony. It follows that a ruler whose reign amounted to only a few days could be said to have "appeared as king" no less than a Thutmose III or a Ramses II. The heir appeared as king, therefore, immediately after and in consequence of the death of his predecessor. This was his accession, his primary appearance as king. Thereafter, while he reigned, he could be said to have "appeared as king," and to be (now) continually visible as king. The metaphor becomes clear when the underlying imagery of the sun's rising and setting is taken into account.

[40] Concerning this frequent expression for the accession of a king, see Sethe, *Übersetzung und Kommentar* . . ., I, 121; II, 180; A. Volten, *Zwei altägyptische politische Schriften* (*An. Aeg.* 4 [Copenhagen, 1945], 43.

The use of the same expression with reference to the coronation is understandable. Here too the ruler was "appearing (to his court and people) as king" in his royal costume with his crown. But there is a distinction, and it seems to lie in the verb *ḫʿy* itself. At his coronation a king "appeared" just as a god "appeared" in all his finery at his own yearly festival. The king's coronation was the royal festival par excellence, and hence the presence of such adverbial adjuncts as "as king" and "upon the throne of Horus."[41] But it was a festival (*ḫʿy*) nonetheless, and consequently the verb *ḫʿy* was quite appropriate. It is inevitable that the Egyptians' use of the same verb to express the idea of accession should create confusion for us moderns, but it is most improbable that the Egyptians experienced our confusion. They probably understood clearly that "to appear" in the sense of "to come to the throne" signified the king's automatic "appearance" on the death of his father, the use of the word being drawn directly from the image of the rising sun; while "to appear" in the sense of "to be crowned" owed its particular shade of meaning to the locution describing the festal "appearance" of a god's statue.[42]

The belief that, in practice, considerable time elapsed between accession and coronation may be more or less correct; but there are no grounds for the assumption that the same interval was required by theory. The myth underlying the institution of kingship knows nothing of such an interval. In the calendar of festivals there are not two widely separated days on which Horus "appears as king," but one, and that is the day immediately following the death of his father Osiris, viz. the first day of the first month of *proyet*.[43] In examples cited above, the accession of Horus (*ʿḥʿ Ḥr*, cf. no. 62) is closely linked with his receiving of the crowns, and this, after all, is what is to be expected. The legitimacy of Horus is visibly demonstrated by the sprouting of the crown from his head, and this miracle must needs occur when he becomes king. Hence the accession day is the logical time to crown the king. It would seem, then, that the "appearance" of a king refers to a single indivisible occurrence, viz. his entry into the kingship on his accession day, at which time ideally he was to be outfitted with the crowns.

[41] See above, example 17.

[42] Cf. Frankfort, *Kingship and the Gods*, 102f.

[43] Gardiner, *JEA* 2 (1915), 124.

One is permitted to wonder whether the ideal did not work out in practice more often than scholars have thought. The presupposition that the ceremonies envisaged by the Dramatic Text of Senwosret I, the Hatshepsut reliefs, and the Haremhab coronation inscription reflect the normal round of ceremonies at every king's accession has coloured many recent scholarly investigations. If this presupposition is valid, and if the Dramatic Text, in particular, actually does set forth the coronation rite per se,[44] then the conclusion is forced upon us that indeed a long period must have elapsed between accession and coronation. Otherwise the elaborate preparations necessitated by the latter could not have been made. But the validity of this presupposition is by no means self-evident. Each of the monarchs in question came to the throne under far from normal circumstances, and it is not unlikely that rare rituals were resurrected or new ones instituted for them. Senwosret I was beset by rebellion at the inception of his reign; and Hatshepsut, in plain terms a usurper, was constantly at pains to justify her position. If we are to believe her, she underwent two coronations, one while her father yet lived (depicted at Deir el-Bahri), and another in the second regnal year of her stepson Thutmose III.[45] Neither can be labelled an "accession day," and with neither did she commence to date regnal years. As for Haremhab, he was the first "orthodox" monarch after the Amarna heresy. His coronation smacks of the miraculous, and was probably in large measure a unique ceremony designed to lend extraordinary divine sanction to his reign. Nor can the "archaisms" of the Dramatic Text and the Hatshepsut reliefs be cited as evidence of the longstanding use of such rites. In the first place, it is within the realm of probability that what has mistakenly been called "archaic" is in actual fact "archaizing." In the second place, a single ancient prototype, perhaps used only occasionally in remote antiquity, if complete enough to be copied, would have sufficed to give an archaic flavour. Again, in the case of the Dramatic Text, it is doubtful whether we can speak of a "coronation." It is true that in one of the scenes the

[44] It is noteworthy that neither the verb *ḫ'y* nor the noun occurs in that part of the text concerned with the crowning of the king. Helck has argued convincingly (*Orientalia*, 23 [1954], 383ff.; cf. especially 410) that this papyrus has nothing to do with the coronation.

[45] Schott, *Nachr. Gött.* (1955), 212f.

king is crowned; but such "coronations," i.e. the formal placing of the crown upon the king's head, must have taken place frequently throughout a monarch's reign, in fact whenever he was decked out for a festival in which he participated. One of the most important duties of the *imy-ḫnt* priests was concerned with just such crownings.[46] But this particular ceremony of the Dramatic Text need not necessarily be equated with the *first* coronation of the king when the crown was first placed formally upon his head.[47]

At a change of reign in ancient Egypt the usual procedure was probably the following. As soon as the old king died his heir automatically "appeared as king" and was hailed as such. As soon as he could, he would have donned the crown and sat upon the throne. There is no reason to believe that the Egyptians took these expressions metaphorically. Undoubtedly, if the heir was present in the palace at the time of the death of his predecessor (which situation must usually have obtained), he would have sat upon the throne and undergone a formal coronation at once. There would have been little need for preparation; under normal circumstances *ḫry-ḥb* priests and *imy-ḫnt* priests and most of the great dignitaries would be close enough to the palace to present themselves before the day of accession had passed. Actually, then, it may be misleading to speak of accession and coronation as taking place always on two different days. Under abnormal circumstances this may have been the case, but surely not always. Undoubtedly the accession was followed months later by an elaborate rite dramatizing the myth of the kingship, but there is no evidence to connect such a celebration with the *ḫʿy-nsw*, "the appearance of the king."

5. "Appearance(s) of the king (*ḫʿy-nsw*)"

(87) *ḫʿy-nsw mst Mn,* "appearance of the king, carving (of a statue) of Min": Palermo Stone, 2/9.

46 Cf. K. Sethe, *Ägyptische Lesestücke* (Leipzig, 1924), 75, and Gardiner's remarks in *JEA* 39 (1953), 26; see also W. Helck, *Untersuchungen zu den Beamtentiteln des ägyptischen alten Reiches* (*Äg. Forsch.* 18 [Glückstadt, 1954]), 29.

47 In fact, in the case of Senwosret I this equation cannot be made, since his actual coronation must have taken place a decade before his accession to sole rule, when he was made coregent. The Dramatic Text, however, reflects a time when the king's predecessor (i.e. Amenemhet I) was dead.

(88) *ḫʿy-nsw ḫʿy-bit ḥb-sd,* "appearance of the king of Upper Egypt, appearance of the king of Lower Egypt, *sd*-festival": Palermo Stone, 3/3.

(89) *ḫʿy-bit sp tpy pḥrr ḥp,* "appearance of the king of Lower Egypt, first occurrence of the running of Apis": Palermo Stone, 3/12 (cf. also 4/6, 10, 12, 14).

(90) *ḫʿy-nsw pğ šs ḥwt-Ḥr,* "appearance of the king of Upper Egypt, stretching the cord (i.e. laying out the ground plan) for the 'Castle of Horus' ": Palermo Stone, 4/2.

(91) *ḫʿy-nsw ḫʿy-bit smꜣ-tꜣwy pḥr ḥꜣ inb,* "appearance of the king of Upper Egypt, appearance of the king of Lower Egypt, unification of the Two Lands, circuit of the walls": Palermo Stone, 5/7 (cf. also 5/8, 10).

(92) *in isft ʿḥꜣy n.n čs.n.i im.s m ḫʿt.i.* "it is the rebels (?)[48] who fight for us; I recruited some of them at my appearance": Papyrus Petersburg 1116A, 59f.

(93) *tpy ꜣḫt wp-rnpt tpy rnpwt ḥtpt n ḫʿ-nsw ḫʿ-bit,* "the first month of *akhet,* New Year's day; the first of the years of peace, of the appearance of the king of Upper Egypt and the appearance of the king of Lower Egypt": *Urk.* IV, 262.

(94) *ḥꜣt-sp 1 tpy šmw sw 4 ḫpr swt ḫʿt-sꜣ-nsw Čḥwty-ms ʿnḫ ğt r nḥḥ,* "regnal year 1, first month of *shomu,* day 4; there occurred the appearance of the king's son, Thutmose, living for ever and ever": *Urk.* IV, 180.

(95) [ ] *čs Ḥwʿ m ḫʿt-nsw ḥr-sꜣ Ḫꜣsḫt imntt,* "[the army reached (?)] the height of Hua on coronation day, behind western Khaskhet": *Urk.* IV, 1735.

(96) *tpy šmw sw* 26 *hrw n ḫʿ-nsw n nsw-bit Wsr-mꜣʿt-rʿ Mry-ʾImn,* "first month of *shomu,* day 26; the day of the royal appearance of the king of Upper and Lower Egypt Usermare Maiamun (Ramses III)": H. H. Nelson, *Medinet Habu. III. The Calendar, the "Slaughterhouse" and Minor Records of Ramses III* (OIP 23 [Chicago, 1934]), Pl. 152:553.

(97) *tpy prt sw 1 hrw n Nḫb-kꜣw n ḫʿ-nsw n nsw,* "first month of *proyet,* day 1; the day of *Nekheb-kau,* of the royal appearance of the king": *ibid.,* Pl. 163:1191.

[48] *Wb.* I, 129:13; *contra* Volten, *Zwei altägyptische politische Schriften,* 29.

(98) *ḥꜣt-sp 31 ꜣbd 1 šmw sw 26 ỉrt ḫꜥy-nsw n Pr-ꜥꜣ*, "regnal year 31, month 1 of *shomu*, day 26; the celebration of the royal appearance of Pharaoh": J. Černý, *Catalogue des Ostraca hiératiques non littéraires de Deir el-Medineh* (IFAO, Documents des Fouilles [Cairo, 1935]), no. 55, vo, 1/2.

(99) *ꜣbd 1 šmw sw 26 wsf ḫꜥ Wsr-mꜣꜥt-rꜥ*, "first month of *shomu*, day 26; idle, the appearance of Usermare": G. Botti and T. E. Peet, *Il Giornale della Necropoli di Tebe* (Turin, 1928), Pl. 53:26.

(100) *ḥꜣt-sp 2 ꜣbd 3 šmw sw 15 hrw pn ỉrt ḫꜥ-nsw*, "regnal year 2, third month of *shomu*, day 15; on this day occurred the celebration of the royal appearance," Černý, *Catalogue des Ostraca hiératiques . . .* no. 44:9.

(101) *tpy prt sw 1 ḥb n Ḥr* [ ] *sꜣ* [*Wsỉr*] *sꜣ ʾIst ḫꜥ-nsw Ḥr-bḥdty mry Rꜥ rḫyt*, "first month of *proyet*, day 1; festival of Horus [ ] son of [Osiris] son of Isis, royal appearance of Hor-Behdety, beloved of Re and mankind": M. Alliot, *Le Culte d'Horus à Edfou au temps des Ptolémées* (Cairo, 1949), 216.

With section 5 we leave the vagaries of the earlier examples, and encounter a specific event designated by the expression *ḫꜥy-nsw*, the "appearance of the king." The Old Kingdom examples seem to reflect a ceremony at which the king appeared in his regalia as king of Upper Egypt or Lower Egypt, or both. Such a ceremony, however, at that period seems to have had no strong connexion with the inception of a king's rule, since it would appear that one need not have been celebrated in the first year of the reign.[49] Nor can the *ḫꜥy-nsw's* of the Palermo Stone (cf. nos. 87 to 91) be anniversaries of the king's accession, for they do not occur in every year-rectangle but are scattered, often irregularly, throughout the reign. The best solution is to consider them as festivals in honour of the monarch as king, in which he appeared in his royal costume and was worshipped by the people.[50] The passage from Hatshepsut's coronation inscription (above, no. 93) appears to be a conscious attempt to emulate the Old Kingdom usage; but unless the syntax is ignored, it seems to denote not a specific festival but the entire reign of the queen.

The remainder of the examples share little in common with those of the Palermo Stone. The passages from New Kingdom texts, in

[49] Cf. Palermo Stone, 2/3.

[50] Cf. below, no. 102.

contrast, designate the accession day or its anniversary. The date ix, 4 of Thutmose III's *ḫ'y-nsw* (no. 94) has been shown to be the first day of each of his regnal years,[51] and the like has been demonstrated for Ramses III's *ḫ'y-nsw* of ix, 26.[52] In no. 100 the date of the *ḫ'y-nsw*, viz. xi, 15, marks the beginning of the second regnal year of Ramses IV.[53] Thus it appears that Egyptian kings of the New Kingdom commenced dating their regnal years on the day on which they celebrated their *ḫ'y-nsw*. Now if in the New Kingdom a system of regnal years (different from the civil year) was employed everywhere for dating purposes—and there is incontrovertible proof that it was[54]—it stands to reason that the regnal years of each king must have begun with his accession, not with a delayed coronation. Otherwise there would be in each king's reign a span of a few months at the beginning (ending on the day of coronation) which would not be covered in the dating system. That such gaps did not occur is proved by business documents, which follow the date of one king's decease with the beginning of the first regnal year of the new king.[55] *Ḫ'y-nsw*, therefore, can refer to nothing other than the king's accession.[56]

6. "Festival(s) of the appearance (*ḥb n ḫ'w*)"

(102) *hꜣ.f r wiꜣ nb stp sꜣ 'q.f ḥr wꜣwt 'ḥ Šm' m ḥbw nb n ḫ'w*, "he descended into every barque (as?) king's escort (?),[57] he entered

[51] K. Sethe, *ZÄS* 58 (1923), 39ff.

[52] Černý, *ZÄS* 72 (1936), 114f.

[53] *Ibid.*, 110f.

[54] For the New Kingdom system of regnal-year dating, see D. H. Haigh, *ZÄS* 9 (1871), 72f. (who seems to have been one of the earliest scholars to point out that in the New Kingdom a reign did not begin on New Year's day); G. Daressy, *RT* 34 (1912), 52; Gardiner, *JEA* 31 (1945), 23f.; Sethe, *ZÄS* 58 (1923), 39; Helck, *Studia Biblica et Orientalia*, III, 113f.

[55] Cf. Daressy, *RT* 34(1912), 45f.; Gardiner, *RAD*, 30.

[56] See Gardiner, *JEA* 31 (1945), 24; cf. Schott, *Nachr. Gött.* (1955), 201. It is dangerous to use the term "Krönungstag" for "accession day" (see Morenz, n. 5 above), unless one first makes clear that one believes the two were identical. The confusion that can result from a failure to clarify the terminology is seen to best advantage in Borchardt, *Mittel*, where the terms "Krönung" and "Thronbesteigung" alternate in the most bewildering fashion.

[57] Or something similar. Presumably here the word is a noun. For a discussion of the term, see Sethe, *Übersetzung und Kommentar* . . ., II, 388; J. Spiegel, *ZÄS* 75 (1939), 119f.; A. H. Gardiner, *Notes on the Story of Sinuhe* (Paris, 1916), 110.

upon the ways of the southern palace at every festival of appearance": *Urk.* I, 83.

(103) *ḥ3t-sp 1 3bd 3 prt sw 21 hrw n ḥb n ḫ'w,*[36] "regnal year 1, third month of *proyet,* day 21; the day of the festival of appearance": *Urk.* IV, 81.

(104) *tpy šmw sw 4 ḥb ḫ'w-nsw n nsw-bit Mn-ḫpr-r' 'nḫ ḏt,* "first month of *shomu,* day 4; festival of the royal appearance of the king of Upper and Lower Egypt Menkheperre, living for ever": *Urk.* IV, 177; cf. *Urk,* IV, 648.

(105) *ḥ3t-sp 23 3bd 4 3ḫt sw* 1 *hrw n ḥb ḫ't-nsw,*[36] "regnal year 23, fourth month of *akhet,* day 1; the day of the festival of the royal appearance": W. Helck, *JNES* 14 (1955), Pl. 2.

The passage cited in no. 102 is of Fifth Dynasty date and supports the view, mooted above, that in the Old Kingdom a "festival of (royal) appearance"[58] was not necessarily commemorative of the coronation. The fact that several such festivals are alluded to here indicates that a fairly large number might occur in the reign of one king.

The remaining examples have to do with the anniversary of the date of accession. The date in no. 104, viz. ix, 4, is precisely that of Thutmose III's accession; and the date of no. 105, viz. iv, 1, is known to be the first day of each of Amenhotpe II's regnal years, and hence the date of his accession.[59] By most scholars it is accepted that the date of no. 103 is that of Thutmose I's accession. Thus there is a good deal of likelihood that when a "festival of royal appearance" is mentioned in New Kingdom texts, the anniversary of the accession is intended.[60]

In summary, the results obtained are as follows. It is clear that in a large number of cases the contexts in which *ḫ'y* is used are too vague to permit a decision as to whether the reference is to a coronation or an accession. The tripartite formula frequently found (see

[58] The context seems to indicate that the *ḫ'w* referred to is that of the king and not of a god.

[59] In the case of Amenhotpe II the picture is clouded by the fact that he may have enjoyed a short coregency with his father, and perhaps commenced dating by his own regnal years while his father was still alive. For a discussion, see *JEA* 51 (1965), 107ff.

[60] Helck, *Studia Biblica et Orientalia,* III, 113.

p. 19) could conceivably allude to any of the following: (1) a ceremony that took place on the accession day, (2) a coronation subsequent to the accession, or (3) any number of subsequent festivals throughout a reign at which the king "appeared." There are, however, a sizable number of examples that can refer only to the act of accession. In a few, *ḫ'y* (or *ḫ't*) seems to be used of the reign itself. It has further been shown to be likely that, where *ḫ'y* is used in a context in which a coronation is described, its use derives from the well-attested employment of *ḫ'y* to denote a festal appearance of a god. It has nothing to do with the act of crowning, and should not be paraphrased by the English word "coronation." The initial (formal) coronation of the king may have followed some little time after the accession, but there is no reason to assume that this was a general rule, or that the coronation could not take place on the day of accession. That is not to deny that the elaborate ritual that had to be performed at every accession lasted long after the first day of the new king's reign. But one should not confuse this ritual with the modern rite of coronation as exemplified, say, in the British monarchy. Finally, as is clearly shown by the examples in sections 5 and 6, *ḫ'w-nsw* and *ḥb n ḫ'w* in the New Kingdom denote exclusively the act and the day of accession, and have nothing to do with the concept of coronation per se.

2

The Family of Ahmose: The Seventeenth Dynasty

This chapter contains a discussion of the Seventeenth Dynasty under three headings: (1) the number and identity of its members; (2) the length of the rule of the dynasty; and (3) the date of the expulsion of the Hyksos.

A discussion of the history and chronology of the Eighteenth Dynasty necessarily involves the Seventeenth, for two reasons. First, the royal family of the two dynasties is the same: Ahmose, the king who in Manetho's lists stands at the head of the Eighteenth, is a full-blooded scion of the Seventeenth. Manetho has placed him at the head of a new dynasty only because he put an end to Hyksos rule in Egypt and inaugurated a period of independence. It has been pointed out, however, that if Manetho had to make a break somewhere in the royal line, he could have done so with some justification before Thutmose I, since this king was probably not a son of his predecessor Amenhotpe I and his chief wife.[1] The second reason for discussing the Seventeenth Dynasty is that the event with which the Eighteenth

[1] K. Sethe, *ZÄS* 36 (1898), 25ff.; *idem, Thronwirren*, §73; *idem, APAW* (1932), no. 4, 9; Bilabel, *Geschichte*, 14, n. 1; cf. Meyer, *Geschichte*, II, 1, 76 and A. Scharff, *Ägypten und Vorderasien* (Munich, 1950), 123. The tradition that places Ahmose at the head of a new line seems to be at least as old as the Nineteenth Dynasty; cf. S. Sauneron, *CdE* 26 (1951), 46ff.

Dynasty begins, viz. the war against the Hyksos, is not confined to the reign of Ahmose, but began early in the Seventeenth Dynasty, and, as the Egyptians themselves represented it, continued to be prosecuted well into the reign of Thutmose III.[2] The triumph of Ahmose marks nothing more than the culmination of the first stage of the conflict.

1. The number and identity of the members of the Seventeenth Dynasty

What Manetho intended by his Seventeenth Dynasty—what kings he included in it and how many years he allotted them—is, at least on the evidence of his epitomizers, impossible to determine. According to Africanus the Seventeenth Dynasty consisted of forty-three shepherds and forty-three kings of Thebes (ruling simultaneously?) and lasted for 151 years.[3] Eusebius[4] has shifted the Hyksos from the Fifteenth to the Seventeenth Dynasty, mentioning Salatis, Bnon, Archles, and Apophis as belonging to the latter, without making any reference to the Thebans. The number of years for the Hyksos given by Eusebius, viz. 103, is sufficiently close to the 108 years allotted to the *ḥqȝw-ḫȝswt* in the Turin papyrus[5] to arrest attention, and is perhaps connected in some way with this datum. While there is doubtless some information of value regarding the Hyksos dynasty in this misplaced passage of Eusebius, his work is worthless in the present investigation. Africanus, on the other hand, is too brief and too garbled to be of any help. The Turin canon, whose testimony for the Seventeenth Dynasty would have been most valuable, is almost totally lost at this point. Thus, since no reliable king lists are available, the monuments must serve as our sole guide in reconstructing the Seventeenth Dynasty.

2 K. Sethe, *ZÄS* 47 (1910), 73ff.

3 Waddell, *Manetho,* 94.

4 *Ibid.,* 94ff. Eusebius, by assigning Salatis and the others to the Seventeenth Dynasty, has clearly made an attempt to bring the Hyksos down closer to the beginning of the Eighteenth Dynasty; his own Fifteenth Dynasty, from which he has removed the Hyksos, thus becomes wholly artificial; cf. E. Meyer, *Ägyptische Chronologie* (Berlin, 1904), 84.

5 X, 21; see G. Farina, *Il Papiro dei Re Restaurato* (Rome, 1938), Pl. X, p. 56; also A. H. Gardiner, *The Royal Canon of Turin* (Oxford, 1959), Pl. III. For a discussion of the figures given in Manetho for the period of the Hyksos, see Gardiner, *JEA* 5 (1918), 43, n. 6.

The ancestry of Ahmose on the distaff side, in contrast to the males of the line, is easily reconstructed. The pertinent information is supplied by the stela erected by Ahmose at Abydos to commemorate his construction of a cenotaph for his grandmother.[6] In line 8 of this text the king, in answer to his wife, says: "I indeed have remembered the mother of my mother, the mother of my[7] father, the great king's wife, king's mother Tetyshery (in cartouche)." Since from other documents[8] Ahmose's mother is known to have been Ahhotpe, the following genealogy is certain:[9]

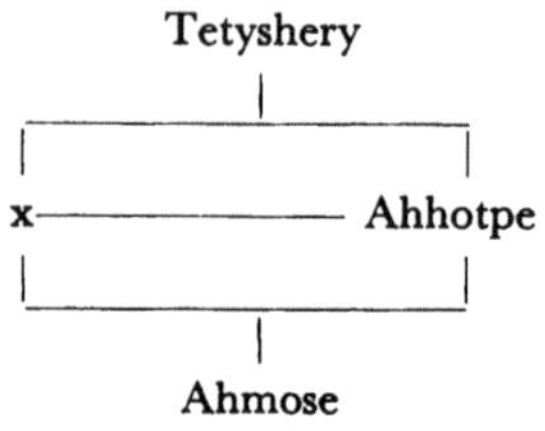

Ahmose's ancestry was carried back one generation further when in 1908 Daressy published his discovery of the mummy bandages of Tetyshery.[10] On these her parents were given as Čenna and Neferu, both of whom bore lowly titles[11] and were clearly commoners. That Tetyshery represented the first generation of the female line from which Ahmose sprang is scarcely to be doubted. The purity of descent to which the queens of the Eighteenth Dynasty could lay claim[12]

6 See Gauthier, *Livre,* II, 159 (III) for bibliography.

7 The cutter omitted  after *it,* whether intentionally or unintentionally is hard to tell; in any case the sense is clear, and the present translation is the only one possible.

8 Cf. the stela of Yuf: P. Lacau, *Stèles du Nouvel Empire* (*CCG* [Cairo, 1909–26]), Pl 6, line 2.

9 It was drawn up long ago and no subsequent discoveries have in any way modified it; cf. G. Daressy, *ASAE* 9 (1909), 137; R. Weill, *JA* (1910), 561; Gauthier, *Livre,* II, 159, n. 2.

10 *ASAE* 9 (1909), 137f.; for photographs of the bandages, see M. A. Murray, *Ancient Egypt* (1934), 67f. (Fig. 4, A–C).

11 Neferu was a *nbt pr*, and Čenna a *s'b.*

12 Would this be a fictitious claim? Was the unbroken succession historical, or was it ever interrupted? In the inscription from Karnak in which Ahmose gives the office of second prophet of Amun to his wife Ahmose-Nofretari, the latter is made to state: "he (the king) clothed me when I was a nobody (*iw nn wny.t*), he

continued throughout seven generations at least, from Tetyshery to Hatshepsut II,[13] and perhaps longer. When the earliest known member of the line is found to have been of low birth, we may well suspect that we are not only at the beginning of the reginal descent, but at the beginning of the royal line itself; in other words, we may suspect that Tetyshery's husband, whoever he was, was a commoner himself before he assumed the cartouches. Admittedly the truth of the last statement is doubtful in view of the scarcity of evidence, but it may well be that the hiatus in the line of Theban kings caused by the Hyksos advance into Upper Egypt was followed by a completely new family of kings.[14]

---

made me powerful when I was poor (*nḥm.kwt*)": E. Drioton, *BSFE* 12 (1953), Pl. facing p. 11; A. Hariri, *ASAE* 56 (1959), Pl. facing p. 202, lines 19–20. *Nn wny.i*, lit. "I did not exist," finds a semantic parallel in *iwty sw*, "a non-entity, pauper": Gardiner, *Grammar*³, 203:2. For *nmḥ*, "poor man," as the designation of one of the lowest (free) social classes, as well as its adjectival use to indicate poverty in general, see the references in R. A. Caminos, *Late Egyptian Miscellanies* (Oxford, 1954), 10; W. Helck, *Zur Verwaltung des mittleren und neuen Reichs* (Leiden, 1958), 122f.; Hariri, *op. cit.*, 178. The question is: Are these expressions in some way rhetorical or hyperbolic? Do they reflect a historical situation otherwise unattested? Or must we conclude that Ahmose-Nofretari was of low birth and station before her marriage to Ahmose? In the latter case the title which she bears *passim*, "king's daughter" (Gauthier, *Livre*, II, 183ff.), would have to be taken in the same way as "king's son" in about the same period of Egyptian history, viz. as the designation of a close relationship between the king and its bearer, though not a blood relationship. In Ahmose-Nofretari's case the title would indicate an adoption into the royal house, in consequence of which the queenly line could at least be represented as unbroken. On the other hand it is equally possible, and perhaps more probable, that the queen's words should be rendered "when I was orphaned" (for *nmḥ*, "to be an orphan," see *Wb* II, 268: 14f.; R. O. Faulkner, *A Concise Dictionary of Middle Egyptian* [Oxford, 1962], 133). Thus her statement would hark back to the reversal of her own and her family's fortunes on the death of Taʿo II, at which time she may well have suffered financial impoverishment (cf. H. Kees, *Das Priestertum im ägyptischen Staat vom neuen Reich bis zur Spätzeit* [Leiden, 1953], 5), but it would *not* be an indication of plebeian birth.

[13] It is denied by some that Hatshepsut II belongs to this line: *HSE* II, 128.

[14] There is no evidence that the kings—not to mention the queens (*pace* P. E. Newberry, *PSBA* 24 [1902], 285ff.)—of the Seventeenth Dynasty were directly related to the Sobkhotpes and the Antefs of the Thirteenth and Sixteenth Dynasties. The New Kingdom royal lists are against such a connexion (see n. 27, below), since they frequently omit kings of the Second Intermediate Period prior to Seqenenre.

Who were the father and grandfather of Ahmose? To the knowledge of the present writer they are mentioned by name nowhere in Ahmose's inscriptions. There is, however, a fairly large group of texts that mention royal persons who must be dated shortly before the time of Ahmose, and some of whom were undoubtedly his immediate ancestors.

The husband of Ahhotpe, Ahmose's mother, is named on the statue of Prince Ahmose.[15] An inscription on the plinth of the statue calls for "invocation offerings of bread, beer, beef, and fowl and every good thing on which the god lives, for the *ka* of the eldest king's son Ahmose, deceased." Flanking this central column are two shorter vertical columns of inscription. The one on the right reads: "it is the great king's daughter,[16] the beautiful one who is joined to the white crown[17] Ahhotpe, who makes his name to live"; and the column on the left is identical save for the substitution of "the good god, son of Re Taʿo (in cartouche), living eternally" in place of Ahhotpe and her titles. A similar inscription on the right side of the throne proclaims that "it is his sister who causes his name to live, the great king's daughter[16] Ahmose." While the fact that Ahhotpe and the girl Ahmose share the title "great king's daughter" might lead one to suppose that they were sisters, the position of Ahhotpe's name opposite that of Taʿo, as well as the fact that she is a queen, shows clearly that she is Taʿo's wife.[18] Taʿo, then, must be (King) Ahmose's father and, like his wife, a child of Tetyshery.

The name Taʿo is accompanied in many contemporary inscriptions by the praenomen Seqenenre.[19] Because of this fact some scholars have postulated that there was a single king Seqenenre Taʿo,

[15] U. Bouriant, *RT* 11 (1889), 159; bibliography in Gauthier, *Livre,* II, 159 (11), and H. E. Winlock, *JEA* 10 (1924), 255, n. 6; photo, *ibid.*, Pl. 18–20, and C. Aldred, *New Kingdom Art in Ancient Egypt* (London, 1951), Pl. 2.

[16] *Sꜣt-nsw wrt;* on this rare title, see *Wb* III, 412:4.

[17] *H̱nmt ḥḏt nfr* (?): *Wb* III, 378:20.

[18] R. Weill, *JA* (1910), 561f.; G. Maspero, *Les Momies royales de Déir el-Bahari* (Cairo, 1884), 625ff.; *idem, Histoire,* II, 78. Gauthier makes Ahhotpe the daughter of Taʿo (*Livre,* II, 159); but see Winlock, *JEA* 10 (1924), 256, n. 1.

[19] Gauthier, *Livre,* II, 156ff.

husband of Ahhotpe and father of Ahmose.[20] By far the majority of nineteenth-century scholars, however, distinguished three Taʿos, at least two of whom bore the praenomen Seqenenre.[21] Partial support for this view was found in the occasional inclusion, within the cartouche of the nomen, of the epithets "great (*ʿꜣ*)" and "brave (*qn*)," and Papyrus Abbott, with its specific reference to the tombs of two kings named Seqenenre Taʿo,[22] could always be cited as more concrete proof that there were more Taʿos than one. However, the hypothesis that there were three Taʿos will not stand the test. The epithets sometimes added to the nomen are not a valid criterion.[23] For a given royal name of the Eighteenth Dynasty one might just as easily distinguish two kings solely on the basis of the presence or absence within the cartouche of such epithets as "ruler of Thebes (*ḥqꜣ Wꜣst*)" or "ruler of Heliopolis (*ḥqꜣ 'Iwnw*)." It is a fact that during the Seventeenth and early Eighteenth Dynasties neither the epithets nor the titulary of a king were rigidly fixed. Kamose, in fact, employed two and perhaps three epithets, which at times took the place of his personal name in the second cartouche.[24] But there is no reason whatsoever to postulate that there were three kings named Kamose!

The evidence of the Abbott papyrus is far more solid. The scribe of this document records that a group of inspectors during the reign of Ramses IX visited *inter alia* two tombs belonging to two kings named Seqenenre Taʿo. The fact struck the scribe as being so singular that he noted specifically that two kings Taʿo were involved.[25]

[20] Weill, *JA* (1910), 577; hesitantly, K. C. Seele, *When Egypt Ruled the East* (2nd ed., Chicago, 1957), 28f.; L. Borchardt, *ZÄS* 50 (1912), 120; Gardiner, *JEA* 5 (1918), 43, n. 3; Drioton-Vandier, *L'Egypte*[4], 298f., 330.

[21] Gauthier, *Livre*, II. 156ff.; Maspero, *Histoire*, II, 78 (but cf. 76, n. 2); Meyer, *Geschichte*, II. 1, 47f.; W. M. F. Petrie, *History*, II, 5ff.; Wiedemann, *Geschichte*, 300ff.

[22] Papyrus Abbott, III: 8ff.; T. E. Peet, *The Great Tomb Robberies* (Oxford, 1930), II, Pl. 2.

[23] Winlock, *JEA* 10 (1924), 244.

[24] *Ibid.*, 264; on the supposed epithet "ruler of the south" (*ḥqꜣ rsi*), see Weill, *BIFAO* 32 (1932), 48 (with figure).

[25] Papyrus Abbott III: 10; Peet, *The Great Tomb Robberies*, II, Pl. 2.

Present-day scholars have been more influenced by this passage than their predecessors, and nearly all of them concede the existence of two Taʿos.[26] The concession, moreover, removes the difficulty of having to fit the two generations of queens to three generations of kings: Tetyshery and Ahhotpe can now take their places as the consorts of Taʿo I and Taʿo II respectively. But while it is not at all unusual to have successive rulers bearing the same personal name, it is strange that their praenomina should be the same. The royal lists of the New Kingdom name only one Seqenenre Taʿo,[27] and only one king of this name is represented by a sarcophagus and mummy in the Deir el-Bahri cache.[28] A praenomen that occurs sporadically in the lists and must be assigned to the Seventeenth Dynasty is Senakhtenre.[29] On the offering table in Marseilles,[30] which contains the most orderly of the New Kingdom lists with the exception of the Abydos and Memphis canons, Senakhtenre stands immediately before Seqenenre. He is also the earliest king mentioned on the table. This is of importance, because the author of the document seems to be interested in tracing back the fictitious "line" of Eighteenth and Nineteenth Dynasty kings no farther than the founder of the Seventeenth Dynasty. These facts, noted first by Daressy,[31] and

[26] M. Alliot, *JNES* 9 (1950), 209; A. H. Gardiner, *Egypt of the Pharaohs* (Oxford, 1961), 163; *HSE* II, 9; A. Scharff, *Ägypten und Vorderasien im Altertum* (Munich, 1950), 119; J. Vandier, *JS* (1944), 167; Winlock, *JEA* 10 (1924), 245; *idem, The Rise and Fall of the Middle Kingdom in Thebes* (New York, 1947), 149. Hayes (ch. 2 of *CAH* II [1962], 32ff.) postulates a Senakhtenre *and* two Seqenenres. Meyer (*Geschichte*, II, 1, 47) makes the two Taʿos brothers, a logical conclusion if the epithet *ʿ3* is to be translated "elder."

[27] List of Khabakhent (*LD* III, Pl. 2a; P–M I[2], 7), no. 3; list of Anhurkhaou (*LD* III, Pl. 2d; P–M I[2], 422), bottom no. 5; list of Arğanen (P–M I[2], 384), top no. 2; Marseilles offering table (H. K. Brugsch, *Monatsberichte Berlin Akad.* [1858]), no. 2; Karnak list of Thutmose III (J. Prisse, *Rev. Arch.* 2 [1845], Pl. 23), left, 4th register, no. 7. Strictly speaking, none of these are lists, but rather rows of statues arranged for the reception of offerings in a mortuary cult. Nevertheless their orderliness reflects, and is doubtless derived from, a true king-list.

[28] Maspero, *Les Momies royales . . .*, 527ff.

[29] Karnak list of Thutmose III (see n. 27), left, 4th register, no. 6; Gauthier *Livre*, II, 168f.

[30] For bibliography, see n. 27 above and also Gauthier, *Livre*, II, 162 (V).

[31] *RT* 13 (1890), 146.

elaborated upon by Winlock,[32] support the conclusions: (a) that Taʿo I's praenomen was Senakhtenre, which could have been confused by the scribe of papyrus Abbott with the very similar Seqenenre, and (b) that Senakhtenre Taʿo I was the founder of the house of the Seventeenth Dynasty.[33] The resultant family tree is generally accepted today as:

Senakhtenre Taʿo I — Tetyshery

|

Seqenenre Taʿo II — Ahhotpe

|

Nebpehtetre Ahmose

Of the remaining royal names which must be assigned to the Seventeenth Dynasty, only that of Kamose remains to be discussed.[34] Two problems centre around this name: first, how many kings bore it, and second, what is his (or their) position in the dynasty? Since the unity or plurality of the kings "Kamose" must first be decided, we begin with this problem.

The personal name Kamose (in cartouche) is found on various monuments in conjunction with three different Horus names. This strange phenomenon has given rise to the theory that there were two

[32] *JEA* 10 (1924), 221; *contra* H. Stock, *Studien zur Geschichte und Archaeologie der 13. bis 17. Dynastie Ägyptens* (Äg. Forsch. 12 [Gluckstadt, 1942]), 76 and 78, who seems to believe that Seqenenre is the original and Senakhtenre corrupt.

[33] A name Sekhentnebre (in cartouche) is found in the list of Khabakhent (bottom, no. 3) between Kamose and Ahmose (for bibliography see n. 27 above). Maspero believed that he was a "secondary king" reigning about the time of Seqenenre or Ahmose (*Les Momies royales . . .*, 638f.; *Histoire*, II, 77, n. 4 of p. 76). Daressy ingeniously identified Sekhentnebre with Senakhtenre, the former name, according to him, having arisen from a bad heiratic transcription of the latter: *RT* 13 (1890), 146; *Recueil d'études égyptol. dédiées à la mémoire de Champollion* (Bibliothèque de l'Ecole des Hautes Etudes, 234 [1922]), 291.

[34] On Sekhentnebre, see preceding note. The Kheper-ka-re of the Karnak list (left, 4th register, no. 8) and the list of Chester Beatty, IX (A. H. Gardiner, *Hieratic Papyri in the British Museum, Third Series* [London, 1935], Pl. 55), who follows the kings of the Seventeenth Dynasty, I take to be Sesostris I of the Twelfth Dynasty.

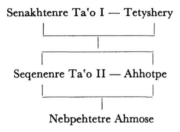

(*sic!*) kings named Kamose.[35] The distribution of the Horus names becomes clearer when the information available is presented in tabular form (see Table I). That the two stelae (II and IV) come

TABLE I

	I *Kamose's inscription from Ahhotpe cache*[36]	II *Stela and Carnarvon tablet*[37]	III *Karnak base*[38]	IV *New stela*[39]
Praenomen				
W3ḏ-ḫpr-rʿ	×	×[40]		×
Horus names				
Sḏf3-t3wy	×			
Ḫʿ-ḥr-nst.f		×		
Nfr-ḫ3b-t3wy			×	
Nbty name				
Wḥm-mnw		×	×	
Golden Horus				
Shr-t3wy		×		
Personal name				
K3-msi	×	×	×	×

[35] Gauthier, *Livre*, II, 169, n. 7, and *Griffith Studies* (London, 1932), 3ff.; also Weill, *JA* (1910), 567f, *JA* (1913), 538, and *Recueil . . . Champollion*, 35. I cannot see that the positions of Weill and Gauthier are logically sound: if three distinct Horus names exist, why not postulate that there were three kings? But if it is admitted that one of the two Kamose's could have changed his Horus name midway through his reign, is it not conceivable that he might have changed it a second time? Weill later conceded the possibility that there were three kings Kamose (*BIFAO* 32 [1932], 51), but his indecision in the whole problem was, and is still, an embarrassment to those who would espouse his theory. It is strange to note that even after the discovery of the second Kamose stela Montet can still seriously weigh the possibility that there was more than one Kamose: *CRAIBL* (1956), 119.

[36] W. von Bissing, *Ein thebanischer Grabfund aus dem Anfang des neuen Reichs* (Berlin, 1900); earlier bibliography in Maspero, *Histoire*, II, 95, n. 6; Daressy, *ASAE* 21 (1921), 129ff.; Gauthier, *Livre*, II, 165f.

[37] Gardiner, *JEA* 3 (1916), 95ff. (with plates); Lacau, *ASAE* 39 (1939), 245ff. (with Pl. 37).

[38] H. Chévrier, *ASAE* 29 (1928), 136; photos in H. Gauthier, *Griffith Studies*, Pl. Ia and Weill, *BIFAO* 32 (1932), Pl. IV.

[39] M. Hammad, *CdE* 30 (1955), 198ff., Fig. 15; L. Habachi, *ASAE* 53 (1956), 195ff., plate facing p. 202.

[40] Gardiner, *JEA* 3 (1916), 97; Lacau, *ASAE* 39 (1939), 263.

from the reign of the same king is strongly suggested by the following considerations: (a) the praenomen *Wꜣǧ-ḫpr-rʿ* is found on both; (b) IV is clearly the continuation of another text, and fits on to II nicely;[41] (c) the method of cutting and colouring of signs is the same in both stelae;[42] (d) in both texts the name "Kamose" is written curiously with the sign  ;[43] (e) both inscriptions are largely narrations by the king in the first person; (f) the air of braggadocio pervading II is found throughout IV also. The Kamose of I is also to be identified with the Kamose of the stelae. Not only is his praenomen again *Wꜣǧ-ḫpr-rʿ*, but at least in some cases his personal name shows an accompanying  ,[44] which must be an abbreviation of  .[45] The Kamose of III remains. Unfortunately his praenomen is missing (if it ever was included), and the extant cartouche does not contain  . But his *nbty*-name, *Wḥm-mnw*, is identical with that of II, and the shape and cutting of the hieroglyphs have marked affinities with those of the two stelae. In short, there is every likelihood that the Kamose of III is the same as the Kamose of I, II, and IV.[46]

Once again the conclusion that there was but one Kamose is not new. It was drawn long ago, and has continued to be held by nearly all scholars, in spite of the ingenuity of Weill and Gauthier.

The problems connected with Kamose are singular in that, while not one piece of conclusive evidence is known, enough circumstantial evidence is at hand to force a single, clear-cut conclusion in all cases. The truth of this assertion is no more apparent than in the problem of assigning a place to Kamose in the Seventeenth Dynasty. No monument known at present gives the names of Kamose's parents,

41 The end of the extant portion of II finds Kamose at Nefrusi just north of Hermopolis, in Middle Egypt; the opening of IV is obscure, but Kamose has penetrated at least as far north as the Faiyum, and is probably within sight of Avaris; see Montet, *CRAIBL* (1956), 114ff.

42 Habachi, *ASAE* 53 (1956), 199.

43 For II, see Lacau, *ASAE* 39 (1939), Pl. 37, line 11; for IV, see Habachi, *ASAE* 53 (1956), plate facing p. 202, lines 21 and 34; in line 24 the praenomen *Wꜣǧ-ḫpr-rʿ* is also accompanied by this sign.

44 E.g. the "lance head" (really a sword?): Gauthier, *Livre*, II, 165 (I); Weill, *JA* (1910), 565; Winlock, *JEA* 10 (1924), 263.

45 Lacau, *ASAE* 39 (1939), 266.

46 The alternative—accepted by Gauthier (*Griffith Studies*, 8)—is that there were two Kamoses with almost identical titulary, whose reigns were virtually consecutive. Gauthier makes his two Kamose's brothers!

wife, or offspring; but the evidence, such as it is, points only one way. This evidence will now be tabulated. (1) On the Marseilles offering table[47] the praenomen *W3ǧ-ḫpr-rʿ* occurs between Seqenenre and Ahmose.[48] (2) The party of inspectors, whose perambulations are described in the Abbott papyrus, visited the tomb of Kamose after those of the two Taʿos.[49] If the order of tombs in this papyrus is significant, as Winlock believes, the position of Kamose's tomb in the necropolis may reflect his position in the dynasty. (3) A graffito from Toshke[50] places the nomen and praenomen of Kamose "given life" beside the nomen and praenomen of Ahmose.[51] (4) Both Kamose and Ahmose contributed grave goods to the burial of queen Ahhotpe.[52] (5) Ahmose apparently buried Kamose since articles bearing his cartouche seem to have been found in Kamose's coffin.[53]

Only one conclusion is possible: Kamose succeeded Taʿo II and was an immediate predecessor of Ahmose. Only this hypothesis will satisfy all the facts. He could have been a brother of Taʿo II, but more likely, in view of the structure of his name, he was a brother of Ahmose.[54] The following genealogy is the one generally accepted

[47] See bibliography in n. 27 above.

[48] The ubiquitous Nebhepetre (Montuhotpe II) immediately precedes Ahmose, but this of course implies no chronological proximity, Montuhotpe II and Ahmose are grouped together in New Kingdom lists merely because they accomplished similar feats, viz. reunification of a divided land. In the list of Chester Beatty, IX, Kamose occurs just before Ahmose (see reference in n. 34 above). The position of Kamose in other lists does not appear to be significant: in the Arǧanen list he occurs between two queens, Ahmose and Sentsonb, and in the Khabakhent list he turns up between "Sekhentnebre" and Prince Binpou. For references see n. 27 above.

[49] Papyrus Abbott, III: 12; Winlock, *JEA* 10 (1924), 222 and 262.

[50] P–M VII, 95; T. Säve-Söderbergh, *Kush*, 4 (1956), 57 and n. 14.

[51] Until such time as the graffito is examined carefully, it is impossible to state whether the two sets of cartouches were carved at the same time; see Säve-Söderbergh, *ibid.* Hence the present writer would reserve judgment on Griffith's belief (*AAAL* 8 [1921], 6; quoted by A. J. Arkell, *A Short History of the Sudan to 1821* [2nd ed., London, 1961], 80) that Ahmose was associated with his brother as successor-designate while the latter was alive.

[52] Winlock, *JEA* 10 (1924), 254.

[53] Daressy, *ASAE* 12 (1912), 64ff.

[54] Weill, *JA* (1910), 565f., *JA* (1917), 141; Winlock, *JEA* 10 (1924), 262; Daressy, *ASAE* 12 (1912), 68. Like so many other sound conclusions regarding the history of this period, this was the product of Maspero's research in *Les Momies royales . . .* (628f.).

by modern scholarship, and there seems to be still no reason to modify it:

Senakhtenre Ta'o I — Tetyshery

Seqenenre Ta'o II — Ahhotpe

(prince) Ahmose(†) | (princess) Ahmose | Kamose | Ahmose I

2. The Length of the Rule of the Seventeenth Dynasty

There is very little evidence by which to determine the length of rule of the Seventeenth Dynasty. Only one dated contemporary text is known (the first Kamose stela), and apart from the fantastic figure of 151 years given in Africanus, no canon of kings offers us any figure, reliable or otherwise. Again the discussion is forced back on scattered pieces of circumstantial evidence; but each piece, it will be seen, harmonizes with the others to present a reliable index to the approximate length of the dynasty.

(1) *The Seventeenth Dynasty embraces two human generations.* This has already been noted above. Tetyshery, the founder of the line of Eighteenth Dynasty queens, was the grandmother of Ahmose. It has been demonstrated that she probably marks the generation contemporary with the coming to power of the Seventeenth Dynasty.

(2) *Tetyshery, wife of the founder of the Seventeenth Dynasty, survived into the early years of the Eighteenth.* Winlock was the first to publish evidence that Tetyshery was still alive in the early years of Ahmose's reign.[55] This evidence is in the form of a stela, purchased by Petrie, which shows clear traces of "the king's mother Tetyshery (in cartouche)" behind her grandson. The stela once contained a date, but the year number is now destroyed. Winlock[56] conjectured that the year was an early one, and he is probably right. There is no evidence, however, that Tetyshery lived to see the Hyksos expelled,

55 *Ancient Egypt* (1921), 14ff.; for a photo see M. A. Murray, *ibid.* (1934), 67, Fig. 3.

56 *Ancient Egypt* (1921), 16.

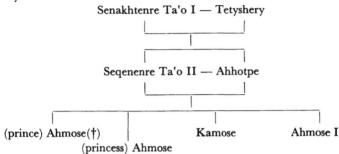

as Winlock also believes.[57] He bases his belief on a papyrus of farm accounts from the early Eighteenth Dynasty, published by Erman,[58] which mentions an "estate (*pr*)" of Tetyshery. Since the papyrus is said to have come from a village of Abusir, and since the only villages named Abusir seem to lie north of the Faiyum in the Memphite area, the estate in question could have been given to Tetyshery only after the apex of the delta was in Theban hands, i.e. after the Hyksos were expelled. But it is impossible to check the true provenience of the papyrus; it may well have been brought to the Memphite region (if it really was found there) from some other part of Egypt. Moreover, is it so improbable that this was an estate of Tetyshery's mortuary temple, bequeathed to her cult after her death? However, one need not resort to such a priori arguments. The new Kamose stela makes it plain that even before Ahmose's time the Hyksos were already confined to the delta. The estate could easily have been bestowed on the dowager queen during Kamose's reign.

(3) *Seqenenre Taʿo II was killed (or murdered) in the prime of life, between the ages of thirty and forty.*[59] It would seem likely, *ipso facto,* that he did not enjoy a long reign. But since there is no indication at what age he came to the throne—he may have been only a child—this fact is of itself of little use. It is unknown how many, if any, of his children, who numbered at least five, were born before he acceded to the throne.

(4) *The highest known date for Kamose is regnal year 3.*[60] Kamose has left relatively few monuments, and his make-shift burial shows that

[57] *Ibid.,* 14ff.

[58] *ZÄS* 37 (1900), 150ff.

[59] Maspero, *Les Momies royales . . .,* 528; see Winlock, *JEA* 10 (1924), 249, n. 2 for other references.

[60] Carnarvon tablet, 1; Karnak stela, 1 (references in n. 37 above). The date on the stela—note the form 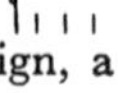 and cf. Lacau's remarks in *ASAE* 39 (1939), 249f.—is carved *over* an *ʿnḫ*-sign, a fact which explains the absence of *ḥr ḥm n,* "under the majesty of". Thus when the text was first carved no thought was given to the date of the exploit; the author intended nothing more than a simple *vivat.* At some later time, however, it was deemed desirable to supply a date to the inscription. Perhaps this is an indication of the growing realization among the Thebans that, now that the Hyksos rule had been permanently repudiated, they themselves were truly independent, and were justified in dating events by the regnal years of their own king. Even though the text does not specify year 3 as the date of the campaign, there can scarcely be any doubt that this is what it refers to.

death came suddenly and unexpectedly.[61] It is not certain that he left any children on his death, or in fact that he had even taken a queen.[62] The six years allotted him by Petrie[63] must be viewed as a maximum estimate. In actual fact he probably did not long survive his famous campaign against the Hyksos, which seems to have taken place in his third regnal year.[64] Ahmose-si-Abina of El Kab does not mention Kamose at all, but passes directly from Seqenenre, under whom his father served, to Ahmose I.[65]

(5) *Awoserre Apophis, who once held Upper Egypt as far as Gebelein,*[66] *i.e. before the rise of the Seventeenth Dynasty, was still on the throne at the end of Kamose's reign.* The position of Apophis in the list of Hyksos kings, even the order of the list itself, has always been a subject for debate. The Manethonian sources show slight confusion. In Josephus[67] the order of the first six Hyksos rulers is given as Salatis, Bnon, Apachnan, Apophis, Iannas, and Assis. Africanus[68] records substantially the same six in his Fifteenth Dynasty in the following order: Saites, Bnon, Pachnan, Staan (=Iannas), Archles (=Assis?), and Apophis. Eusebius,[69] who seems to have used Africanus or a source used by Africanus as a base, names only four of these kings,

[61] Winlock, *JEA* 10 (1924), 262.

[62] At first glance the "god's-wife Sat-Kamose (in cartouche)" of the Khabakhent list (top row, no. 10) might appear to be a daughter of Kamose, or perhaps a granddaughter (see Maspero, *Les Momies royales* . . ., 629); but in fact nothing is known regarding her parentage; see also Daressy, *Recueil . . . Champollion*, 295. The supposition that Ahmose-Nofretari was at one time Kamose's queen (Maspero, *Histoire*, II, 78) also lacks proof, and is opposed by the gist of Ahmose's donation stela from Karnak; see n. 12 above.

[63] Petrie, *History*, II, 15.

[64] See above, n. 60.

[65] V. Loret, *L'Inscription d'Ahmès fils d'Abana* (Bibliothèque d'Etudes, 3 [Cairo, 1910], 1, lines 4–5.

[66] Daressy, *RT* 14 (1892), 26; Weill, *JA* (1911), 13; Gauthier, *Livre*, II, 140 (III). Von Bissing has always refused to believe that the Hyksos ever held Upper Egypt (see *AfO* 11 [1936], 328, n. 13; *OLZ* 47 [1944], 90; Gardiner was at one time inclined towards the same view: *JEA* 3 [1916], 110); yet he has not offered a single convincing argument as to how traces of their occupation got to the upper portions of the valley. His explanation of the Gebelein blocks which bear the names of Khayan and Apophis—"Die Stücke aus Gebelein . . . werden wohl verschleppt sein"—is weak in the extreme.

[67] *Contra Apionem*, I, 14, §§79–81.

[68] Waddell, *Manetho*, 90.

[69] *Ibid.*, 94ff.

and assigns them to his Seventeenth Dynasty; his order is as follows: Saites, Bnon, Archles, and Apophis.[70] It will be seen at once that the only major difference between Josephus and Africanus here is the position of Apophis: the former puts him fourth, the latter sixth. Most scholars have placed greater confidence in Josephus than in Africanus, since he claims to quote from Manetho, and most likely had the Aegyptiaca (or parts thereof) before him.[71] Christian or Jewish chronography, which is reflected in Africanus, removed Apophis, it is claimed, to the end of the list in order better to accommodate Jewish presuppositions regarding the chronology of the Israelite sojourn.[72] Apophis is connected specifically with the patriarch Joseph (and *ipso facto*) with the beginning of the sojourn) in a tradition preserved in Syncellus,[73] which undoubtedly had its origins in Hellenistic times. According to this tradition Joseph came to Egypt as a slave in Apophis's fourth regnal year, and was made ruler of Egypt in his seventeenth year. But as Erman pointed out, long ago,[74] whoever computed these dates had before him *already* a version of Manetho in which Apophis stood last in the list of Hyksos rulers. We must reckon, then, with two ancient variants of Manetho, neither of which can be evaluated properly without referring to older, i.e archaeological, sources.

The Turin canon is very fragmentary in column X, where the names of the Hyksos rulers once occurred, but what has been preserved is helpful. The total is haply intact and reads: "[Total rulers] of foreign lands, 6; they ruled 108[75] years" (X: 21). It is thus clear that the Manethonian tradition of six kings goes back at least as far as the Nineteenth Dynasty, the date of the Turin canon, and probably much earlier. The one name preserved in the canon, however. *Ḫ3mwdy*, the last of the six, corresponds to none of the names in

[70] The order Syncellus gives (*ibid.*, 96), which inserts Apophis before Archles, I take to be a corruption of Eusebius's original list. The Armenian version and the Book of Sothis both assign Apophis to the fourth and last position.

[71] R. Laqueur, *apud* Pauly-Wissowa-Kroll, *Real-Encyclopedia der classischen Altertumswissenschaft* (Stuttgart, 1928), 27, col. 1064ff.; see esp. 1087.

[72] Lacqueur, *ibid.*, col. 1088.

[73] Waddell, *Manetho*, 238.

[74] *ZÄS* 18 (1880), 125ff.

[75] For this reading of the numeral, upon which doubt has been cast (cf. R. A. Parker, *JEA* 28 [1942], 68), see now Gardiner, *The Royal Canon of Turin*, 17.

Manetho.[76] It resembles neither Assis nor Apophis. It is always possible, of course, that the Hyksos kings had a second name by which they were popularly known, but here we lack any proof whatsoever.

The remains left by the Hyksos themselves are confusing. Of Manetho's list only two names, Iannas (Ḫayan)[77] and Apophis, appear on contemporary monuments.[78] The latter, though sparse, are sufficiently impressive to suggest that these two and the dynasty to which they belonged wielded great power. Besides Iannas and Apophis, however, a plethora of royal names occurs, mostly Semitic, on seals and scarabs of contemporary date. The fact that none of these can be assigned certainly to Manetho's Fifteenth Dynasty, coupled with the unequivocal statement of Africanus that the Sixteenth and Seventeenth Dynasties also included "shepherd" kings,[79] led almost all scholars to the conclusion that there were two phases of Hyksos occupation: the period of the "great Hyksos" (the six kings of Fifteenth Dynasty) followed by a period of "late Hyksos," which corresponded to the weakening of foreign rule and the rise of the Seventeenth Dynasty. A diligent examination of the scarabs and seals of the period seemed to support this broad bifurcation,[80] as did the apparently sound demonstration that a Hurrian element was found in Egypt in the "late Hyksos" period, but not in the earlier.[81]

[76] Farina's suggestion (*Il Papiro dei Re Restaurato,* 55) that *Ḫ3mwdy* is preserved in the garbled form *Kertos* (Book of Sothis: Wadell, *Manetho,* 240) is rather doubtful. In any case Kertos in the Book of Sothis is succeeded by Aseth, and is thus not the last in the list. Helck's suggested equation of *Ḫ3mwdy* with the *Ḫndy* of Petrie, *Scarabs and Cylinders with Names* (London, 1917), Pl. 19, is also surrounded by doubt, though it seems more probable: *Die Beziehungen Ägyptens zu Vorderasien im* 3. *und* 2. *Jahrtausend v. Chr.* (Wiesbaden, 1962), 105, n. 6. Helck is correct, however, in dating this seal to the Second rather than to the First Intermediate Period, as Frankfort did: *JEA* 12 (1926), 92.

[77] Identification first proposed by Naville, *Bubastis* (EEF 8 [London, 1891]), 25f. Helck (*Beziehungen Ägyptens zu Vorderasien,* 93) is now doubtful.

[78] Albright's belief (*BASOR* 146 [1957], 31) that he has found Salatis (written *Za-a-lu-ti*) in a seventeenth-century Hittite text is naturally of great interest, but, as he himself confesses, the possibility is somewhat "remote."

[79] Cf. K. Galling, *ZDPV* 62 (1939), 96f.

[80] H. Stock, *Studien . . .,* 42ff., 64ff.; see also Albright, *BASOR* 168 (1962), 41, n. 23.

[81] R. M. Engberg, *The Hyksos Reconsidered* (SAOC 18 [Chicago, 1939], 19, 35.

There seemed to be no objection to assigning "Apophis the great" with a praenomen Awoserre to the "great Hyksos," and seeing in him a transitional stage between the barbarous conquerors and the semi-Egyptianized "late Hyksos."[82] The Apophis of the Seqenenre tale was either dismissed as a fictional character, or identified with one of the "other" Apophids, distinguished by the praenomina Nebkhopesh(?)re and Aqenenre.[83] Those few who believed that the Hyksos kings numbered six and only six, like Winlock[84] and Gardiner,[85] were roundly criticized.[86]

Seldom has such an elaborate theory been so completely demolished by a single piece of new evidence as has this reconstruction of the Hyksos period by the discovery of the second Kamose stela. Awoserre Apophis, far from being one of the earliest rulers, was the adversary of Kamose, and undoubtedly the protagonist of the Seqenenre tale.[87] It thus becomes highly likely that Africanus's version of Manetho, which places Apophis last in the list, is the original; the alternative—that two Hyksos reigns intervened between Apophis and the expulsion in the middle of Ahmose's reign—has, at present, little in its favour.[88] Apophis, with a reign of something over thirty-three years,[89] during which time he changed his praenomen twice,[90] witnessed the collapse of his house and was perhaps still the

[82] Stock, *Studien* . . ., 46.

[83] Gauthier, *Livre*, II. 141ff. (6 and 7).

[84] *The Rise and Fall of the Middle Kingdom* . . ., 97ff.

[85] *JEA* 5 (1918), 43, n. 6; Gardiner states that Müller (in *Studien zur Vorderasiatischen Geschichte*, 16ff., a work not available to me) shared this view also.

[86] Cf. the reviews of Winlock's *Rise and Fall* . . . by Säve-Söderbergh in *Bib. Or.* 6 (1949), 87ff., and by Faulkner in *JEA* 34 (1948), 124.

[87] Cf. Säve-Söderbergh, *Kush*, 4 (1956), 61.

[88] Yet Helck (*Untersuchungen zu Manetho*, 37; *MDIAK* 17 [1961], 109) and Hayes (*CAH* II, ch. 2 [1962], 24) continue to assert that Apophis was followed by two short-lived successors. If the current arrangement of the Turin fragments is accepted, and if the highest possible restoration of the four partly preserved year totals is made, the presence of two ephemeral kings at the end of the dynasty becomes more credible. But in any case the probability is not impressive.

[89] A. B. Chase, L. Bull, and H. P. Manning, *The Rhind Mathematical Papyrus, B.M.* 10057 *and* 10058 (Oberlin, 1929), II, photo 1, col. 2.

[90] There is nothing unlikely in this, especially in view of the fact that among contemporary Seventeenth Dynasty kings modifying the titulary was something of a fad. Those who believe in three Apophises must explain the singular fact that

adversary of the Egyptians at Sharuhen. With this revelation the "late Hyksos" vanish like mist. The true explanation of the Semitic and assured Egyptian names that occur in cartouches during the Hyksos period must be sought in the widespread feudal system in vogue during the Middle Bronze Age.[91] These "kings" were really feudal lords, contemporaries and vassals of Apophis and others, the same kind of "kings," in fact, of whom it is said in a Mari letter that ten or fifteen "follow" Hammurabi of Babylon, but twenty Yarim-lim of Yamkhad.[92] One would dearly like to know how many kings "followed" Apophis!

The Gebelein blocks[93] show that Apophis held Upper Egypt at some point in his reign. The fact that Khayan is also mentioned at the same site suggests that the Hyksos occupation of the south continued from the reign of Khayan into the first years of the reign of Apophis. On the other hand, Apophis is now known to have been still reigning at the end of the Seventeenth Dynasty. The only conclusion that can be drawn from these facts is that the Seventeenth Dynasty, if, as seems likely, its inception post-dates the Hyksos

---

Aqenenre and Nebkhopesh(?)re are very seldom mentioned on scarabs (one example of Nebkhopeshre is given in Petrie, *Scarab*, Pl. 22 [17A]), while Awoserre has a great number to his name; cf. Weill, *XIIe Dynastie, Royauté de Haute-Égypte et domination Hyksos dans le Nord* (Bibl. d'Étude, XXVI [Cairo, 1953]), 125. Hayes (*CAH* II, ch. 2 [1962], 24), who makes Aqenenre Apophis one of the ephemeral Hyksos rulers who occupied the throne just before Avaris fell, does not attempt to explain how it is that a dagger with his name on it was found at Thebes: W. R. Dawson, *JEA* 11 (1925), 216f. Nor does the inscription of Aqenenre on a table of offerings (A. Kamal, *CCG* [1909], 61; Weill, *JA* (1911], 8ff.) fit particularly the last scion of "a dynasty tottering on the verge of ruin": "Live Horus, 'Pacifier of the two lands,' the good god, Aqenenre; (this is) what he made for his father Seth, lord of Avaris, when he had placed all lands beneath his feet . . . ." The simplest solution is to make "Aqenenre" and "Nebkhopesh(?)re" early praenomina of Awoserre Apophis. Nebkhopesh(?)re, known from the sword of Nehmen, the retainer (Daressy, *ASAE* 7 [1906], 115ff.), and a flint knife (Weill, *JA* [1911], 14), may be the earliest of the three.

[91] J. M. Munn-Rankin, *Iraq*, 18 (1956), 68ff.; Hayes (*CAH* II, ch. 2 [1962], 19) pictures these kinglets as "chiefs of the many different Asiatic tribes banded together under the leadership of the Great Hyksos." See also Helck, *Die Bezichungen Ägyptens zu Vorderasien*, 94.

[92] G. Dossin, *Syria*, 19 (1938), 117.

[93] See above, n. 66.

occupation of the south,[94] was itself shorter than, and was contained within, Apophis's reign of $33+x$ years.

We conclude from this discussion that the Seventeenth Dynasty covered something less than the normal length of two human generations. Twenty years would seem to be a judicious estimate, but even this may be too much.[95]

3. The Date of the Expulsion of the Hyksos

Without a doubt this date was recorded on a triumphal stela similar to those of Kamose. Until such time as the record comes to light, however, speculation alone must suffice.

The autobiography of Ahmose-si-Abina, besides being the fullest record of the expulsion of the Hyksos, also contains the best indication of the point in Ahmose's reign when this event took place. Ahmose does not say in which reign he was born, but states that he had "his upbringing"[96] in El Kab, "my father being a soldier of the king of Upper and Lower Egypt Seqenenre."[97] He himself became a soldier "in the time of" Ahmose I. There is no indication in the text as to how much of the reign had elapsed before this event took place. Ahmose does make clear, however, that he entered the service "while I was a lad (*šri*), before I had taken a wife, while I (still) slept in a —."[98] In spite of our ignorance of the last expression,

[94] Thus most probably Winlock, *Rise and Fall*..., 2 and 148f.

[95] Cf. Säve-Söderbergh, *JEA* 37 (1951), 62, n. 4: "... it seems necessary to allow at least more than one generation for Kamose and dynasty 17...."

[96] *'Ir.n.i ḫprw.i m dmi n Nḫb*, following Gardiner's translation in *JEA* 5 (1918), 49 and n. 1. The difficulty stems from the fact that this particular use of *ḫprw* seems to be a *hapax*: see *Belegstellen* to *Wb* III, 266:14. Gardiner is followed here, as against De Rougé (*MAIBL*, 1st ser., III [1851], 109f.) and Schaeffer (*ZÄS* 42 [1912], 102), because his rendering seems to make better sense. Moreover, if, as De Rougé and Schaeffer believed, the meaning is only "I was born," one might have expected *msy.i* (passive *sḏm.f*): cf. the Sebakkhu stela, K. Sethe, *Aegyptische Lesestücke* (Leipzig, 1924), 83:1.

[97] Loret, *L'Inscription d'Ahmès fils d'Abana*, 1, line 5. The wording seems to imply that Ahmose's childhood was spent, in part, under Seqenenre; for *iw* with noun subject in a circumstantial clause, see Gardiner, *Grammar*³, §117:1.

[98] *Śmt* (or *šmꜣt*?) *śnw*, lit. "a *smt*-fabric of net." This has been taken to mean a costume worn by children: cf. De Rougé, *MAIBL*, 1st ser., III (1851), 151ff. "costume des enfants"; *Wb* IV, 119:10 "... Kleidung des Unverheirateten (beim Schlafen)"; Loret, *L'Inscription d'Ahmès fils d'Abana*, 19, "manteau, couverture";

it seems clear that Ahmose is stressing his extreme youth. There follows an allusion to his "founding a house (*grg.n.i pr*)," i.e. establishing a household, a process which included not only courtship and marriage but also the acquisition of a house and property, and perhaps also the begetting of children.[99] Thus the time that intervened between his becoming a soldier as a boy and his founding a household can scarcely have been less than about four years, and may well have been a decade or more. Ahmose continues his autobiography with the account of his transfer to the ship "North" and his infantry duty in the entourage of the king. There follow these episodes: (1) the beginning of the siege of Avaris (8); (2) his further transfer to the ship "Appearance in Memphis" (8–9); (3) a battle of the Djedku-canal (?) (9–10);[100] (4) another battle "in this place" (10–11); (5) a third battle "south of this town" (*rsi n dmi pn*)" (11–13);[101] (6) the spoiling of Avaris, at which point we are probably to understand that the Hyksos had been driven out of the Delta. Again in this part of the text the reader is not told the length of time covered by the narrative. Although it is within the realm of possibility that the time that elapsed between his "founding a house"

cf. also Breasted, *ARE* II, 6, n. *e*. B. Grdseloff identified the first word with *smȝt*, "phallic sheath," and translated ". . . je dormais avec l'étui attaché(?)" (*ASAE* 43 [1943], 365). Apart from the fact that children of ancient Egypt were not likely to don any costume at bedtime, the sleep of the young would be distinguished from that of the adults rather by what they slept *on*, i.e. the kind of bed. Hence Gardiner's "hammock of net" seems to me *a priori* more acceptable than any of the above translations. (*JEA* 5 (1918), 49, n. 5).

99 What is involved in the expression *grg pr* is well illustrated by the Ptahhotpe passage beginning 326ff. (Dévaud's numbering; Z. Žaba, *Les Maximes de Ptahhotep* [Prague, 1956], 41ff.); cf. also Papyrus D'Orbiney 9:2ff. (Gardiner, *Late Egyptian Stories* [Bibl. Aegypt. I [Brussels, 1932], 18f.); Chester Beatty V, vs. 2:6ff. Gardiner, *Hieratic Papyri in the British Museum, Third Series*, Pl. 26).

100 Concerning this body of water, see Gauthier, *DG* VI, 137.

101 A peculiar locution if El Kab is meant (see Maspero, *Histoire*, 87)! Cf. Breasted, "A New Chapter in the Life of Thutmose III" (*Untersuchungen*, II, 2), 26a; *idem*, *ARE* II, 7, n. *d*. It would seem rather that Avaris is intended; see Albright, *JPOS* 2 (1922), 121f. Nevertheless, it should not be imagined that a withdrawal of the Egyptian army as far south as El Kab would have been unlikely. The new Kamose stela shows that part of the Hyksos strategy was to involve the Egyptians on their southern frontier with the Nubians, and on one occasion Kamose was forced to withdraw to Esneh to repulse an incursion: lines 4ff. (for references, see n. 39 above).

and the seizure of Avaris was only about a couple of years, the impression remains that it was longer.[102] It has been suggested that the five battles recounted correspond to five campaigning seasons, the entire siege in consequence being of four years' duration;[103] and to judge from the traditional impregnability of Avaris, this hypothesis is not unlikely.[104]

The following table enables one to visualize the distribution of events in, and the relative length of, the early part of Ahmose's reign down to the expulsion of the Hyksos:

1.	From Ahmose's accession to the entry of Ahmose-si-Abina into the army	unknown
2.	From the latter event to his "founding a house"	min. *ca.* 4 years, max. *ca.* 10 years.
3.	From the latter event to the beginning of the siege	unknown
4.	Duration of the siege	min. *ca.* 1 year, max. *ca.* 4 years.
5.	From the capture of Avaris to the actual withdrawal of the Hyksos	unknown (if any)

On the length of period 1 nothing can be said. If there was a period 5, its length may have been only months or even weeks. Period 3 may have been longer, since it comprises Ahmose's promotion to the "North" and his service as an infantryman. On a minimal estimate, therefore, scarcely less than six years in Ahmose's reign had passed before Avaris was taken, and this landmark in Egyptian history would have to be placed in his seventh regnal year. On the maximal estimate, over fifteen years had elapsed, and the seizure of Avaris would fall, at the earliest, in regnal year 16. The upper limit must be year 17, for the following reason. In year 22 Ahmose was employing cattle captured among the *Fnḫw* to haul stone for him in the Turah quarries.[105] Prior to year 22, yet after the expulsion of the Hyksos, the following events must be inserted: (a) the three-year

[102] Note especially that the two promotions recounted in this part of the text came, according to Ahmose, on account of his valour. In other words he had to prove himself in each post. This in itself suggests a fairly lengthy passage of time.

[103] Breasted, *ARE* II, 7, n. *h*.

[104] Cf. Josephus, *Contra Apionem*, I, 14, §78; one late tradition, though in fact erroneous, declares that Avaris proved too strong for Ahmose, and that he was forced to conclude a treaty with the Hyksos: *ibid.*, §88.

[105] *Urk.* IV, 25.

siege of Sharuhen;[106] (b) the Nubian campaigns;[107] (c) the campaign into Djahi (i.e. central Syria), on which presumably these cattle were taken.[108] Five years is probably a conservative estimate for such momentous events.

The conclusion to the above discussion is that the expulsion of the Hyksos occurred between years 7 and 17 of Ahmose's reign, the evidence tending to favour a higher rather than a lower date within this range. The present writer would opt for year 15 or thereabouts.[109]

106 Ahmose's biography, line 15.

107 *Ibid.*, lines 16ff.

108 Louvre Statue of Ahmose-pe-Nekhbet: Sethe, *Urk.* IV, 35.

109 Helck (*Beziehungen Ägyptens zu Vorderasien*, 101) opts for year 10.

3

The Coregencies of the Early Eighteenth Dynasty

The word "coregency" appears often in Egyptological works, but only rarely does a definition accompany it. Because of the nature of the case things could scarcely be otherwise. Some term must be used for the diarchy, which is historical fact; yet we must confess at the same time almost total ignorance of the circumstances that forced the adoption of this form of government, in a given instance. The paucity of evidence may still continue to hamstring attempts to probe deeper into the nature of the Egyptian coregency, and it is probably this utter lack of data that explains the silence of modern scholars on the subject.[1]

This is not the place for a detailed examination of the phenomenon of the Egyptian coregency. Our interest in the subject extends only so far as it has a bearing on relative or absolute chronology. Hence it will suffice for present purposes to draw a broad, formal distinction between what appear to be two basic types of coregency. First there is that sort of dual administration in which "junior" and "senior" partners—to borrow Simpson's terminology[2]—both possess the titulary and symbols of full kingship, with the single exception that the junior partner defers to the senior in matters of regnal year dating.

[1] A notable exception is the work of W. K. Simpson on the coregencies of the Twelfth Dynasty: *JNES* 15 (1956), 214ff.

[2] *Ibid.*

In this type of coregency the junior partner begins dating his own regnal years with the death of his predecessor. The second type of coregency differs from the first in that, *inter alia,* the junior coregent numbers his years from the inception of the coregency, while the senior partner continues to count his own regnal years from the beginning of his own reign. Thus the years of such a coregency can be said to be "double-dated," and monuments giving equivalent dates according to the two systems are sometimes found. The second type of coregency seems to have been most popular under the Twelfth Dynasty. The first, because it is more difficult to detect, cannot be said to have been fashionable during any single period.

To the chronologist interested in absolute chronology the first type of coregency is of little moment. Since the dated years of senior and junior partners do not overlap, it is possible to add the two reigns together and arrive at a correct total. The second type, however, vitally interests him for the simple reason that unless the exact amount of "overlap" between the dated years of the two reigns is known, the addition of the regnal years will result in an inflated total. Only a double-dated inscription can indicate that one is dealing with the second type of coregency, and unfortunately such inscriptions are relatively rare.

For the first five kings of the Eighteenth Dynasty the evidence of coregencies of either type is extremely slight.

For a coregency of Ahmose with Amenhotpe I there is scarcely any evidence. Their cartouches are occasionally found juxtaposed,[3] but no double-dated inscriptions occur, and the biographies of men who lived through the two reigns do not even hint at a coregency.

There is a little evidence for a coregency of Amenhotpe I and Thutmose I. From the time of Sethe[4] the scholarly consensus has been that Thutmose I was not a son of Amenhotpe I, his predecessor, but acquired his claim to the throne probably through his marriage to Ahmes, who may have been a sister of Amenhotpe I.[5] It would

[3] Cf. G. Legrain, *Répertoire généalogique et onomastique du musée du Caire* (Geneva, 1908), nos. 15 and 17.

[4] *Thronwirren,* §§1–5; *ZÄS* 36 (1898), 25ff.; *APAW* (1932), no. 4, 9.

[5] *Thronwirren,* §5; *APAW* (1932), no. 4, 10; *HSE* II, 54; Hayes, "Egypt: Internal Affairs from Tuthmosis I to the Death of Amenophis III," in *CAH* (1962), II, 5; Meyer (*Geschichte,* II, 1, 76) is, perhaps rightly, doubtful.

have been sensible of Thutmose to contrive to have himself made coregent with his brother-in-law in order to strengthen his claim. And this is precisely what the evidence of certain blocks from Karnak seems to indicate. The blocks come from a shrine of Amenhotpe I which once stood somewhere inside the enclosure of the Amun temple.[6] On the south face of the shrine Thutmose I, with cartouches and royal accoutrements, is shown three times: on the left in an *atef*-crown with his *ku* making a libation before Min; in the centre, in the white crown, running a race before Amun; and on the right, again before Min, making a libation in a bag wig. If this relief were carved, as seems likely, while Amenhotpe I was still alive, a good case could be made for a coregency. But whether it is accepted as evidence or not, it is fairly certain that no coregency of the second type was ever enjoyed by these two monarchs. The circular letter announcing the accession day of Thutmose I, i.e. the day from which he dated his regnal years, makes no mention of Amenhotpe I, and the only reasonable conclusion is that he had already passed away, leaving Thutmose I as the sole ruler.

The present discussion takes for granted that Sethe's ingenious theory regarding the succession of the three Thutmosids and Hatshepsut is finally disproved. Almost entirely on the basis of the erasures of Hatshepsut's name and figure, and their replacement by those of Thutmose I, II, or III,[7] Sethe evolved a picture of the dynastic feud in which all four contestants vied with each other for the throne and alternated in the kingship in the most bewildering fashion. His entire structure was built on the single premise that, whenever a name is found cut *over* an earlier one, it must have been the owner of the superimposed name who effected the erasure and recutting. There is no reason to accept this as a general rule. In the case of Sety II of the Nineteenth Dynasty, his superimposed cartouches in the tomb of Twosre were certainly cut *after* his death, he thus having had nothing to do with the usurpation.[8] Thutmose III's hatred for his aunt and his piety towards his father and grandfather adequately account for the erasures of Hatshepsut's name at Deir el-Bahri and elsewhere.

[6] H. Chevrier, *ASAE* 47 (1947), 167, Pl. 24 and 26.

[7] Sethe admitted the overriding importance of this evidence to his theory; cf. *APAW* (1932), no. 4, 54ff.

[8] Cf. Gardiner, *JEA* 44 (1958), 16.

Prior to Sethe's publication of *Thronwirren*, Thutmose III seems generally to have been credited by scholars with the hacking of Hatshepsut's name and whatever recutting there was;[9] and this must be accepted today as historical fact.[10]

There seems at present to be no evidence of a coregency of Thutmose I and Thutmose II.[11]

Some evidence exists which may possibly show that Thutmose II and Thutmose III were for a short time coregents. In Thutmose III's building inscription on the seventh pylon at Karnak, the king states: "the rule of the two lands, the throne of Geb, the office of Khepry were pre-ordained for me, at the side of my father, the good god, the king of Upper and Lower Egypt, Okheperenre, given life for ever."[12] Sethe construed the preposition *r-gs*, "at the side of," as almost equivalent to "as coregent of," and offered this passage as evidence for a coregency.[13] However, it seems just as likely that *r-gs* is here to be rendered "in the presence of,"[14] and construed with the verb. We should then have merely a description of a formal proclamation in court, when the king was present, of the appointment of the heir apparent.[15] A second piece of evidence in the form of a hieratic graffito comes from the step pyramid complex.[16] The date (year 20) is ascribed to both Hatshepsut and Thutmose III, in that order; then follow the words: "now his majesty was . . . king with his(?) father, exalted(?) upon the Horus throne of the living, like Re every day." If "his majesty" is a reference to Thutmose III, then this would seem to be an obvious reference to a coregency he enjoyed

[9] Cf. the reference in note 7; also E. Naville, *Deir el-Bahari: Introductory Memoir* (London, 1896), 27. There are no grounds for Naville's contention (*ibid.*, 11; *ZÄS* 37 [1899], 48f.) that it was Ramses II who was responsible for the cutting of the names of Thutmose I and II over those of Hatshepsut; cf. Sethe. *ZÄS* 36 (1898), 37ff.; *APAW* (1932), no. 4, 56.

[10] For a résumé of Sethe's theory, and of the rebuttals it has called forth, see Drioton-Vandier, *L'Egypte*[4]. 381f.

[11] The coregency Sethe postulated, based as it was upon the spurious evidence of erasures, must be rejected: *APAW* (1932), no. 4, 70.

[12] *Urk.* IV, 180.

[13] *APAW* (1932), no. 4, 69.

[14] Cf. Gardiner, *Grammar*[3], §198.

[15] Sethe (*APAW* [1932], no. 4, 69) recognized this as a possible alternative translation, but in the end rejected it.

[16] C. M. Firth and J. E. Quibell, *The Step Pyramid* (Cairo 1935), I, 80 (F).

with Thutmose II. The possibility cannot be ruled out, however, that it is Hatshepsut who is being referred to, and that the allusion is to her fictitious coronation by her father Thutmose I. As to the type of coregency of Thutmose III and his father, no definite statement can be made for lack of evidence. However, the fact that in texts of the earliest date in Thutmose III's reign no mention is made of Thutmose II tends to suggest that the coregency, if it is historical, was of the first type and that Thutmose III began numbering his years only on the death of his father.

For the first five reigns of the dynasty there is thus no evidence of any coregency of the second type, or, in other words, no reason to suppose that any of the dated years of any king overlapped the reign of his predecessor.

THE REGNAL YEAR DATING OF HATSHEPSUT'S REIGN

In her Deir el-Bahri inscription Hatshepsut states that she received the accoutrements of kingship and was crowned by her father on New Year's day in an unspecified year.[17] This ceremony was termed an "appearance of the king of Upper and Lower Egypt," and from the information given in the inscription, it must have taken place during Thutmose I's reign. Yet Hatshepsut, throughout the reign of Thutmose II[18] and even in the early regnal years of Thutmose III,[19] bore only the titles of a princess and a queen. Then in Thutmose III's second regnal year,[20] on the twenty-ninth day of the sixth month, Amun confronted Hatshepsut in public, proclaimed her king of the two lands, and had her crowned in the chapel of *mꜣʿt*.[21] This latter incident, recorded in an as yet unpublished inscription of the queen at Karnak, has generally been taken as a more historical account than that of the Deir el-Bahri texts;[22] and so it undoubtedly is. The two accounts are not necessarily mutually exclusive, however,

[17] *Urk.* IV, 262.

[18] *HSE* II, 80, Fig. 43; *Urk.* IV, 144; S. Schott, *Nachr. Gött.* (1955), 202f.

[19] *Urk.* IV, 201.

[20] It can scarcely be any other reign, in view of Hatshepsut's status during Thutmose II's floruit.

[21] Schott, *Nachr. Gött.* (1955), 212f.

[22] *Ibid.*, 213; Hayes, "Egypt: Internal Affairs from Tuthmosis I . . .," in *CAH* (1962), II, 7.

and the Egyptians, if they thought about it at all, probably had little difficulty in construing the coronation of year 2 as a reaffirmation of Hatshepsut's earlier appointment. Nor is one justified in writing off the Deir el-Bahri account as pure fabrication. It is highly likely that an actual occurrence lies behind it, perhaps a formal presentation by Thutmose I of his daughter to the court, or even a proclamation that Hatshepsut was the "heiress." It is to be noted in this connexion that even under Thutmose II, when she was still a princess and queen, Hatshepsut bore the title of "great crown princess" or "heiress (*iry-pʿt wrt*)."[23] Although in monuments subsequent to year 2, Hatshepsut is formally called "king" and is depicted as a man, the popular designation "queen" was not given up. The ostraca from Deir el-Bahri prove that this appelative continued to be applied to her, as "pharaoh" was to Thutmose III.[24] This curious fact shows very clearly the equivocal nature of Hatshepsut's reign: despite the vigorous protestations of her kingship, she remained something of an interloper, a provisional regent, as long as she lived.

Although we possess two dates for Hatshepsut's coronation, viz, i, 1 and vi, 29, she used neither as a point from which to date regnal years. Of the day which Hatshepsut counted her "accession" day we know nothing. As has long been realized, the first day of her regnal years is shown by the Karnak obelisk inscription to be somewhere between vi, 1 and xii, 30.[25] This would accommodate vi, 29, but it would also fit ix, 4, the day of Thutmose III's accession. And that Hatshepsut did indeed equate her own regnal years with those of her stepson is easily proved.[26] In a number of inscriptions from her reign[27] the date is followed by the names of both Hatshepsut and Thutmose III in such a way that both are made to share the regnal year. In one singular inscription from Sinai, the regnal year (11) is made out to belong to Neferure, the daughter of Hatshepsut.[28] This

[23] Cf. *Urk.* IV, 192. For this title in the New Kingdom, see *Wb.* II, 415; 22–23; Gardiner, *AEO* I, 14*ff.; *idem*, *JEA* 39 (1953), 10; W. Helck, *Orientalia*, 19 (1950), 416ff.

[24] Hayes, *JEA* 46 (1960), Pl. 9, no. 2:10; Pl. 10, no. 5, recto 3; Pl. 10, no. 6, recto 8; Pl. 11, no. 14, recto (*passim*).

[25] *Urk.* IV, 356f.

[26] Cf. Sethe, *Thronwirren*, §17; *idem*, *APAW* (1932), no. 4, 23.

[27] *Urk.* IV, 393; 1377f.; Firth-Quibell, *The Step Pyramid*, I, 80.

[28] A. H. Gardiner and J. Černý, *The Inscriptions of Sinai* (London, 1952–55), Pl. 68:179.

probably does not reflect a separate reign, but rather an attempt on Hatshepsut's part to credit her stepson's reign to her daughter, the heiress.[29] As such, the attempt appears to have been unsuccessful, since no other monuments exist which are similarly dated.

The date of Hatshepsut's death (less likely, her "removal") is not indicated on any monument. Manetho credits a certain queen Amesses who has often been equated with Hatshepsut,[30] with twenty-one years, nine months of reign.[31] If this period is reckoned from the accession of Thutmose III, it brings us to a point at the end of the fifth month in his twenty-second regnal year. It is certainly worthy of note that the enigmatic date on the Armant stela is year 22, vi, 10.[32]

[29] See further below, p. 85.

[30] Wiedemann, *Geschichte*, 306; Sethe, *Thronwirren*, §5; Gauthier, *Livre*, II, 236, n. 2; G. Maspero, *RT* 27 (1905), 16; Meyer, *Geschichte*, II, 1, 78; Sethe, *APAW* (1932), no. 4, 6; W. Helck, *Untersuchungen zu Manetho*, 40; J. Von Beckerath, *OLZ* 54 (1959), 10; G. Fecht, *ZDMG* 35 (1960), 120.

[31] Waddell, *Manetho*, 100; E. Hornung, *Untersuchungen zur Chronologie und Geschichte des neuen Reiches* (Ägyptologische Abhandlungen, 11 [Wiesbaden, 1964], 33f.

[32] Sir R. Mond and O. H. Myers, *The Temples of Armant* (London, 1940), Pl. 88.

4

The Reign of Hatshepsut

It is stated by many historians that Hatshepsut's reign was of a peaceful nature, devoid of wars.[1] Occasionally one is left with the impression that the author feels this is how the queen intended it, in other words that she pursued a conscious policy of non-aggression. Little positive evidence is ever advanced in favour of this assumption; it seems to be taken more or less generally as a self-evident truth.

In 1957 Habachi published a text,[2] a graffito from the island of Sehel, which provides a specific and unequivocal description of a war undertaken by Hatshepsut. The writer, one Tiy,[3] says: "I followed the good god, the king of Upper and Lower Egypt ⸢Makare⸣,[4] may she live! I saw when he (*sic*) overthrew the Nubian bowmen, and when their chiefs were brought to him as living captives. I saw when he razed Nubia, I being in his majesty's following. . . ." Taking this graffito in conjunction with other scattered phrases at Deir el-Bahri,[5] in Senenmut's tomb,[6] and on Djehuty's

[1] Cf. for example, A. J. Arkell, *A History of the Sudan to 1821* (London, 1961), 87; Drioton-Vandier, *L'Egypte*[4], 339, 398; A. H. Gardiner, *Egypt of the Pharaohs* (Oxford, 1961), 189; Hayes, *CAH* II (1962), ch. 9, 18; T. Säve-Söderbergh, *The Navy of the Eighteenth Egyptian Dynasty* (Uppsala, 1946), 17; A. Scharff, *Ägypten und Vorderasien* (Munich, 1950), 126.

[2] *JNES* 16 (1957), 99ff.; p. 100, Fig. 6.

[3] 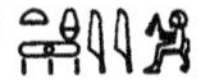 .

[4] Hacked but visible: Habachi, *JNES* 16 (1957), 101.

[5] *Ibid.*, 102.

[6] *Ibid.*, 104.

stela,[7] Habachi concluded that there was indeed a war during Hatshepsut's time in the south, and that the queen herself was actually at the scene of hostilities. Even this evidence, however, has been treated with scant respect by more recent writers.[8]

It is the present writer's conviction that, as so often is the case in dealing with historical sources for ancient Egypt, the haphazard of preservation has given us a rather lop-sided view of Hatshepsut's reign. The evidence for foreign campaigns is more plentiful than is sometimes thought; and it may well be that the reason there is not more is because Thutmose III destroyed it so as not to invite comparison with his own military successes.

The first and major piece of evidence is the inscription of Tiy. This has been dealt with fully by Habachi,[9] and so will not detain us here.

A second piece of evidence, which in the light of Tiy's text takes on new importance, is the thoroughly conventional scene from Deir el-Bahri which shows the Nubian god Dedwen leading captive southerners to the queen.[10] In the same part of the temple (the lower colonnade) Hatshepsut is shown as a sphinx crushing her enemies beneath her feet.[11] These are stock scenes, to be sure, and too much weight should not be attached to them.[12] Habachi's new evidence, however, shows that they were by no means without justification.

A more important text of similar content from Deir el-Bahri is the long and unfortunately fragmentary inscription from the lower colonnade.[13] Here there is something more than a conventional reference to Hatshepsut's foreign wars. The text seems to begin with an allusion to Thutmose I's Nubian campaign:

(1) sailing north in victory and might [ ] Okheperkare on his first victorious campaign [lacuna of unknown length] (2) . . . with me. I will cause to sail south [lacuna of unknown length] (3) . . . the chief of [vile] Kush [whom th]ey [brought?] as a living captive; [ ] in his moment, who seizes without anything being

---

[7] *Urk.* IV, 438:10. The passage was wholly preserved when Spiegelberg read the text.

[8] Cf. Gardiner, *Egypt of the Pharaohs,* 189.

[9] *JNES* 16 (1957), 99ff.

[10] E. Naville, *The Temple of Deir el Bahari* (London, 1908), VI, Pl. 152.

[11] *Ibid.,* Pl. 160.

[12] Cf. T. Säve-Söderbergh, *Ägypten und Nubien* (Lund, 1941), 152.

[13] Naville, *The Temple of Deir el Bahari,* VI, Pl. 165.

seized from him.[14] She says: " As [Amun] lives for me and loves me [ ] (4) [lacuna of unknown length] the land in might and valour [ ]... these (?)[15] fortress-towns of [his?] majesty [ ] the garrison of the sovereign raged *(nšny)*.

The better-preserved part of the inscription continues as follows:

(5) . . . as was done by her victorious father, the king of Upper and Lower Egypt, Okheperkare, who seized all lands; [ ] has begun (?) an uproar,[16] those who are in [lacuna of unknown length]. (6) [ ] a slaughter was made among them, the number (of dead) being unknown; their hands were cut off [lacuna of unknown length] (7) [ ] she overthrew [ ] the gods [lacuna of unknown length] (8) [ ] likewise; all foreign lands spoke (?) (their) heart's rage,[17] (but?) they turned back[18] on account of the greatness (?) [lacuna of unknown length] (9) [the enemy?][19] were plotting in their valleys, saying [lacuna of unknown length] (10) [ ] overland, horses upon the mountains [lacuna of unknown length] (11) [ ] the number [of them] was not known [. . . Amun, lord] of Karnak, who leads me. . . .

Other scattered phrases refer to the fact that "she has destroyed the southern lands," and claim that "all lands are beneath her feet."

Enough has been translated to show that this inscription is dealing with a military campaign, which not only is compared with the first campaign of Thutmose I but also has some direct connexion with it.[20] Since that particular venture was concerned with Nubia, and since in the present text we have a reference to the "southern lands," it would seem that the scene of the hostilities recorded here was in the south. The occasion for the punitive expedition involved plotting on the part of the Nubians, and perhaps an attack upon an Egyptian garrison.[21] The queen dispatched(?) her army south, a great slaughter was made, and captive chiefs(?) were brought back.

14 On the supposition. which is by no means certain, that the middle fragment on the bottom line of Naville's plate belongs here.

15 Cf. *Urk.* IV, 138:16.

16 Emending 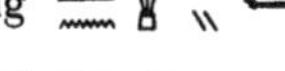 to  .

17 *Nšt-ib:* cf. *Wb* II, 337:10, 340:24.

18 *Ḥs.ny.n;* perhaps a strange writing of the *sḏm.ny* form: Gardiner, *Grammar*[3] §486, obs. 2.

19 Something similar; determinative 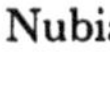 .

20 Sethe, *APAW* (1932), no. 4, 70, n. 2.

21 Cf. the occasion for Thutmose II's Nubian campaign: *Urk.* IV, 137ff.

We have less evidence for Asiatic campaigns, although some does exist. The possibility cannot be ruled out that the inscription just discussed contained references to other campaigns, and one in Asia may well have been among them. In another text of Hatshepsut,[22] hacked and modified by Thutmose III, it is said that "her arrow is among the northerners." A more explicit statement, cast in the form of a divine prophecy addressed to the child Hatshepsut, states: "you shall seize the chiefs of Retenu by violence, those left over from your father('s reign); your catch shall be men by the millions, the plunder of your arm; your captivity men by the thousands for the temples."[23] Hatshepsut is thus to consolidate the Asiatic conquests of her father. It is true that these phrases smack of stock promises and boasts, but the allusion to the work of Thutmose I makes prima facie evidence for some historical basis.

A number of officials have also left records, datable to Hatshepsut's reign, which allude to foreign expeditions. From Sinai comes a stela of Thutmose III's thirteenth regnal year[24] whereon the official responsible for the inscription calls himself "a follower of his lord in the foreign land of [ ]." This kind of expression is well known as a designation of service on a military campaign. Similarly Anebny, the overseer of the royal armoury, is called in a statue inscription "a follower of his lord, in his footsteps, in the southern and northern foreign lands."[25] Djehuty in his stela also mentions the conquests of the queen, whom he says he saw on the battlefield collecting booty.[26]

The inscriptions of Tiy and Djehuty make it plain that the queen herself actually led a Nubian expedition; but there is evidence that Thutmose III also was not inactive as a general during the period of his stepmother's rule. By the time of his first Syrian campaign he had already captured Gaza, a victory which must have been achieved in some unrecorded campaign during Hatshepsut's lifetime.[27] In a

[22] Naville, *The Temple of Deir el Bahari*, VI, Pl. 167.

[23] *Urk. IV*, 248.

[24] A. H. Gardiner and J. Černý, *The Inscriptions of Sinai* (London, 1952–55), Pl. 61:180.

[25] *Hieroglyphic Texts in the British Museum*, Pl. 34, lines 9–10.

[26] *Urk.* IV, 399.

[27] This is the only reasonable explanation of the appelative applied to Gaza in the annals of year 23, "the town which the ruler had taken (*dmi mḥ.n pꜣ ḥqꜣ*):" *Urk.* IV, 648. Cf. A. Alt, *PJB* 10 (1914), 67 and n. 2; surely this is not a *name* that the Egyptians gave to Gaza: see Bilabel, *Geschichte*, 32, n. 3.

rock inscription from Tombos dated to year 20 Thutmose III is called "the good god, who overthrows him who has attacked him."[28] In an adjacent passage Amun is termed "one who gave victory". It seems that in these generalizations there is the reflection of a campaign, albeit perhaps a minor one, led by Thutmose III around his twentieth year against Nubia. It is rather doubtful whether this campaign, or another undertaken while Hatshepsut still lived, is the one alluded to in the Armant stela. The passage in question[29] reads as follows: "he bagged a rhinoceros by archery in the southern land of Nubia, after he had journeyed to Maw to seek him who had rebelled against him in that land. He set up his stela there as he had done at the ends [ ]." Säve-Söderbergh seems to believe that the stela alluded to here is none other than the Gebel Barkal stela, and that the entire episode is to be dated to year 47.[30] Yet immediately following the section translated comes the description of the first Asiatic campaign, introduced by the following: "his majesty did not delay in journeying to the land of Djahi to slay the rebels who were in it, and to reward those who were loyal in it. . . . His majesty returned (*scil.* to Djahi) whenever the need arose(?)."[31] Two considerations force one to accept these words, not as vague generalizations, but as a cursory description of the first campaign (year 22–23). First, his purpose was to slay rebels, and the grounds for the first campaign were precisely the same, viz. that it was necessary to quell the rebellion that had broken out against his majesty.[32] Second, the phrase "his majesty returned whenever the need arose(?)" is intelligible only if the precedent for such action has been described just previous, and to Thutmose the precedent in this case was his first campaign. Now it is true that the author of the Armant stela did not follow strictly the chronology of the reign. It seems, however, that exceptionally, as in the present case, the order of events is to be accepted at face value. The expression "his majesty did not delay . . ." is explicable only if it is construed with what precedes. The delay denied by the author would have been thoroughly understandable if the king had been 1000 miles up the Nile in Kush. The use of this

[28] Säve-Söderbergh, *Ägypten und Nubien*, 209, Fig. 16.

[29] Cf. R. Mond and O. H. Meyers, *The Temples of Armant* (London, 1940), Pl. 88, lines 8ff.

[30] *The Navy of the Eighteenth Egyptian Dynasty*, 6, n. 1.

[31] *R tnw sp.*

[32] *Urk.* IV. 648.

locution is thus a strong argument that the order of events is unassailable; in other words, that a campaign into Nubia took place not long before the first Asiatic expedition of year 23.

Further confirmation may be elicited from the pylon inscriptions at Armant.[33] Here a rhinoceros is represented along with his astounding measurements, and the legend identifies him as "the catch of pharaoh in the country of vile Kush on his first campaign of victory." The exceptional interest in this beast evidenced by the relief and text calls to mind the statement just translated in the stela that stood in the same temple. If the text on the pylon does date from the reign of Thutmose III,[34] the only conclusion possible is that a Nubian campaign had taken place before the battle of Megiddo, and had been designated as the first. Later, after Hatshepsut died, and Thutmose's Asiatic campaigns completely eclipsed his earlier victories, the Nubian battles were forgotten, and the campaigns were numbered afresh beginning with Megiddo.[35]

In summary, there is reliable evidence to prove the historicity of at least four military campaigns or series of campaigns during the two decades Hatshepsut ruled Egypt alone. These are: (1) the campaign against Nubia led by the queen herself, probably early in the reign; (2) mopping-up operations in Palestine and Syria, also probably early; (3) the capture of Gaza by Thutmose III, probably later in Hatshepsut's floruit; (4) the campaign against Nubia by Thutmose III, shortly before the queen's death.

It is just possible that we should increase this list to six. If the long Deir el-Bahri text alludes to a different campaign from that described by Tiy, a second Nubian war must be inserted somewhere before no. 3; and if Thutmose III's Tombas inscription is considered as not pertaining to the campaign on which he shot the rhinoceros, there will be another Nubian expedition (*c.* year 20) to be accommodated between nos. 3 and 4.

The evidence cited above shows clearly that the belief that Hatshepsut undertook no foreign wars is simply untrue. During the two decades of her reign both she and the nominal ruler Thutmose III

[33] *Urk.* IV, 1248.

[34] Thus, e.g. Hayes, *CAH* II (1962), ch. 9, 27; also Helck (see preceding note).

[35] A similar renumbering of campaigns seems to have been attempted in Amenhotpe II's reign; see D. B. Redford, *JEA* 51 (1965), 122.

carried out military ventures of no mean proportions. Yet Hatshepsut's reign continues to be characterized as a conservative, reactionary throwback, imbued with the isolationist, non-aggressive tendencies of the Old and Middle Kingdoms. Wilson's assessment of the reign is representative of this widespread view:[36]

The reigns of Hat-shepsut and of Thut-mose III contrast strongly in the activities of the state. She records no military campaigns or conquests; he became the great conqueror and organizer of empire. Her pride was in the internal development of Egypt and in commercial enterprise; his pride was in the external expansion of Egypt and in military enterprise. This was a conflict between the older concept of the Egyptian state, an isolated and superior culture, which needed to express no major concern about other countries because no other country presented an important challenge to Egypt, and the new concept of the Egyptian state, a culture which felt obliged to assert its superiority by capturing and holding foreign territory. . . . Our theory . . . is that there was a choice to be made and that two different parties chose differently, Hat-shepsut's faction in terms of the lesser effort of earlier times and Thut-mose III's faction in terms of a new and major international venture. . . . Thut-mose III rejected the pattern of the past by making military activity regular and purposeful. . . . Hatshepsut gave Egypt internal glories instead of external victory. . . . In foreign affairs she repeated the traditional pattern from the past. . . . The unusual prominence given to this venture [the Pwenet expedition] has meaning as an expression of policy, that Egypt should cultivate more intensively the friends she already had and let the unfriendly Asiatics suffer from their own stubborn hostility because Egypt would not deal with them. Hat-shepsut was demonstrating the feasibility of the old pacific and tolerant policy of the past.

Thus the tenor of Hatshepsut's activity is understood by Wilson as the result of a conscious policy; her reign appears to us moderns to have been peaceful, conservative, and isolationist because she so intended it to be.

Quite apart from the texts cited earlier in the present chapter, the interpretation of Hatshepsut's reign as a reaction against imperialism is based largely on an *argumentum e silentio*. Without any other evidence to guide us it is dangerous to argue that what *did happen* was also what was *hoped would happen,* i.e. that the course of history is itself a clear reflection of premeditated policy. The military achievements of Hatshepsut are bound to suffer eclipse through the unfortunate circumstance that her reign was followed by the most brilliant imperialist expansion in Egypt's history. But the contrast, seen *post*

[36] J. Wilson, *The Burden of Egypt* (Chicago, 1951), 174ff.

eventum, should not lead us to conclude that Hatshepsut at the time actually shunned militarism; after all she did not live to see her nephew's successes, and she was scarcely clairvoyant. If it is true that Thutmose III's campaigns contrast most strikingly with her efforts in the military sphere, an even greater contrast must appear between the reign of Thutmose and those, say, of Haremhab and Sheshonk I. Solely on the basis of extant texts we should have to conclude that the reigns of the latter two monarchs were almost devoid of foreign wars. Yet will anyone assert that Haremhab and Sheshonk, soldiers both, consciously espoused a policy of "eschewing military endeavour and concentrating on peaceful goals"?[37] Not only is the preservation of ancient Egyptian texts spotty, and *ipso facto* unreliable in the over-all impression they convey, but also we cannot afford to forget that what a ruler finds expedient to do may not always be what he would like to do. Although it seems from what has been preserved from her reign that Hatshepsut occupied herself most of the time with peaceful pursuits, the evidence presented above shows that she did undertake, and at least once led in person, military campaigns abroad. No one is justified in asserting that this military activity was not in accord with her intended policy, or that she pursued it reluctantly. If one continues to insist that her floruit seems unusually peaceful, I must answer that there are two very probable reasons for its being so: (a) she was a woman, and thus found it rather inconvenient to lead an army of men in the field,[38] and (b) the world situation did not call for the use of exceptional military force during her lifetime.

A conflict between an isolationist-conservative party propounding a policy of traditional "non-aggression" and an outward-looking, imperialist party does not seem to the present writer to be the key to Hatshepsut's reign. But if the lines were not drawn between traditionalist and imperialist, where were they drawn? Or were there any lines at all, save those that separated the personalities of Hatshepsut and Thutmose III? Was it, indeed, nothing more than a power struggle between two divine giants, or were there other political ramifications?

37 *Ibid.*, 175.

38 T. Säve-Söderbergh, *Pharaohs and Mortals* (New York, 1957), 97.

The family of the Seventeenth and Eighteenth Dynasties had risen to power through victory in war, and much fighting had made its members by nature belligerent and ruthless in their personal dealings. During the war of liberation the Theban kings, like their Eleventh Dynasty predecessors under similar circumstances, had surrounded themselves with military men; the nation was on a war footing, and the king and his council formed the general staff. The same situation in regard to the royal family and court obtained throughout most of the dynasty, a fact which, as Aldred has seen,[39] explains the predominance of the military in high places at Amarna.

Although the king was the real head of state, and commander-in-chief of the army, the queen stood surprisingly close to him in both these departments. She was well informed on matters of state, exercising considerable influence over the heir presumptive and presumably over her husband as well;[40] and she even commanded her own body of troops![41] Nor did her influence decline with the passing of her husband: the queen-mother and dowager queen retain their position of authority vis-à-vis the son and grandson, and on the monuments are shown together with the king, sometimes to the exclusion of his queen.[42] This matriarchal streak is one of the most striking features of the early Eighteenth Dynasty. The stubbornness and driving ambition of the queens could not help but precipitate a conflict with the males of the family, at least if the women persisted in grasping after what logically must have been their ultimate aspiration, viz. the crown. After five generations of rule this is precisely what happened.

Matriarchy in popular jargon is often applied rather loosely to a number of unrelated social phenomena.[43] It is sometimes used of matriliny, i.e. descent and inheritance through the female line; but true matriarchy in the sense of female dominance of family affairs is not invariably linked with matriliny. Nor strangely is the avunculate, i.e. the influence of the maternal uncle in the rearing of the

[39] *JEA* 43 (1957), 30f.

[40] Cf. Tushratta's letter to Tiy, EA 26.

[41] Cf. the texts cited above concerning Hatshepsut; also *Urk.* IV, 21.

[42] M. A. Murray, *Ancient Egypt*, 1934, 67, Fig. 3; C. Aldred, *New Kingdom Art in Ancient Egypt* (London, 1952), Pl. 4.

[43] See R. H. Lowie, *Primitive Society* (New York, 1947), 64ff.; 166ff.; 180ff.; M. Titiev, *Introduction to Cultural Anthropology* (New York, 1959) 266ff., 280ff.

offspring. In fact, although the entire mother-clan may predominate more or less in the relations of a young family, it is rarely the wife herself whose voice is heard. Matronymy also is often connected with matriarchy, but the mere naming of the child by the mother's family has no bearing on whether or not the wife rules. Matriarchy in its strictest sense is never found. The Khasi of Assam approach very close to it; yet even here, where matriliny, matrilocal residence, feminine ownership, the avunculate, and a good deal of feminine rule are tolerated, the husband rules his family undisputed.[44] In short, it would seem advisable to refer in sociological contexts to a "matriarchal tendency" rather than matriarchy. By matriarchal tendency is meant the importance given by a society to either the person, the biological function, the legal status, or the will of its female members.

With such a definition matriarchal tendencies are found to be relatively common in various parts of the ancient and modern Near East. Matriliny and matronymy are both found sporadically among the modern bedouin of the Fertile Crescent;[45] and among their ancient forbears of the eighth century B.C. the Assyrian conquerors encountered tribes ruled by queens.[46] There is some evidence to suggest that even in more sedentary groups of West-Semitic-speaking peoples, including the Hebrews, matriarchal tendencies occurred rather often,[47] although in general they were overshadowed by the dominant patriarchal organization of the early Semites.

Coming now within the geographical sphere of Egypt's influence, we find matriarchal tendencies strong in Nubia and Kush from ancient through modern times, at least in ruling families. The queen mother in the royal house of seventh century Napata held a dominant and respected position,[48] and the passage of time did nothing but enhance the power of this member of the family. By the time of the kingdom of Meroe the matrilineal descent of the heir designate was apparently the rule, and not infrequently a succession of queens is found occupying the Meroitic throne for long periods.[49] Among the

[44] Lowie, *ibid.*, 189f.

[45] J. Morgenstern, *ZÄW*, NF, 8 (1931), 46ff. Cf. in this connexion the queen of Sheba in 1 Kings 10.

[46] Cf. Pritchard (ed.), *ANET*², 284, 286, 291.

[47] Morgenstern, *ZÄW*, NF, 6 (1929), 91ff.; *idem*, *JBL* 78 (1959), 322ff.

[48] Arkell, *A History of the Sudan to 1821*, 127.

[49] *Ibid.*, 157ff.

more modern Beja, women occupied a similarly important position. Not only did matriliny prevail, but also occupancy of the throne by a woman was relatively common.[50] It is by no means improbable that the ancient Medja (the progenitors of the Beja)[51] were signalized in their social mores by the same feminine dominance, and that matriarchal tendencies were rather widespread among the tribes of ancient Nubia.

During the Seventeenth Dynasty a good deal of contact took place between the peoples of Nubia and the Egyptians of the incipient Theban kingdom. Egyptian freebooters and adventurers drifted south out of Upper Egypt into the wilds of the trans-cataract region to hire themselves as soldiers to the king of Kush,[52] while an opposite movement brought Nubian mercenaries of Medja extraction into the service of the Seventeenth Dynasty.[53] In numbers the latter migration far outweighed the reverse movement of Egyptians. At numerous sites in Upper Egypt as far north as Asyut the Medja have left behind the remains of their settlements and their shallow pan-graves.[54] So large was the body of Medja mercenaries present in Egypt at this time that they formed a whole contingent of the army Kamose led north against the Hyksos.[55]

It is inconceivable that so sizable a settlement of Nubians inside the narrow confines of the "head of the south" should have left the culture of the tiny Theban state unaffected. Although the extent of the influence will probably never be known correctly, not a few of the distinctive features of New Kingdom society and religion may have appeared through contact with Nubia.

In particular one wonders what contacts or connexions the royal family of the Ta'o's had with the land and people south of the first cataract. A number of ethnic strains have at various times been postulated for this family, but none has had widespread acceptance. Older scholars used to suggest a tincture of Negro blood on the basis of the black (or blue) complexion of Ahmose-Nofretari in certain

[50] J. L. Burckhardt, *Travels in Nubia* (London, 1819), 278 and 503.
[51] See Gardiner, *AEO* I, 73*ff., esp. 80*.
[52] B. Gunn, *ASAE* 29 (1929), 5ff.; Säve-Söderbergh, *JEA* 35 (1949), 50ff.
[53] Säve-Söderbergh, *Ägypten und Nubien*, 135ff.
[54] *HSE* II, 39ff.
[55] Carnarvon Tablet, 12: Gardiner, *JEA* 1 (1914), Pl. 12.

New Kingdom tomb paintings, but scarcely anyone will hold this view today.[56] Likewise the suggestion of E. Meyer[57] that Ahhotpe I was of Cretan origin is given little credence, though the title "mistress of Hau-nebu"[58] is intriguing. A more recent view, that of Helck, would have it that the Seventeenth Dynasty had a Hurrian background.[59] Such a postulate is not as fantastic as might at first appear, at least not if one accepts Helck's further thesis that a dominant element in the Hyksos movement was Hurrian. The extent of Hurrian involvement in the movement is, however, very problematical (certainly Engberg's conclusions[60] are baseless), Semites and Aryans probably comprising most of the horde.[61] That the Seventeenth Dynasty was of Hurrian origin is thus not very likely.[62]

It must be admitted that we have virtually no reliable evidence regarding the origin of the Seventeenth Dynasty. Of the family of Taʿo I we know nothing; of his wife's, scarcely more than that she was the daughter of commoners.[63] But given the broad historical picture of Upper Egypt in the first half of the sixteenth century, one must admit that the theory mooted below emerges not entirely without support. It is not unlikely, in view of the heavy influx of Nubians into Upper Egypt, that the family of the Seventeenth Dynasty could boast of a large admixture of Nubian blood. We have already noticed the prominent position occupied by women in the family; but there is also the evidence of personal names compounded with *iʿḥ*, *kꜣ*, and *Ǧḥwty*. These theophorous names presuppose a strong attachment to

[56] Cf. on this problem Maspero, *Histoire*, II, 98f., n. 10.

[57] *Geschichte*, II, 1, 55.

[58] *Urk.* IV, 21.

[59] *Die Beziehungen Ägyptens zu Vorderasien* (Wiesbaden, 1962), 102ff.

[60] *The Hyksos Reconsidered* (Chicago, 1939), *passim;* cf. A. Alt, *Die Herkunft der Hyksos in neuer Sicht* (Berlin, 1961), 18f.

[61] From the evidence of the personal names there can be little doubt of the Semitic element: cf. Alt, *op. cit.*, 5, n. 3; S. Yeivin, *JEA* 45 (1959), 16ff.

[62] Helck's assertion (*Die Beziehungen Ägyptens zu Vorderasien,* 103) that the predominance of the moon in personal names of the Seventeenth and Eighteenth Dynasties is to be connected somehow with the Hurrian god Kushuh is doubtful. His further contention that the Eighteenth Dynasty name Sapair (*Sꜣ-pꜣ-ir;* Gauthier, *Livre,* II, 188ff.) is really a transliteration of the Hurrian name *Šapari* is doubtful. In Egyptian syllabic orthography *Šapari* would probably become  (cf. W. F. Albright, *The Vocalization of Egyptian Syllabic Orthography* [New Haven, 1934], 54f. and 49).

[63] Above, p. 30.

a lunar cult, and there is no reason to believe that it was a Hermopolitan or a Theban one.[64] The moon cult flourished in Nubia too,[65] and personal names of the Second Intermediate Period compounded with lunar elements are found in Nubia.[66] Moreover, the early Eighteenth Dynasty image of the royal family as carrying on the traditions of the Twelfth Dynasty[67] finds no explanation if the Seventeenth Dynasty was of Theban origin—the connexions of the Twelfth Dynasty were all with the Faiyum area. But if the Taʿo's were in whole or in part of Nubian origin, an explanation could easily be found in the strong impression left by the Amenemhet's and Senwosret's in Nubia, where the forts they had built continued to be used during the Hyksos period, and where their deified persons were already ranked alongside the local pantheon.[68] A family that originated in a land where the Twelfth Dynasty had already become a legend would take the reigns of power in Thebes imbued with a sense of mission, a desire to resurrect the glorious, united Egypt of the Middle Kingdom.

While the Nubian origin of the Seventeenth Dynasty must of necessity remain entirely hypothetical, the matriarchal tendency in the family is a fact. Both Tetyshery and Ahhotpe I wielded great authority vis-à-vis their husbands and children, and the latter openly threw her weight into the politico-military sphere by quelling an incipient rebellion, perhaps at the time her husband Taʿo II perished.[69] Great as the influence of these two queens was, however, it was not until the arrival of the third generation that the exalted status of the queen was formalized.

After some fifteen years of fighting under Ahmose, Egypt paused, breathless but not fatigued. She had rid herself of foreign domination

[64] Gardiner, *Egypt of the Pharaohs*, 174f.

[65] Cf. Thoth "lord of *Tꜣ-i-sꜣ-ti*" (*Urk*. IV, 1486); the lunar god of Soleb whom "Nebmare, Lord of Nubia" apparently assimilated (below, p. 97, n. 45); there is some possibility that Dedwen also had lunar connexions; cf. S. A. B. Mercer, *The Religion of Ancient Egypt* (London, 1949), 225. On the identity of Dedwen as a bird of prey, see Kees, *Der Götterglaube im alten Ägypten* (Leipzig, 1941), 45; also H. Gauthier, *Revue Egyptologique*, NS, 2 (1920), 1ff.

[66] Säve-Söderbergh, *JEA* 35 (1949), 50ff.

[67] See below, pp. 78f.

[68] Cf. Säve-Söderbergh, *JEA* 35 (1949), 54, Fig. 2, line 2.

[69] Cf. *Urk*. IV, 21.

in the north, had completely discomfited, though not annihilated, the Kushite kingdom in the south, and now could rest in the assurance that if any further fighting were to take place it would not be on her soil. It was time to rest and take stock. War must be followed by reorganization and rebuilding. There must also be, after the present dangers of counterattack and famine had been obviated, a spiritual reassessment and a formulation of new policy. To the ancients the spiritual and the political were all bound up with man's relationship to his gods.

The family of Ahmose, the former Seventeenth Dynasty, was now firmly established in Thebes, and their feeling of affinity with the local god Amun was strong. Since the rebellion against the Hyksos had begun right in Thebes, it was Amun himself who had rebelled against the Hyksos Baal. And if Thebes had won, had it not been Amun who had triumphed over Baal? *Ipso facto* Amun was destined to receive the booty, and the free-will gifts of king and people besides. Ahmose set about to embellish the small provincial shrine that had survived from Middle Kingdom times, and presented to the gods the spoils of his wars and all sorts of cultic paraphernalia. Overnight, as it were, Amun of the backwoods, so long impoverished during the years when Thebes was cut off from the products of Asia and Kush, found himself the possessor of vast riches undreamed of two generations earlier. Ahmose had begun a historical process which, centuries later, would culminate in the monstrous spectacle of the fabulously wealthy "king of the gods" dictating to the earthly king through his priesthood.

It is not to be believed that Ahmose failed to realize the latent power he was bequeathing to Amun by catapulting him to the pinnacle of the pantheon. His purpose was to tie the cult closely to the kingship by reserving for the monarch the right to choose the high priest of the god. The control of the second highest office in the priestly hierarchy, that of second prophet, would be in the hands of the queen, who could appoint whomsoever she pleased.[70] Nevertheless, Ahmose was creating a second power within the state, which could, and finally did, challenge Horus for the rule; and none of his precautionary measures would avail then.

[70] Cf. the stela granting Ahmose-Nofretari this right; for references, see above pp. 30f., n. 12.

The third generation of the line of queens appears during the reign of Ahmose in the person of Ahmose-Nofretari. This strong-willed woman, the king's full sister, probably had a good deal to do with delineating in formal terms the exact status of the queen. She is called "female chieftain of Upper and Lower Egypt," which is possibly a direct reference to her political authority. A more important title created for her was that of "god's-wife (*ḥmt-nčr*),"[71] and herein we touch upon a fundamental theological doctrine of the Eighteenth Dynasty, enunciated under this its first king. The queen was the repository of that power which, when bestowed at birth upon her offspring, distinguished him from all other quasi-royal progeny as the rightful heir to the throne. Other royal relatives, even the king himself, did not really figure in determining the succession: the queen was the heiress, and the right to the throne passed through her. In order better to ensure the purity of the line, the doctrine had it that on the night of the conception the god Amun had become incarnate in the person of the reigning king and had impregnated the queen with divine seed. By virtue of this fact the queen could call herself "god's-wife,"[72] and her offspring could justifiably maintain that in a mystical sense he was truly the "son of Amun."[73] Since Amun had thus by choice selected the queen, she became his favourite and functioned in his temple. The entire feminine staff of the shrine was under her supervision, exactly as, in an earthly family, the servant girls were subservient to the mistress of the house. The queen had her own palace and her own estate,[74] and presumably the king would be obliged to present himself at her apartments if he wished

[71] See C. E. Sander-Hansen, *Das Gottesweib des Amun* (Copenhagen, 1940), 20; the epithet was applied to Ahhotpe posthumously.

[72] *Ḥmt-nčr;* I understand this title as implying first and foremost a consummated marriage with the god, and not merely as designating the office of high-priestess (though the title secondarily entailed the duties of such an office).

[73] *Sꜣ-'Imn;* as an epithet, see *Wb* III, 408:13. Cf. the description of Amenhotpe in Ramessid times as "son of Amun, the divine seed, eminating from his body": *JNES* 22 (1963), 31, Fig. 1, lines 6 to 8. *Sꜣ-'Imn* is found as an epithet already on a seal of the Seventeenth Dynasty; cf. G. Legrain, *Répertoire généalogique et onomastique du Musée du Caire* (Geneva, 1908), no. 6; and the concept has its roots in the Middle Kingdom.

[74] I. Hariri, *ASAE* 56 (1959), plate facing p. 202, lines 17–18.

to visit. Here was matriliny and matrilocal residence with a vengeance![75]

Ahmose-Nofretari proved to be a fertile god's-wife. She bore at least four sons, of whom all but one predeceased their father.[76] The surviving heir when Ahmose died was one Amenhotpe, who must have been but a child at the time. His mother ruled for him for about six or seven years,[77] and the impression she left on subsequent generations was a lasting one. But although she was *de facto* ruler of the land, she did not seize the throne and proclaim herself king. To the end of the period of regency she remained the queen-mother and first god's-wife, filling in until her son came of age.

The title of god's-wife stood in danger of passing into obsolescence. It had been bestowed, undoubtedly in anticipation, on three daughters of Ahmose-Nofretari in turn,[78] but two had died prematurely, and the third had apparently no chance to prove herself.[79] It was then given to a fourth daughter, named after her maternal grandmother Ahhotpe, who was married to Amenhotpe her brother, but who died apparently childless.[80] Consequently it was conferred—almost in desperation, one might imagine—on yet another daughter named, with a typical Egyptian lack of imagination, Ahmose. Yet throughout this spate of premature deaths the doctrine of Amun's progeniture

[75] On the subject of the god's-wife see Sander-Hansen, *Das Gottesweib des Amun passim.*

[76] In their probable order: Si-amun (G. Maspero, *Les Momies royales de Déir el-Bahari* [Cairo, 1884], 538; Gauthier, *Livre,* II, 190f.), Ahmose-onkh (Hariri, *ASAE* 56 [1959], plate facing p. 202), Amenhotpe, and Ahmose Sapair (Gauthier, *Livre,* II, 188ff.). Both Si-amun and Ahmose-onkh at one time held the distinction of being eldest (surviving) son, and therefore probably died before their father. Amenhotpe was thus probably the third son, unless Sapair preceded him but died before his elder brothers.

[77] Does the appearance of a new viceroy of Kush, Turo, *c.* year 7 of the reign (J. H. Breasted, *AJSL* 25 [1908], 108) signalize the coming of age of the young king?

[78] Sander-Hansen, *Das Gottesweib des Amun,* 6 (nos. 3 to 5).

[79] Unless, indeed, Sander-Hansen's no. 5, Sat-Kamose, is to be relegated to third position, perhaps as a daughter of King Kamose, who lived on into Ahmose's reign and held the title for a short time subsequent to Ahmose-Nofretari.

[80] She was not a "king's-mother" as Gauthier claims (*Livre,* II, 207 [A,1]; 208 [A,4]). The texts cited by Gauthier belong respectively to Ahmose-Nofretari (cf. P–M I², 250) and Ahhotpe I (cf. Maspero, *Les Momies royales . . .,* 545).

of the heir remained firm, and even when Amenhotpe realized that a son would not be born to him, it survived unshaken.

Towards the close of his reign Amenhotpe chose one of his generals, a certain Thutmose, to succeed him; and to that end he married him off to Ahmose and elevated him to the throne as coregent. The choice of a rank commoner should not provoke any wonder on our part, for the Egyptians acquiesced most blandly. The practice of looking outside the royal family for a successor is, in any case, quite in keeping with matriliny as it appears in ancient royal houses. From the Levant comes evidence that sometimes a king would ignore his own sons when it came time to select the next occupant of the throne, and choose from among his able warriors. The heir designate would then be obliged to marry the king's daughter to legitimize his claim to the throne. Thus it would be possible to find whole dynasties in which no king was related to any other, the blood relationship passing only through the line of queens.[81] Thutmose employed the same method of selection. His sons Amenmose and Wadjmose, born by an earlier(?) wife[82] before his elevation to the throne, were passed over in favour of an obscure individual, named Thutmose too, the king's son by a concubine. His eldest daughter by Ahmose, named Hatshepsut, was formally proclaimed heiress and prospective god's-wife, and the boy Thutmose was joined to her in wedlock. This pattern of selection was rapidly becoming the norm when Thutmose II penetrated into a dark corner of the harem to bring forth another concubine's son, again a namesake, as his successor.[83] But this time the selection encountered opposition.

The queens who had occupied the position of god's wife since the passing of Ahmose-Nofretari had been non-entities, but Hatshepsut was made of the same fibre as her grandmother. Probably already in her girlhood she nursed the hope of one day reviving the former

[81] Cf. Morgenstern, *ZÄW*, NF, 6 (1929), 108; *JBL* 98 (1959), 322ff.

[82] Not likely by Ahmose, since Amenmose was old enough in his father's fourth year to hold the rank of general: *Urk.* IV, 91.

[83] Thutmose III's mother Isis has been considered a concubine because there was no indication of a royal parentage or even an impressive titulary. In her son's mortuary temple, however, she is called "great king's-wife, his beloved, mistress of south and north, great heiress, god's-wife and king's-mother": G. Legrain, *ASAE* 7 (1907), 134; H. Ricke, *Das Totentempels Thutmosis' III* (Cairo, 1939), 30, n. 5.

glories of her line. At first, however, she had no secret designs on the throne; and the fact that later, as her half-brother's queen, she had excavated a tomb for herself equipped with paraphernalia for a *queenly* burial shows that no craving for the kingship yet gnawed at her entrails.[84] But the line of queens was to revive, and her daughter Neferure, the heiress, was to take a prominent part in the rule. For this purpose the title god's-wife was bestowed upon her. Hatshepsut may have naïvely assumed that her designs for her daughter were shared by Thutmose II, or it may have been that an agreement had been reached regarding the succession which the king's dramatic appointment of Thutmose III abrogated. In either case Hatshepsut was outraged by Thutmose III's accession, but she waited for her moment to strike.[85]

One account of Thutmose II's settlement of the succession comes from Thutmose III himself.[86] In an inscription written decades later he tells how as an acolyte in the Temple of Amun he was singled out by the god on a festival day. The barque of Amun was proceeding around the hall on the shoulders of its priestly bearers when all at once it halted, and by some sign the divine occupant indicated his choice of the child Thutmose. At this point the king's account tells of how he was whisked off to heaven and presented with his titulary in the presence of the gods themselves. What actually happened next is not known, but our ignorance is unimportant. What matters is that, according to Thutmose, his reign began under the aegis of Amun.

Despite the apparent originality of Thutmose's text, the extant sources show that this miraculous occurrence was supposed to have been a repetition of one that had taken place at the beginning of

[84] H. Carter, *JEA* 4 (1917), 107ff.; W. C. Hayes, *Royal Sarcophagi of the Eighteenth Dynasty* (Princeton, 1935), 12ff.

[85] To postulate a previous agreement between Hatshepsut and Thutmose II regarding the succession of Neferure, which was broken at the last moment by Thutmose II, on his own initiative and to the chagrin of the queen, seems to me to be the best explanation of two facts: (a) that the king chose an utterly obscure child of the harem as successor, whereas the precedent of Amenhotpe I of choosing a stalwart commoner outside the family was before him, and (b) the rapid and early take-over by Hatshepsut, with Neferure being thrust into a prominent role.

[86] *Urk.* IV, 157ff.

Thutmose I's reign. There is at Deir el-Bahri a fragmentary inscription,[87] of over twenty lines originally, which was carved by Thutmose III[88] over an earlier text of Hatshepsut. In the original scheme of decoration Hatshepsut carved her text behind a figure of herself(?), shown in front of her father, who sat in a kiosk on a dais. What information the queen wished to convey by her inscription is not immediately apparent, save that it was of a nature extremely objectionable to Thutmose III. He removed it completely, and in its place wrote out a "coronation" inscription, which purports to give the circumstances surrounding Thutmose I's accession to the throne. What remains of the text bears a remarkable affinity to Thutmose III's own coronation account.[89] In short, Thutmose is claiming for his grandfather the same divine ordination as he says he enjoyed himself. The question is: Which king in actual fact was elevated to the throne by such a staged theophany? Or was the gimmick, proved once in the case of Thutmose I, used again by his son to substantiate his choice of successor? Another possibility that suggests itself is that

[87] Naville, *The Temple of Deir el Bahari*, VI, Pl. 166; cf. also Sethe, *APAW* 1932 (no. 4), 78ff.; Helck, *Studia Biblica et Orientalia*, III, 115.

[88] Naville, *The Temple of Deir el Bahari*, VI, 9.

[89] These affinities are best appreciated in a table of comparisons:

Deir el-Bahri text	*Karnak text of Thutmose III*
[ ]*ʿḥʿ.ti*[ ]; "[ ] standing [ ]" (1).	*ʿḥʿ.kwi m wȝǧyt mḥtt;* "while I was standing in the northern hall . . ." (*Urk.* IV, 157:13).
[ ] *nfrw.f; wn.in.f ḥr pẖr* [ ]; "[seeing?] his beauty; then he proceeded around [ ]" (3).	[ ] *ḥr pẖr wȝǧyt ḥr gswy.sy;* "[this god] proceeded round the hall on its two sides" (*Urk.* IV, 158:8).
nčr pn ẖnw; "this god halted" (4).	*iw.f ẖnw;* "he halted" (*Urk.* IV, 158:12).
[ ] *rn nb mnḫ n* [ ]; "[ ] every effective name of [ ]" (4?).	*wd.⟨f⟩ n.i nḫbt ǧs.f;* "he himself set a titulary for me" (*Urk.* IV, 160:11).
[*snḫt.n.f*] *rn.*[*f m*] *Kȝ-nḫt, di.n.f* [ ]; "[he empowered his] name as 'Mighty Bull,' he caused [ ]" (6).	*snḫt.n.f wi m Kȝ-nḫt, di.n.f ḫʿw.i m-ẖnw Wȝst;* "he empowered me as 'Mighty Bull'; he caused me to appear in Thebes" (*Urk.* IV, 160:13).
rdi.n.f n.f pḥt[*y.f . . .*]; "he granted him [his] strength [ ]" (7).	*di.n.f n.i sḫm.f pḥty.f;* "he granted me his might and his strength" (*Urk.* IV, 161:3).

both texts are modelled on an original of Thutmose I, now lost; in other words that Thutmose III is blatantly—and wrongfully—usurping a text of his grandfather.

The correct solution to the puzzle is supplied by the text itself. Portions of the original inscription of Hatshepsut show through the palimpsest, and the words discernible together with the feminine grammatical forms[90] indicate two important facts: (a) that the underlying inscription was also a "coronation" inscription, and (b) that it referred to the queen herself. It is possible, therefore, that the story of the miraculous designation of the heir, as told by Thutmose III of himself and of his grandfather, was originally a creation of Hatshepsut, by and for herself.

It is obvious that the tale is a fabrication. In any case, Hatshepsut did not need to justify her usurpation yet, at least not in this way. An oracle of Amun would suffice, and, accompanied as it would be by "wonders," the impression on the people would be much more dramatic than a banal reinterpretation of history. And so, in the second year of Thutmose III, very close to ten months after the commencement of the new reign, the expected pronouncement by Amun was heard, the wonders were performed, and Hatshepsut became king.[91] Prior to this time she had been known only as "great king's-wife,"[92] and although this designation remained a popular one throughout her reign,[93] she thereafter took over a kingly titulary on formal monuments, and appeared in male form and costume.[94]

There was no opposition. Why should there be? Thutmose was allowed to retain the outward show of kingship, and his aunt even allowed him to appear behind her in reliefs. Among the people he was still referred to as "king" and she as "queen";[95] what more did he want? Nevertheless things had been well planned. While Hatshepsut was still "great king's-wife" her chief steward Senenmut had repaired to the Aswan quarries, and by the time Amun delivered his oracle two enormous obelisks were ready for erection at Thebes.[96]

[90] Cf. *'ḥ'.ti*, line 1.

[91] S. Schott, *Nachr. Gött.* (1955), 212.

[92] *HSE* II, 80.

[93] Cf. W. C. Hayes, *MDIAK* 15 (1957), 80.

[94] On the subject of her masculine appearance in the reliefs, see P. Lacau, *RHR* 143 (1953), 1ff.

[95] Cf. Hayes, *JEA* 46 (1960), Pl. 10:5, recto 3; 6, recto 8; Pl. 11:14, recto 4, 6, 10, 12, 14; also p. 34, n. 1.

[96] Habachi, *JNES* 16 (1957), 88ff.

The allusion to careful planning presupposes that Hatshepsut already had a "party" to support her. There can be no doubt that her chief supporter was her steward Senenmut, a man of low origin, who throughout most of the reign appears to have been something of a power behind the throne.[97] Who the other members of her "party" were we cannot be sure, but certainly her father's chief advisor Ineni was with her, [98] as well as the old soldier and treasurer Ahmose pa-nekhbit.[98] The erstwhile vizier and high priest of Amun, Hapuseneb, also must have lent considerable support.[100] By year 5 he had relinquished his vizierate,[101] but he continued to function as high priest of Amun during most of Hatshepsut's floruit, suffering no diminution of power at all. But perhaps it is misleading to speak of a "party," since this suggests political goals and the espousing of definite policy. As soon as Hatshepsut achieved her coup, all Egypt came over to her, and "Egypt laboured for her submissively."[102] She had a circle of favourites, a motley collection of individuals with no common background and little reason to share political goals. There were the "new men" of humble birth, like Senenmut and his brother Senmen, the first herald Duwa-eneheh,[103] the second prophet of Amun Ipuyemre,[104] and the chief steward Amenhotpe;[105] foreigners, like the engineer Benya, born of Hurrian stock,[106] or Nehsi the treasurer, possibly of Nubian;[107] the old guard, like Ahmose pa-nekhbit and Ineni; landed gentry, like Djehuty of Hermopolis,[108] and Yamu-nefru of Nefrusi;[109] and scions of bureaucratic families like User-amun the vizier,[110] or Sen-nefer the treasurer.[111] These hardly constituted a "party." Indeed, if any could have read the handwriting on the wall, they doubtless would have left the queen's side

97 For bibliography see Helck, *Verwaltung*, 473ff.

98 *Urk.* IV, 59f.

99 *Ibid.*, 34.

100 G. Lefebvre, *L' Histoire des Grands Prêtres d'Amon de Karnak* (Paris, 1929), 72f.; Kees, *Das Priestertum im Ägyptischen Staat vom neuen Reich bis zur Spätzeit* (Leiden, 1953), 11f.

101 Cf. Helck, *Urk.* IV, 1380–4; since in the southern vizierate the long-lived Ahmose was succeeded directly by his son User-amun in year 5, it may have been the northern vizierate that Hapuseneb held.

102 *Urk.* IV, 60.

103 *Ibid.*, 1379f.

104 Kees, *Das Priestertum* . . ., 13.

105 Helck, *Verwaltung*, 479.

106 Cf. Säve-Söderbergh, *Orientalia Suecana* (1960), 54ff.

107 *Urk.* IV, 354.

108 *Ibid.*, 419ff.

109 *Ibid.*, 1453ff.

110 *Ibid.*, 1380ff.

111 *Ibid.*, 528ff.

at once—shocking behaviour for a loyal "party" member (although the latter is admittedly rare)!

The twenty-year reign, auspiciously inaugurated by Amun's oracle, was to be a unique break with the past. Far from conservative—how can a woman who proclaims herself king, thus violating all traditional norms of monarchy, be called conservative?—Hatshepsut showed herself to be an imaginative planner possessed of a rather original taste.

When it emerged from the war of liberation, the Eighteenth Dynasty appeared in many ways to be merely a continuation of the traditional Middle Kingdom. In the official lists[112] the Eighteenth Dynasty kings followed those of the Twelfth Dynasty immediately, while in other groupings of kings Ahmose and family are inevitably grouped with Nebhepetre, Kheperkare, or some other illustrious Middle Kingdom ruler.[113] The image of the king in the early Eighteenth Dynasty, viz. the military generalissimo and civil leader who fights tirelessly to protect Egypt, is precisely that of the late Twelfth Dynasty; and in the admonitory tone in which Ahmose gives his people political advice[114] there is more than an echo of the "instruction of Sehtepibre."[115] This attempt by the Ahmosids to represent themselves as the successors of the Twelfth Dynasty kings and the upholders of the Middle Kingdom tradition is exemplified also in the art and architecture of the early Eighteenth Dynasty. Painting and sculpture, for example, are clearly inspired by Middle Kingdom styles, techniques, and subject matter.[116] The architectural achievements of the age, though admittedly scarce, feature pyramidal tombs for royalty, "cenotaphs" at Abydos, and simple way-shrines for processions, all throwbacks to Middle Kingdom archetypes, executed carefully, yet with little originality. In particular, the

[112] Cf. the Abydos and Memphite canons.

[113] Cf. *LD* III, 2; A. H. Gardiner, *Hieratic Papyri in the British Museum, Third Series: Chester Beatty Gift* (London, 1935), Pl. 53a.

[114] *Urk.* IV, 20.

[115] Sethe, *Aegyptische Lesestücke* (Leipzig, 1924), 68f.

[116] C. Aldred, *New Kingdom Art in Ancient Egypt* (London, 1952), 7f.; W. S. Smith, *The Art and Architecture of Ancient Egypt* (Harmondsworth, 1958), 128.

rudimentary layout of the Middle Kingdom temple is still present;[117] the complex processional temple, so typical of the New Kingdom and later, has not yet come into being.

The first signs of change come under Thutmose I. If we are to postulate for the early Eighteenth Dynasty a conflict over state policy between traditionalists and imperialists, as Wilson and others would have it, then such a conflict must be placed here, around the time when Thutmose I came to the throne. By no means could the new king be termed a "traditionalist". If he did meet with opposition, it must have been weak indeed, for he seems to have had little trouble in putting through his programme for Egypt. Some of his innovations presaged what was to become the norm in succeeding generations. He moved his court to Memphis, where the palace he built was still used by royalty 150 years later;[118] and from here he planned and executed his conquest of Asia. As far as we are able to say, this marked the inception of the Asiatic empire.[119] At Thebes the first attempts were made to transform the provincial shrine of Amun into a large, state temple. An enceinte wall was thrown up around the whole, and a pylon was erected as a grand façade with obelisks, and probably colossi flanking the approach.[120] Across the river Thutmose excavated his tomb in a lonely wady beyond the cliffs, where no earlier king had ever thought of locating his final resting place. A new departure too was the great distance separating the tomb from the mortuary chapel, which was built in the Nile valley. The tomb was rock-cut; the pyramid form, at least for kings, was now to be abandoned permanently.

117 For typical ground plans of the Middle Kingdom, see J. Vandier, *Manuel d'Archéologie Egyptienne* (Paris, 1952–58) II, 2, 621 Fig. 326, 629 Fig. 329, 639 Fig. 332.

118 Cf. the restoration inscription of Tutankhamun: Helck, *Urk.* IV, 2028; see also p. 2109.

119 There is good evidence that Ahmose too had campaigned in Syria (*Urk.* IV, 35), had fought Mitanni (Borchardt, *Mittel*, Pl. 18; Brunner, *MIOF* 4 [1956], 323ff.), and had hunted wild animals(?) in Asia (*HSE* II, 44). It is most unlikely, however, that this attempt at empire-building lasted; both Hatshepsut and Thutmose III in their inscriptions indicate Thutmose I as the real founder of Egypt's empire in the Levant.

120 Cf. Ineni's biography, *Urk.* IV, 55ff.

This spirit of innovation and the willingness to modify the norm were accentuated during the reign of Hatshepsut. Although there exist a few doubtful precursors of the terraced temple she built at Deir el-Bahri, the originality of the design cannot be gainsaid. Likewise the works of art from her reign, although again owing a debt to the Middle Kingdom, display the imprint of an individual novel taste, which must be none other than that of the divine being who occupied the Horus-throne.

In so far as we can speak of the policies of the queen's administration (and it is a justifiable inference that royal inscriptions, stereotyped as they sometimes are, do convey the specific aspirations of the monarch), we must conclude from her repeated references to it that a building programme had top priority. "[She shall build] your chapels and sanctify [your] houses," Amun had prophesied to the gods concerning the child Hatshepsut;[121] and the gods themselves had addressed the princess with the words "you shall refound it (the land), you shall repair what is in ruins in it, you shall make your chapels your monument. . . ."[122] Hatshepsut was later to boast that she it was who rebuilt the ruins left by the Hyksos in the north: "I have repaired what was destroyed, I have raised up what was in pieces ever since the Asiatics had been in Avaris in the Delta, nomadic bands being among them, overthrowing what had been made. . . .[123]

But new foundations have to be provided with endowments, and Hatshepsut was not blind to the need of bolstering Egypt's economy. Running a close second to the building programme were the economic measures taken by the queen. Trade with foreign countries was furthered, not only with the African lands to the south, but also with the Levant and the islands of the sea. And what could not be acquired through trade was seized by military conquest.

We have already pointed out the error of the widespread notion that Hatshepsut's reign had a decidedly pacific tinge. The texts show that the army had an important role to play in Hatshepsut's design to rebuild Egypt. She was proud of the state of preparedness of her forces, a state that she rigidly maintained: "my troops,[124]

[121] *Urk.* IV, 217; cf. also 290.

[122] *Ibid.*, 247.

[123] Gardiner, *JEA* 32 (1946), Pl. 6:36–8.

[124] *Mnfyt* not *mšʿ*; cf. Gardiner, *ibid.*, 46, n. 16.

which were (formerly) unequipped, are (now) well paid since I appeared as king."[125] Her military ventures abroad were designed partly to keep the peace, partly to get rich spoils for Amun. In Hatshepsut's own eyes she was pursuing the same military policy as her father; indeed, she represented her Asiatic campaigns as merely the fulfilment of the operation left incomplete at Thutmose I's death.[126] To the modern ear this sounds like propaganda, and, with a strict definition of the term, such it undoubtedly is. But it is another thing to assert that the queen intended to deceive people by it. There is no evidence to suggest that she did not actually believe that she was carrying out the expressed will of her father and deviating not at all from the path he had chosen to follow. Being a woman, and being consumed by the desire to establish her claim and that of her daughter to the throne, she could not help but deviate somewhat, nay considerably, from what Thutmose I would have wished; but she did not think she was deviating.

It is not at all improbable that Thutmose III was thrust into the army as a child at the queen's behest, and that it was part of her grand design that he should take command of the army when he came of age and lead the foreign campaigns, while she looked after internal affairs. There is no reason to suppose that Thutmose chafed at his being relegated to the army, or that he in any way differed with his aunt in matters of foreign policy involving the army. In fact, when he eventually took over the reigns of government on the queen's death, his military policy proved to be merely an extension of her own. The sole difference was that he pursued it more ruthlessly and logically, devoting himself for twenty years body and soul to its fulfilment. To keep the peace, Thutmose reasoned, one had to raise the frontier at the farthest possible distance from the homeland and keep it there. And to ensure a steady flow of wealth into the treasury the intervening territory had to be administered with rigour. To require a simple oath from the vassals was insufficient. Their children had to be carted off to Egypt, and governors installed in their territories. A woman could not accomplish all this; a matriarchate could not meet Egypt's imperial needs.

[125] *Ibid.*, Pl. 6:15.

[126] Cf. the Deir el-Bahri text quoted above, p. 60.

Despite the vigour with which she prosecuted her programme for Egypt, an aura of illegitimacy always surrounded the person of Hatshepsut. Desperately she tried to mask it, asserting her rights over and over in the official inscriptions. She had two means of doing this: first by stressing her legal right as successor to her father and, second, by emphasizing the mystery of her divine parentage. To stress the legality of her succession she resorted to an obscure incident that had occurred when she was a girl, and transformed it out of all recognition. The original incident itself was probably nothing more than Hatshepsut's "coming-of-age," at which time Thutmose I presented her to the court as the heiress. Twenty years later, however, it sounded like this:

Said his majesty (Thutmose I) to her (Hatshepsut): "Come, O glorious one, whom I have placed in my embrace, that you may witness the arrangements (made) for you in the palace . . . that you may receive the honour of your double crown . . . you shall be mighty in the two lands, you shall seize the rebellious. You shall appear in the palace, your forehead adorned with the double crown. . . ." His (text, my) majesty had brought to him the royal nobles, the dignitaries, the companions, the courtiers of the residence and the leaders of the commons. . . . There occurred a sitting of the king himself in the audience chamber on the west side, while these people were prostrated in the court. Then his majesty said to them, "This daughter of mine, Khnumetamun Hatshepsut—may she live!—I have appointed as my successor, upon my throne. It is she, in fact, who shall sit upon this marvellous dais. She shall direct the commons in every sphere of the palace; it is she, indeed, who shall lead you. Obey her words, unite yourselves at her command. . . ." The royal nobles, the dignitaries, and the leaders of the commons heard this proclamation of the promotion of his daughter, the king of Upper and Lower Egypt, Makare—may she live eternally! They kissed the earth at his feet when the word of the king fell upon them. They thanked the king of Upper and Lower Egypt Okheperkare—may he live eternally!—and then went forth rejoicing. . . . All the commons of all the hamlets of the residence heard, and they came rejoicing; hamlet after hamlet announced it in his name, troop after troop [exulted?], leaped, danced for the great joy in their hearts. They repeatedly proclaimed the name of her majesty as king . . . they realized that she was indeed the daughter of a god. . . .[127]

The incident has now become, in this Deir el-Bahri text, the formal proclamation of Hatshepsut as king. Her assumption of power in the second year of Thutmose III had been merely the finalizing of her

[127] *Urk.* IV, 255–60.

appointment as ruler, an appointment made by none other than her father, the revered Okheperkare Thutmose I.

Her divine filiation was emphasized partly by her own assertions and partly by Amun's testimony. The following scattered phrases, taken from the Karnak obelisk, exemplify the type of asseveration she was constantly using:[128] "I have done this (i.e. erected the obelisks) out of a loving heart for my father Amun. . . . I did it under his command, it was he who led me. I did not conceive any works without his agency; it was he who gave the directions. . . . I am truly his (Amun's) daughter, the one who glorifies him. . . ." On the successful completion of the Pwenet expedition Amun is made to say: "Welcome, my sweet daughter, my favourite, king of Upper and Lower Egypt Makare, the maker of my beautiful monuments. . . . You are king. . . . You satisfy my heart at all times. . . . I have given you all countries, all foreign lands, that your heart may be happy with them. Long ago I prophesied them for you: 'the ages of the future shall see it'—concerning these many years. . . ."[129] The better to impress the populace with her divine descent, the mystery of her birth and the paternity of Amun were set forth in a series of reliefs in the Deir el-Bahri temple. The account traced the history of the queen from the time when Amun designated Hatshepsut's mother, Ahmose, as the chosen vessel, through the miraculous birth and her childhood, concluding with her coronation at the hands of the gods. In part, at least, it was an old story, some of the episodes in the tale being found already in Middle Kingdom texts.[130] But it was shaped by the queen to her own needs, and probably contains not a little new material.

Her courtship of the Amun cult created a situation the seriousness of which Hatshepsut probably did not appreciate. The strong reliance the queen was placing on Amun to strengthen her position was resulting in a sharp rise in status for the god's chief ministers. Suddenly the two highest offices in the priesthood took on a political importance that the founder of the dynasty, Ahmose, had specifically tried to prevent. Hapuseneb, the first prophet, bore the titles "overseer of prophets of Upper and Lower Egypt" (Kultusminister),

128 Breasted, *ARE* II, §316ff.

129 A. De Buck, *Egyptian Readingbook* (Leiden, 1948), I, 49.

130 Breasted, *ARE*, II, 95, n. *c*.

"overseer of temples," "overseer of every office of the estate of Amun" (i.e. executive manager of the estate), "great chief in Upper Egypt", and "overseer of Upper Egypt."[131] Some of these titles were also borne by his later contemporary, Ipuyemre, the second prophet.[132] Thus jurisdiction over all phases of the operation of the Amun cult, both sacred and secular, the control of cults and temples of all other gods, as well as a position of authority in the civil administration were in the possession of the Amun priesthood.[133] But this was nothing but the culmination of the process that had begun when the Seventeenth Dynasty triumphed over the Hyksos. The rise in the fortunes of Amun was commensurate with the absolute power of the royal house. The king triumphed over the Asiatics on the battlefield, but it was Amun who gave the victory. The situation contained a conflict in embryo: two divine giants could not both share the spotlight. In a land where the rule had been monarchic, sooner or later there was bound to be a clash for power. Just where, in actual fact, did the right to govern lie, with Amun or with the king? With a transcendent being, removed from man, whose will was interpreted by a group of human beings, or with a god incarnate, living upon earth? To translate from theological jargon, the rule of Amun would mean oligarchy, the rule of Pharaoh, monarchy. Hatshepsut had unwittingly strengthened the "oligarchs" in her efforts to bolster a hybrid form of monarchy!

Six generations after the inception of the dynasty the matriarchal tendencies of the royal family had burgeoned out into a true matriarchy. The succession itself, and not merely the power to legitimize succession, was now to pass through the queens. The practice of bypassing heirs, both male and female, in favour of an arbitrary

[131] Lefebvre, *L'Histoire des Grands Prêtres d'Amon* . . ., 230f.

[132] Kees, *Das Priestertum* . . ., 11ff.

[133] The marked aggrandizement of the Amun cult under Hatshepsut gives the lie to the belief that her reign was a renunciation of foreign war (Wilson, n. 36 above), or that she refused to prosecute the Asiatic war because she disdained to be the heir to the Hyksos empire (Helck, *Die Beziehungen* . . ., 118). Of all Egyptian cults, that of imperial Amun was most vitally concerned with the pursuance of the war in Syria, for, as the champion of that war, his status and wealth both depended on it.

choice on the part of the king was to be given up. Hatshepsut's successor would be her eldest offspring, and that was her daughter Neferure. Upon her was bestowed a titulary befitting a ruler, "lady of the two lands, mistress of Upper and Lower Egypt."[134] The reign itself, in fact, was made over to her name, and we have a text dated anomalously to "regnal year 11 under the majesty of the god's-wife, Neferure, may she live!"[135] A relief above the text shows Neferure, Hatshepsut, and, significantly, Senenmut, who may well have been the "evil genius" behind this and many other novel moves.

Hatshepsut was making a supreme effort by the sheer weight of her personality to modify the basis of Egyptian kingship and succession. But her personality was not sufficient, and her ancillary measures were not thorough enough. Nor were they logically conceived: her assumption of *kingly* attributes was, in fact, a concession to patriarchy.

The queen's situation was hopeless. She belonged to an older generation than Thutmose III, and could not hope to outlive him. Much less could she hope that he would assist Neferure in preserving a matriarchal form of rule. Already in the seventh year of the reign the boy king had signalized himself in some obscure way, perhaps by making an endowment to the temple of Amun.[136] As a youth in his early twenties he again embellished the cult of the king of the gods in year 15.[137] At the same time he was beginning to insinuate his own friends and contemporaries into high office. Many of these, like Yamu-nedjeh the herald[138] and Menkheperraseneb the high priest of Amun,[139] were men of lowly origin, who had somehow come to the attention of the young king. A good number speak in their inscriptions of their military connexion with the crown,[140] and these must have been they with whom Thutmose first came in contact in the days of his army training. But while the "new men" are very numerous in Thutmose's entourage, many of the older families

[134] Gauthier, *Livre*, II, 251:4.

[135] Gardiner-Černý, *The Inscriptions of Sinai*, Pl. 68:179.

[136] Gardiner, *JEA* 38 (1952), Pl. 5:26 and p. 12.

[137] *Urk.* IV, 172.

[138] *Ibid.*, 940.

[139] *Ibid.*, 926.

[140] Min, the treasurer: *ibid.*, 1027ff.; Yamu-nedjeh: *ibid.*, 1370; May, *ibid.*, 1372; Nakht, the royal messenger: Gardiner-Černý, *The Inscriptions of Sinai*, Pl. 57:181; Min-mose, the engineer: *Urk.* IV, 1441ff.

of officials are represented too.[141] Understandably, only a few of the parvenus from Hatshepsut's coterie were accepted by the new king.[142]

Sometime after year 16 Senenmut disappeared. Whether his fate was a natural death or a fall from favour and assassination, we do not know. If the latter, and if Hatshepsut was responsible, we can only conclude that she was unwittingly following a sudden whim of rage, for the disappearance removed her chief supporter. With the death of Neferure about the same time all her hopes regarding the succession and the permanence of the matriarchy must have been dashed. Thutmose III, a man in his prime and a born soldier, quickly filled the vacuum created by the departure of Senenmut and Neferure, and Hatshepsut must have been forced to adopt a conciliatory attitude towards him if she wished to salvage anything. Thutmose now appeared more frequently beside Hatshepsut in reliefs and texts,[143] and, as we have seen, was delegated the task of undertaking the foreign wars. The latter were becoming more numerous and ominous. Gaza and certain Nubian principalities rebelled; but their sure defeat did not deter others from raising the standard of revolt. In Asia Kadesh was the chief fomenter of insurrection, and already she was forming an alliance of all the states of Palestine and Coele-Syria, doubtless in preparation for an attack upon Egypt when Hatshepsut died.[144]

[141] Cf. the family of southern viziers to which Rekhmire belonged: Helck, *Verwaltung*, 435ff.

[142] One of the few appears to have been the treasurer Tiy; cf. *JNES* 16 (1957), 99ff. Another was Djehuty the herald; Davies, *Griffiths Studies*, 279ff.

[143] Cf. Gardiner-Černý, *The Inscriptions of Sinai*, Pl. 14:44, 57:181, C. M. Firth and J. Quibell, *The Step-pyramid* (Cairo, 1935), I, 80(F); Sethe, *Urk*. IV, 1066 (Thutmose III alone); *Urk*. IV, 1375 (Thutmose III alone).

[144] To postulate such subversive action while Hatshepsut yet lived is the only way to account for the sudden appearance of the coalition within months of Thutmose III's assumption of sole rule. It is interesting that Thutmose III represents himself as prosecuting the war against the Hyksos (*Urk*. IV, 648). Was it the design of Kadesh to retake Egypt and re-establish the Hyksos hegemony? And why did Kadesh take the lead? Had the impetus for the original Hyksos invasion come likewise from the middle Orontes? If so, in the context of the Middle Bronze political situation in the Levant, the kingdom of Qatna, the close neighbour of Kadesh, must have been the prime mover.

According to a likely hypothesis, the passing of the queen took place on the tenth day of the sixth month in the twenty-second year of the reign.[145] It was probably a natural death; Thutmose had no reason to hasten her fate. It must have been obvious to everyone that the matriarchy she had established was doomed. For three generations of future rulers at least, and probably for five, the right to the throne would belong to the eldest son; and though the title and rank of "god's wife" would remain in vogue for a time, its incumbents would prove ineffectual.[146] When next a bevy of daughters would necessitate the reintroduction of matriliny, the title "god's wife" would not be pressed into service. That phase, at least, of the mystery of the paternity of Amun would be for ever defunct.

The death of the queen was, of course, followed by the effacement of many of her monuments at the instigation of the king. But Thutmose was motivated not so much by a genuine hatred as by political necessity. His own legitimacy stood in need of demonstration, and his own links with his illustrious grandfather Thutmose I had to be emphasized. To leave the glories of Hatshepsut's reign open to view would, in any case, invite invidious comparison with his own accomplishments, a comparison that the new monarch just would not brook. He had to assure himself at the outset that his aunt's claims and successes, mutually exclusive as he saw them to his own, would survive in the memory of no one. And so one by one her reliefs were hacked out, her inscriptions erased, her cartouches obliterated, her obelisks walled up. Egypt was to know her no more. But did Thutmose remember her? Here and there, in the dark recesses of a shrine or tomb where no plebeian eye could see, the queen's cartouche and figure were left intact.[147] Standing alone before the image of the queen, Thutmose relented. She was, after all, his own flesh. She had not put him to death, or even deprived him of the crown. In the darkness of the crypt, in the stillness of the cella, her cold statues, which never vulgar eye would again behold, still conveyed for the king the warmth and awe of a divine presence.

145 Cf. Drower in *The Temples of Armant,* 183, n. *b.*

146 Sander-Hansen, *Das Gottesweib des Amun,* 7 and 13.

147 P. Gilbert, *CdE* 28 (1953), 219ff.

5

The Alleged Coregency of Amenhotpe III and Akhenaten

The first scholar to suggest that Amenhotpe III and Akhenaten ruled together for a time as coregents was Petrie.[1] He believed that the Amarna letters showed that Amenhotpe III was negotiating with Tushratta for a bride for his son just prior to his death. The girl in question was Taduhepa, Tushratta's daughter, whom Petrie identified with Nefertity. Since Tushratta refers to the marriage in a letter addressed to Amenhotpe III, it is clear that the nuptials took place before the Egyptian king died. But, according to Petrie, Akhenaten's first two daughters do not appear upon their father's monuments until his sixth regnal year, on the basis of which Petrie concluded that the marriage of Akhenaten and Nefertity is to be dated to year 4. This would mean that the two kings were coregents for at least four years. Petrie was even more specific. In his time the highest known date for Amenhotpe III's reign was the thirty-sixth year. Manetho, however, gives only thirty years to this king. The discrepancy was explained by Petrie on the assumption that Manetho gives only the length of Amenhotpe's *sole* reign, his last six years being spent in a coregency with his son Akhenaten.

[1] Petrie, *History*, II, 207ff.

Petrie did not gain a following.[2] Few of the historians writing during the first three decades of the present century gave even formal recognition to his theory. And when early in the thirties Borchardt argued in favour of a coregency, it was on the basis of certain Theban tomb scenes.[3] Since Borchardt's evidence will be examined below, we shall not give the details of his argument here. Suffice it to say that the coregency he postulated was shorter than Petrie's, amounting (in the light of newly acquired evidence) to from three to five years.[4]

It is fair to say that the modern hypothesis of a long coregency between Amenhotpe III and Akhenaten originated among the British excavators of Amarna. Impressed with the "great number of objects bearing the name of Amenhotpe III discovered at Amarna,"[5] Pendlebury[6] and Fairman[7] postulated a coregency "which lasted for some time after the foundation of the city,"[8] i.e. for five or six years at least. Fairman, on the basis of the occurrence of Amenhotpe III's name with the later form of the Aten's name,[9] suggested "that Amenhotpe III was alive (and possibly at Amarna) about the ninth year of Akhenaten's reign."[10] In two subsequent publications[11] Pendlebury opted for a coregency of about eleven years. For support

[2] With the apparent exception of H. Carter, *The Tomb of Tut.ankh.Amen* (London, 1923–33), III, 2ff.

[3] L. Borchardt, *Allerhand Kleinigkeiten* (Leipzig, 1933), 23ff.; *idem, Mittel*, 83.

[4] Borchardt is still followed by F. Cornelius (*AfO* 17 [1956], 307) and K. Jaritz (*MIOF* 6 [1958], 199).

[5] J. Pendlebury, *CoA* II, 102. One feels that the assumption that Tutankhamun was the son of Amenhotpe III has played a more important role in the formulation of the hypothesis than has hitherto been admitted: see H. R. Hall, *JEA* 14 (1928), 76f.; S. R. K. Glanville, *JEA* 15 (1929), 8, n. 2; J. Pendlebury, *Tell el-Amarna* (London, 1935), 9f. The alleged evidence that Tutankhamun considered Amenhotpe III to be his father has not been included in the present discussion since it begs the question how old Tutankhamun was when he died. Note that the weight of this evidence has been greatly lessened by the discovery of an inscription in which Tutankhamun is called the son of King Ay: K. Seele, *JNES* 14 (1955), 179.

[6] *CoA* II, 102. [7] *CoA* II, 103ff. [8] *CoA* II, 102.

[9] On the names of the Aten, and their use in the chronological determination of the events of the Amarna Age, see B. Gunn, *JEA* 9 (1923), 168ff.

[10] *CoA* II, 108.

[11] *Tell el-Amarna,* 10ff.; "Summary Report on the Excavations at Tell el-Amarnah, 1935–1936," *JEA* 22 (1936), 198.

he turned to two scenes in the tomb of Huya at Amarna, which seemed to contain evidence that Amenhotpe III had died around Akhenaten's twelfth regnal year.[12] Both scholars apparently assumed from the beginning that any coregency would entail the overlapping of the dated years of both kings. This was not, however, the view of Albright who, although convinced that Amenhotpe III and Akhenaten had in fact been coregents, refused to concede that "any of the former's thirty-six years were contemporary with the latter's seventeen."[13] Among other scholars whose support was won for the coregency hypothesis before the Second World War we may mention Engelbach and Seele. The former accepted a coregency of at least nine years,[14] being, it seems, largely under the influence of the juxtaposition of Amenhotpe III's name with the later form of the Aten's name on the offering slab from Amarna.[15] Steindorff and Seele went even further, and called for "scarcely less than a dozen years" to be assigned the coregency.[16]

The classic promulgation of the coregency hypothesis is to be found in *The City of Akhenaten* (London, 1951), Vol. III, pp. 153–57. In these pages H. W. Fairman has set forth evidence of two kinds: (a) dated dockets of Amenhotpe III found at Amarna, and (b) inscriptions that associate the names of Amenhotpe III and Akhenaten. All the evidence known at the time of writing was included. After weighing the pros and cons Fairman himself comes out in favour of a nine-year coregency as the "most reasonable interpretation of the known facts."[17] In the wake of Fairman's study a respectable number of scholars have expressed themselves on the side supporting a coregency of some length.[18] One among them, C. Aldred, has added

[12] N. de G. Davies, *The Rock Tombs of El-Amarna* (EEF Archaeological Survey of Egypt, Memoirs 13 to 18 [London, 1903–8]), III, Pl. 1ff. This evidence will be examined in detail below.

[13] W. F. Albright, *JEA* 23 (1937), 193, n. 8.

[14] R. Engelbach, *ASAE* 40 (1940), 134ff.

[15] *CoA* III, Pl. 64:4–6.

[16] G. Steindorff and K. Seele, *When Egypt Ruled the East* (1st ed., Chicago, 1942), 201.

[17] *CoA* III, 157.

[18] F. Giles, *Aegyptus* 32 (1952), 293ff.; W. C. Hayes, *JNES* 10 (1951), 36f.; *HSE* II, 258f. and 280f.; P. van der Meer, *Ex Oriente Lux*, 15 (1957–58), 76ff.; J. Wilson, *The Burden of Egypt* (Chicago, 1951), 213; *idem*, *JNES* 13 (1954), 128; for further references see the following note.

considerably to the body of evidence in favour of the coregency.[19] Rebuttals, on the other hand, have been few. Over twenty-five years ago in a review of Carter's *The Tomb of Tut.ankh.Amen,* Vol. III, Scharff argued, but not at length, against a proposed coregency of six or seven years.[20] In 1954 W. Helck published a more elaborate rebuttal of Fairman's position,[21] and this has stood until recently as the only formal statement against the hypothesis which deals with the problem in detail. To be sure, however, the passing remarks made by those opposed to the hypothesis have been on the increase in the last decade.[22]

Within the last few years three studies have appeared which have to do wholly or in part with the hypothesis of the coregency. The first, the work of F. Giles, is entitled "The Amarna Period: A Study of the Internal Politics and External Relations of the Late Eighteenth Dynasty of Egypt" (unpublished doctoral dissertation, University of London, 1959) and is concerned with the political and religious history of Egypt and the Levant during that period. Giles devotes a lengthy section at the beginning of his work to the coregency of Amenhotpe III and Akhenaten, and comes to the conclusion that a coregency of twelve years best fits the facts. The second work, by E. F. Campbell, is called *The Chronology of the Amarna Letters with Special Reference to the Hypothetical Coregency of Amenophis III and Akhenaten* (Baltimore, 1964). As the title suggests, Campbell is concerned more directly than is Giles with the problem of the coregency. He brings to bear on the subject the results of an intensive study undertaken by Albright and his pupils over several decades. Campbell's decision after careful consideration is that the Amarna

19 See his articles, *JEA* 43 (1957), 114f. and *JNES* 18 (1959), 113ff.

20 *AfO* 10 (1935), 87ff.

21 W. Helck, *MIOF* 2 (1954), 196ff. Many would-be opponents of the coregency theory have been content to be silent; cf., for example, Drioton-Vandier, *L'Egypte*[4], 384f.; A. Scharff, *Ägypten und Vorderasien im Altertum* (Munich, 1950), 141f.

22 Cf. Sir A. H. Gardiner, *JEA* 43 (1957), 13f.; *idem, Egypt of the Pharaohs* (Oxford, 1961), 213; W. C. Hayes, "Internal Affairs from Tuthmosis I to the Death of Amenophis III, Part 1," in *CAH* (1962), II, 12, n. 7; W. Helck, *Untersuchungen zu Manetho* (Berlin, 1956), 68, n. 3; *idem, MDIAK* 17 (1961), 108; W. S. Smith, *The Art and Architecture of Ancient Egypt* (Harmondsworth, 1958), 184ff.; J. Von Beckerath, *OLZ* 54 (1959), 7; G. Roeder, *ZÄS* 83 (1958), 45; W. Helck, *OLZ* 59 (1964), 459ff.

Letters are against the proposed coregency. The third work, the results of a doctoral dissertation like the other two, is *Untersuchungen zur Chronologie und Geschichte des neuen Reiches* (Wiesbaden, 1964) by Erik Hornung. Hornung devotes one chapter to the alleged coregency, and, like Campbell, concludes that the evidence is against it.

Although Campbell's investigation of the Amarna letters with reference to the coregency is in many ways definitive, no similarly intensive examination of all the evidence that has been adduced is at present available. To undertake such an examination is the burden of the present chapter. Since Fairman's compilation of evidence in *The City of Akhenaten*, Vol. III, is the most complete array, his order is followed here, other evidence supplied by Aldred, Giles, and others being added at the end. Following this investigation of the evidence the case for the opposition will be presented. Since this involves in part evidence supplied by the Amarna Letters, ground already covered by Campbell will be trodden again, but in more summary fashion. It is hoped that this scrutiny of the evidence alone, stripped of secondary arguments several stages removed, will help to clarify the problem and point towards a possible solution.

1. From Amarna come two fragmentary wine-jar dockets,[23] one dated to year 28,[24] the other to year 30.[25] Since the only king of the immediate period who ruled twenty-eight years or more was Amenhotpe III, Fairman does not hesitate to assign the regnal years to him. Although he admits that these ostraca "do not automatically indicate the survival of Amenophis III after the beginning of the reign of Akhenaten," he feels that they supply strong support for a coregency. It would be most unlikely, he argues, that wine jars would have been taken to Amarna empty. Moreover, the jars labelled in years 28 and 30 could not have been reused vessels and the labels old by the time they reached Amarna because the old labels would then surely have been replaced by new ones. Therefore, he concludes, wine of years 28 and 30 of Amenhotpe III was being consumed in Amarna. Now, since wine was usually consumed within a few years

[23] Fairman, *CoA* II, 103f.; III, 154; F. Giles, "The Amarna Period," 7; E. F. Campbell, *The Chronology of the Amarna Letters with Special Reference to the Hypothetical Coregency of Amenophis III and Akhenaten* (Baltimore, 1964), 7.

[24] *CoA* III, Pl. 91:168.

[25] *CoA* II, Pl. 58:47.

of bottling in ancient Egypt (the interval between bottling and uncorking in one known case being five years: *TA*, Pl. 23:43) because of the porosity of the wine jars, he feels that the only reasonable conclusion is that Amarna was occupied around, or very soon after, the end of the third decade of Amenhotpe III's reign. But this would mean that years 28 and 30 of that king were close in time to Akhenaten's fifth regnal year, since the building of his new city of Amarna seems to have begun in that year. Thus a coregency approaching a decade in length is suggested.

Fairman's argument will be seen to rest upon the following assumptions: (a) that the dates in question belong to Amenhotpe III's reign; (b) that the dates mark the first and only (dated) occasions on which the containers in question were used; and (c) that shortly after the dockets were written, these containers were to be found at Amarna. If the assumptions should prove correct, Fairman would be justified in his belief that year 28 of Amenhotpe III and year 5 of Akhenaten were not far apart.

Let us examine the assumptions separately. As for the first, it is not absolutely certain that the ostraca date to Amenhotpe III's reign, though admittedly this is a possibility. Giles has suggested[26] that the dates may belong to a successor of Akhenaten. Haremhab's name occurs several times at Amarna,[27] Sety I's at least once,[28] and Ramses II and Merneptah are represented by graffiti in the quarry.[29] In addition, the name of Ramses III was found on blocks from the river temple, suggesting that some building of his once stood on that spot.[30] It could be that a partial occupation of the site occurred during the reigns of some or all of these kings, and that the ostraca were deposited on the site by these later inhabitants. Another possibility is that year 30, at least, refers not to the regnal year of a human king, but to the *sd*-festival of the Aten, who was represented by the Egyptians with the accoutrements of kingship.[31] The difficulty with this view is that, while none of the ostraca from Amarna (or any other

[26] "The Amarna Period," 7.

[27] *TA*, Pl. 11:5; *CoA* III, 12, Pl. 60:3; F. G. Newton, *JEA* 10 (1924), 293; H. Frankfort, *JEA* 13 (1927), 210.

[28] Newton, *JEA* 10 (1924), 293.

[29] *TA*, 4; also Ramses II (scarab): *CoA* III, 63.

[30] L. Woolley, *JEA* 8 (1922), 67f.; *CoA* I, 160.

[31] Cf. the present writer, *JEA* 45 (1959), 35, n. 11.

site for that matter) is specifically dated to the reign of a king whose name occurs after the date, it is virtually certain that the year numbers of the ostraca belong to human reigns. The presence of *ḥȝt-sp* on both the ostraca in question militates in favour of a king's reign. (Is there any evidence that the Aten was credited with a reign dated by regnal years?)

Fairman's second assumption is baseless. There is no way of telling whether the containers to which these dockets belonged were reused. It is quite conceivable that, if they were reused, the jars were provided with no second docket, because the new owner may have been a private individual.[32] It is impossible now to say whether a second docket was in fact added, since both ostraca are now mere fragments. Fairman claims that a second label "would almost certainly have been palimpsest,"[33] but this is quite untrue. Any further docket might just as easily have been added *below* the first, with no attempt being made to erase the earlier inscription.[34] Even if a second docket had been applied so as to obliterate most of an earlier one,[35] the former text might not appear if, as in the present case, only a small fraction of the original docket were preserved.

The third assumption is both unwarranted and unlikely. It is unwarranted not only because there is evidence that upon occasion wine jars could be kept as long as a decade or more before use,[36] but also because Fairman has not disposed of the possibility that the containers had been reused before they were taken to Amarna. The assumption is unlikely since its logical corollary leads to a conclusion from which the two dockets themselves point away. If these wine jars with dockets of years 28 and 30 were deposited at Amarna shortly after they were filled and labelled for the first time, then year 5 of Akhenaten fell reasonably close to year 28 or 30 of Amenhotpe III. It is most surprising, then, that only two dockets dating to these years of Amenhotpe III have been found, and *none* of subsequent

[32] Note that both ostraca come from residential quarters, that of year 28 from the scribes' houses (*CoA* III, 159) and that of year 30 from the southwest quarter of the north suburb (*CoA* II, 51).

[33] *CoA* III, 154.

[34] A good example is *TA*, Pl. 23:43.

[35] Cf., for example, an ostracon from Malqata (W. C. Hayes, *JNES* 10 [1951], 46, Fig. 6, no. 42) "partly covered" by a later docket (*ibid.*, 87; the later one being no. 62).

[36] See W. Helck, *MIOF* 2 (1954), 196f.

regnal years of the same king, which would have been contemporary with the actual occupation of Amarna. Dated dockets for the early period of the new capital's existence are not sparse: years 5, 6, and 7 of Akhenaten are represented by *at least*[37] eighty-nine dated ostraca. Since a further discussion pursuant to these observations would lead into the problem of the lack of inscriptions bearing double datings, a problem that will be taken up below, the present examination of these ostraca will terminate here.

2. Fairman's next piece of evidence is the reliefs of Akhenaten from the temple of Soleb in Nubia.[38] This temple, which is almost entirely the work of Amenhotpe III, possesses a few scenes executed under Akhenaten on the pylon.[39] Fairman's own private copies of the inscriptions show that wherever Akhenaten's cartouches appear, the praenomen (*Nfr-ḫprw-rʿ Wʿ-n-rʿ*) is original, but the nomen *ꜣḫ-n-itn* (Akhenaten) is in surcharge. This can only mean that the pylon was decorated by Akhenaten before his fifth or sixth year. One of the reliefs shows Akhenaten before "Nebmare, Lord of Nubia," a deified form of his father. Since Amenhotpe III is shown elsewhere before this same "Nebmare, Lord of Nubia,"[40] there is no reason to believe that the latter is a deceased manifestation of Amenhotpe III, as Breasted thought.[41] "It is probable, therefore," Fairman concludes, "that at Soleb Akhenaten, as king, is shown before his living father and that these scenes are to be dated to the postulated coregency . . . ."[38]

Helck is not convinced by Fairman's argument. To him, the epithet "Lord of Nubia," which the deified Nebmare bears, makes it plain that this is a statue, and not the king himself: "Amenophis IV opfert hier also vor einer Statue seines Vaters."[42]

It would seem that scholarly debate on the pylon scenes at Soleb has rather missed the point. Whether, for instance, Akhenaten is

[37] Apart from ostraca on which the date is in doubt.

[38] Fairmen, *CoA* III, 154; Helck, *MIOF* 2 (1954), 197; Giles, "The Amarna Period," 8; Campbell, *The Chronology of the Amarna Letters . . .*, 7f.

[39] *LD* III, 110k.

[40] Cf. the scenes on the east face of the north jamb of the door leading to the hypostyle hall: *LD* III, 85a; A. J. Arkell, *A History of the Sudan to 1821* (2nd ed., London, 1961), Pl. 4(b); also the pillar inscription, *LD* III, 87b.

[41] J. H. Breasted. *AJSL* 25 (1908), 87f.

[42] *MIOF* 2 (1954), 197.

shown before his living father or a statue is as meaningless as the question whether the god Amun in neighbouring scenes is the live god or a statue. For the Egyptians, this distinction did not exist. The question should be phrased: Do these scenes depict actual occurrences that have transpired or are expected to transpire on a mundane level, or are they what we "moderns" might call idealized events? The answer must be that they depict idealized events, and as such belong with the vast majority of temple reliefs as imaginative portrayals. Such scenes as the coronation by the gods and the presentation by the god of the sign of life, both of which occur on the Soleb pylon, are decidedly not "historical" in the modern sense of the word.

Fairman wrestles with the problem as to whether, in the scenes showing Akhenaten with his "deified father," the latter is deceased or still living. Like Helck, he is battling a chimera. Akhenaten is standing before one who is essentially a god in his own right, and who is quite distinct from the person of Amenhotpe III. That the god in question is in origin a manifestation of Amenhotpe III is proved by his name "Nebmare." But he is an entity separate from that king, as is shown by the scenes in the same temple in which Amenhotpe III himself stands before him. Akhenaten is thus not standing before his father, but before the god "Nebmare, Lord of Nubia"; and this fact alone has no bearing on whether Amenhotpe III was alive or dead at the time the scenes were carved.

Fairman comes to the crux of the problem only once when he says: "the cult of Amenophis III was certainly not a funerary one, and I have reason to doubt whether it continues after his death."[43] The fact that a king's cult is not funerary does not, of course, mean that it cannot survive his death. The contention that this particular cult did not survive after the death of Amenhotpe III is the only argument that Fairman has drawn in favour of the coregency from the Soleb evidence. If the cult of Nebmare, Lord of Nubia, died with Amenhotpe III and if the pylon scenes showing Akhenaten worshipping this god are original, a good case can be made for the coregency. But here evidence is wholly lacking. Elsewhere, especially at Thebes, the cult of the deified Amenhotpe III continued into

[43] Fairman, *CoA* III, 154.

Ramessid times and even later,[44] and there is no reason to believe that at Soleb the case was any different. Even if there were such a close connexion between the king and his Nubian manifestation that the cult of the latter disappeared with the monarch's death, there would surely be some time lag, no matter how small, between the death of Amenhotpe III and the total extinction of the cult. Evidence for as close a connexion as this is, however, lacking.[45] In the absence of all other indications we must conclude that a large and well-equipped temple such as Soleb would not be closed and its cults disbanded overnight. There would be ample time for the new king to complete the decoration during his first year of reign, before divine service died out. And in fact the temple service did not cease with Amenhotpe III's death. There is evidence that in Tutankhamun's reign Soleb, its temple, and presumably its cults were still flourishing.[46]

Fairman's argument, it must be pointed out, is based on the assumption that the pylon was decorated by Akhenaten. Certainly his nomen and praenomen appear in many of the surviving cartouches. But the question is: Are they original? Fairman states that, while the nomen of Akhenaten is usually in surcharge on the pylon, the praenomen is not. He concludes, therefore, that the pylon was decorated by Akhenaten before his fifth year. Lepsius, in his copy of three of the pylon scenes,[47] shows both praenomen and nomen as original, and Breasted in the early part of the present century seemed to share

[44] Cf. A. Varille, *ASAE* 34 (1934), 11, n. 3; P–M I², 354 (Tomb 277). The deified Amenhotpe III is mentioned in a Nineteenth Dynasty text as one of the gods worshipped at Memphis (Sallier IV, vo. 1:8), and, in the guise of Hapi, is found in Ptolemaic reliefs from Denderah (Petrie, *History,* II, 189). Cf. also A. Rowe, *ASAE* 40 (1940), 42; *HSE* II, 306, Fig. 191.

[45] "Nebmare, Lord of Nubia," to judge from his crescent and disk head-dress, had strong connexions with the moon. Could it be that the deified Amenhotpe III had here assimilated a native Nubian moon god? If such were the case, there would be far less reason for the cult of this composite deity to become extinct on the death of Amenhotpe III than if "Nebmare, Lord of Nubia" were a wholly artificial creation of Egyptian theologians.

[46] A mayor of Soleb is mentioned in Huy's tomb (A. H. Gardiner and N. de G. Davies, *The Tomb of Huy, Viceroy of Nubia in the Reign of Tutankhamun* [EES Theban Tomb Series 4; London, 1926], Pl. 14), and Tutankhamun is known to have embellished part of the temple (cf. the inscription on the granite lion now in the British Museum: I. E. S. Edwards, *Hieroglyphic Texts from Egyptian Stelae etc. in the British Museum* [London, 1939], 8, Pl. 15).

[47] *LD* III, 110k.

this view.[48] Janssen, the scholar who has examined the scenes most recently, gives somewhat different results.[49] These are tabulated below.

Scene	*Content*	*Royal name*
1	Coronation by the gods Uto, Atum?	Illegible
2	Coronation by Horus and Seth (figure of king and text of Horus hacked)	Nomen: Akhenaten over Amenhotpe Praenomen: hacked (illegible)
3	King before "moon god"	Hacked (illegible)
4	(lost)	
5	King before Amun (or Amenhotpe III?)	Hacked (nomen more deeply) Amenhotpe Nebmare (or *vice versa?*)
6	King before Nebmare, Lord of Nubia	Cartouches of Akhenaten over those of Amenhotpe III
7	King before Nebmare, Lord of Nubia	Cartouches of Akhenaten over those of Amenhotpe III
8	(cornice)	Cartouches of Akhenaten (original)

It can easily be seen that Janssen's readings differ markedly from those of the other scholars mentioned. If his results are accepted, it is impossible not to conclude that some scenes at least, if not all, are the work of Amenhotpe III, whose cartouches were only subsequently changed to those of his son. The cornice, it would appear, is the only extant portion of the pylon whose decoration can be attributed beyond doubt to Akhenaten.

To sum up, the pylon scenes showing a king before the lunar deity "Nebmare, Lord of Nubia" have no bearing on whether Amenhotpe III was living or dead at the time of their execution. If it could be shown that the cult of this god did not survive the death of Amenhotpe III, the reliefs on the pylon might become pertinent to the matter of the coregency, but evidence is completely lacking, and it is unlikely a priori that the cult disappeared so soon. Finally, the entire argument of Fairman *may* prove superfluous, if Janssen is correct in reading the original cartouches of scenes 6 and 7 (those in which

[48] *AJSL* 25 (1908), 87ff.

[49] J. Janssen, *Kush,* 7 (1959), 166ff.; for the numbering of the scenes, see 167, Fig. 6.

"Nebmare, Lord of Nubia" appears) as those of Amenhotpe III and not of Akhenaten.

3. A rock relief at Aswan shows two chief sculptors, Men and Bek (father and son respectively), worshipping seated statues of two kings.[50] Men worships a statue of Amenhotpe III, whose two cartouches both contain his praenomen *Nb-mꜣʿt-rʿ*, while Bek worships a statue of Akhenaten (erased). The Aten's name is also present, and the epithets "celebrator of jubilees (*ir ḥb-sd*)" and "lord of all that which the disk encircles (*nb šnnt nbt 'Itn)*" point to a date for the execution of the relief "not earlier than the latter half of the eighth year."[51]

That the relief dates well along in Akhenaten's reign is certain not only from the form of the name of the Aten, but also from the costume worn by the two men. It is equally certain that the objects worshipped are statues of Amenhotpe III and Akhenaten.[52] Since the epithet applied to the statue of the former, "ruler of rulers (*ḥqꜣ ḥqꜣw*)," is also applied to the colossus of Memnon, and since Men is called "overseer of works in the Red Mountain," whence came the Memnon colossi,[53] Varille thinks it probable that the statue depicted in the Aswan relief is one of the two colossi of the king on the west bank at Thebes.[54] It could well be, as Helck has suggested, that "diese Darstellung verewigt die Tatsache dass . . .der Vater des *Bk* eine Statue des Konigs Amenophis III hergestellt hatte. . . ."[55] Whether this is so or not, the mere juxtaposition of statues of two kings is no proof at all that both were alive and reigning at the same time. The fact that Men and Bek, father and son, *both* bear the titles "chief sculptor" and "overseer of works in the Red Mountain" suggests that they held office successively, and that here we have, in idealized portrayal, nothing more than an expression of their faithful service to successive sovereigns.

4. Fairman adduces as his fourth item of evidence the famous stela from Amarna which shows Amenhotpe III, "an old and sick man,"

50 Fairman, *CoA* III, 154; Helck, *MIOF* 2 (1954), 197.
51 Fairman, *CoA* III, 154; B. Gunn, *JEA* 9 (1923), 171.
52 Helck, *MIOF* 2 (1954), 197; P–M V, 249; J. H. Breasted. *ARE* II, 401, n. *d*.
53 *Urk*. IV, 1823.
54 A. Varille, *ASAE* 34 (1934), 15.
55 *MIOF* 2 (1954), 197

with his wife Tiy seated before a pile of offerings.[56] The name of the Aten is in its later form. Presumably the inference to be made is that Amenhotpe III was still alive and resident at Amarna after the eighth year of his son's reign.

The stela was found in fragments in the north and west loggia of the house of Paynehsi (R 44. 2). The style of execution leaves no doubt that the stela dates from the height of the Amarna revolution. It clearly belongs to a class of small private stelae from Amarna which show a king, alone or accompanied by a queen, seated before a table of offerings. The present object cannot, then, be discussed in isolation, but the meaning and purpose of the class as a whole must be investigated.

The fact of the private nature of this class of stela is important. Helck, pursuant to this, has suggested that the owner of the present stela (Paynehsi?) had a personal connexion with the old king.[57] This may well be, but we are still in the dark as to the function of the object. Were all those who owned such stelae in the personal service of the king depicted? Griffith called them "relics of the loyalty and worship accorded by the people to the divine king and his family. . . ."[58] The crucial word here is "relics," and the present writer must conclude that Griffith is here speaking, not of their original function, but of the information they give modern scholarship. Were the stelae cultic objects, or merely memorials (without attempting a close definition of the latter term)? It seems likely that they had something to do with a private, household cult, but it must be admitted that there is no compelling proof of this.

Whether this stela proves that Amenhotpe III was alive and living in Amarna when it was carved is quite another matter. One need only point to the many tomb scenes in which the deceased is shown making an offering to or simply adoring a king or kings long since dead[59] to elicit proof that the cult of the deified king was exceedingly strong. Again, if Amenhotpe III was living at Amarna and was worshipped on the same footing as Akhenaten, a conclusion that must follow from the class of stela, why has only a single example

[56] Fairman, *CoA* III, 155; Helck, *MIOF* 2 (1954), 197; Pendlebury, *Tell el-Amarna*, 11; published by F. Ll. Griffith in *JEA* 12 (1926), 1f. (with plate).

[57] *MIOF* 2 (1954), 197.

[58] *JEA* 12 (1926), 1.

[59] Cf. P–M I^2, 464(3).

been found? The supposition that Amenhotpe III is herein represented as a senile, diseased man, on the threshold of death,[60] seems to have given rise to the belief that his last days were spent at Amarna. An examination of the photo of the stela given in Griffith's article fails singularly to turn up one solitary characteristic of the seated male figure which indicates that the artist wished to represent an aged man. Bent heads and thick necks may belong to old gentlemen, but plenty of youths are cursed with them. Similarly, the relaxed attitude and the paunch are not necessarily signs of old age, and especially at Amarna these are found *passim* in art. The artist is, in fact, portraying the royal couple according to the norms current at Amarna, and the age of the king does not come into question.

I think it can be shown that the Paynehsi stela was carved after Amenhotpe III died. The temple of Soleb was constructed during the last decade of Amenhotpe III's reign. A *terminus a quo* is provided by the scenes depicting the first *sd*-festival,[61] and by the date in one of the scenes of year 30, tenth month, day 1.[62] It seems certain from these facts that it was one of the latest structures to be erected by Amenhotpe III. Its construction doubtless occupied the period from shortly before year 30 to the king's death in year 38. Indeed, the decoration was not quite finished when he passed away, and the finishing touches were applied to the pylon by Akhenaten.[63] To the stage of decoration contemporary with the last years of Amenhotpe III belong the many pairs of cartouches throughout the temple, inscribed *Nb-mꜣʿt-rʿ Imn-ḥtp*. At some subsequent period, after the original decoration was completed, many of the nomens were erased and their cartouches filled with praenomens.[64] Even the nomens on

[60] Fairman, *CoA* III, 154: "... an old and sick man ..."; Pendlebury, *Tell el-Amarna*, 11: "an old man"; Griffith, *JEA* 12 (1926), 1: "in a rather weary and decrepit attitude ... an aged man and fat"; Campbell, *The Chronology of the Amarna Letters* ..., 9: "heavy and flaccid."

[61] P–M VII, 169ff. and above.

[62] Janssen, *Kush*, 9 (1961), 207.

[63] Janssen, Kush, 7 (1959), 169.

[64] Cf., for example, *LD* III, 83a–c; for further examples of the replacement of Amenhotpe III's nomen by his praenomen, see *LD* III, 82e (Sedeinga), and the relief of Men and Bek at Aswan (see above, n. 50). There is even a case of Satamun's name being erased and replaced by *Nb-mꜣʿt-rʿ*: Engelbach, *ASAE* 40 (1940), Pl. 26:2; also Varille, *ASAE* 34 (1934), 654f. For the praenomen of Amenhotpe III on Tiy's shrine, see below.

the lions in front of the temple, which must belong to the latest stage in the construction, were later changed to praenomens.[65] It is possible that at least one nomen of Amenhotpe III on the pylon was afforded the same treatment.[66] The conclusion is obvious. Up to the time when Amenhotpe III's death brought a temporary halt to the nearly completed decoration, the practice continued, as we should expect, of inscribing the king's name unashamedly as 'Nebmare Amenhotpe." Indeed, the very latest inscriptions from his reign show this writing, and no one can doubt that while Amenhotpe III lived his nomen held no repugnance for himself or his subjects.

But the nomen *Imn-ḥtp* was repugnant to Akhenaten, and he subsequently changed not a few into the less offensive praenomen. The resultant designation of his father, of course, was utter gibberish. The unequivocal evidence from Soleb that the mutilation of the nomens there occurred after the entire temple had been finished and almost completely decorated constitutes proof that Akhenaten's practice of emending his father's nomens began only after Amenhotpe III had died. The Paynehsi stela shows two pairs of Amenhotpe III's cartouches. All four are original, and all four contain the praenomen *Nb-mꜣꜥt-rꜥ*. The Paynehsi stela must consequently have been carved only after Akhenaten began to alter his father's nomens. It follows that the stela dates from the period subsequent to the death of Amenhotpe III, and thus it cannot be used as evidence for a coregency.

5. From the royal tomb at Amarna Fairman cites[67] a fragment of the sarcophagus of Meketaten on which the praenomen of Amenhotpe III appears beside that of Akhenaten.[68] Was Amenhotpe III alive when the sarcophagus was prepared for his granddaughter? And does its preparation date from a time after the accession of Akhenaten? Certainly an affirmative answer must be accepted for the second

[65] Edwards, *Hieroglyphic Texts . . .*, 8, Pl. 15. Breasted (*ARE* II, 364, n. *c*) is, of course, wrong in attributing the modification to Tutankhamun.

[66] Janssen, *Kush*, 7 (1959), 168.

[67] *CoA* III, 155; Helck, *MIOF* 2 (1954), 198.

[68] U. Bouriant *et al.*, *Monuments pour servir à l'étude du culte d'Atonou en Egypte: I: Les tombes de Khouitatonou* (MIFAO 8 [Cairo, 1903]), 14ff. and the references quoted on p. 15, n. 1, to which add P–M IV, 236 and Gauthier, *Livre*, II, 351 (xxvii).

question, but not necessarily for the first. The precise date of Meketaten's death cannot be given in the present state of our knowledge. It seems likely, however, that her death postdates her father's twelfth year, when she is shown with her parents and sisters at the reception of foreign tribute.[69] There is no way of knowing exactly when she was provided with mortuary equipment, but it may have been long before her death. Queen Ahhotpe I of the Seventeenth Dynasty died during the reign of her grandson; yet she took to the grave objects manufactured during the reign of her eldest son over three decades earlier.[70] If Meketaten was born before her father's accession, she might already have possessed mortuary equipment when her grandfather died; but Meketaten's birth, like her death, is an event for which no one can fix a certain date.[71]

[69] Davies, *The Rock Tombs of El-Amarna*, II, Pl. 37; for discussion see also K. C. Seele, *JNES* 14 (1955), 174, n. 44; *contra* K. Sethe, *Nachr. Gött.* (1921), 115f., n. 3, and Gunn, *JEA* 9 (1923), 172 and n. 1. A wine-jar docket from Amarna, dated "year 13," mentions a "house (*pr*)" of "the king's-daughter Meketaten.' (*CoA* III, Pl. 86:37). Usually estates and buildings belonging to living members of the royal family incorporated only titles or relationships: personal names were reserved for the designations of property belonging to deceased royalty. In the present case, however, it need not be assumed that Meketaten was dead in year 13, since a docket of year [1]5 (*ibid.*, Pl. 86:39) refers to a house of her sister Meret[aten] at a time when this eldest of Akhenaten's daughters was certainly alive. It is likely that the plethora of female offspring in the king's family necessitated a fuller reference to each daughter by name when her real estate was the subject at hand. There is another ostracon, however (*ibid.*, Pl. 86:38), which mentions Meketaten again, this time with the determinative  added after her name. Does the presence of this sign entitle one to conclude that she had died? Unfortunately the date is not preserved on this ostracon, while the dated example of year 13 is broken away immediately after the sun disk and cartouche ring.

[70] Maspero, *Histoire*, II, 96ff.

[71] Seele states (*JNES* 14 [1955], 171, n. 27): "Meketaten . . . seems to have been born up to year 6." At least five of the girls, however, were born before the change of the name of the Aten in year 8 or 9 (Davies, *JEA* 7 [1921], 5; Aldred, *JEA* 43 [1957], 38, n. 8); consequently the birth of Meketaten seems to be forced back before year 5 at the latest, and *a fortiori* to the earliest years of her father. Her absence in the "earlier" boundary inscription (text A: Davies, *The Rock Tombs of El-Amarna* V, 30, n. 6) may or may not be significant; for a word of caution on the mechanical dating of Amarna monuments by the number of Akhenaten's daughters depicted, see Bouriant, *Monuments* . . ., 22; Aldred, *JEA* 45 (1959), 29, n. 2. Van der Meer (*Ex Oriente Lux*, 15 [1957–58], 79f.) thinks that at least the first three daughters were born before their father's accession.

That the presence of the praenomens of both kings on this sarcophagus proves that they were coregents is far from certain. Helck, who dismisses this piece of evidence briefly but effectively, states: "Die Nennung des Amenophis III auf dem Sarg der *Mkt-'Itn* ist sicher als Betonung des Familienzusammenhanges zu deuten."[72] As will be pointed out below, a similar desire to emphasize family relationships underlies the inclusion of Amenhotpe III's name beside that of Tiy in inscriptions coming from Akhenaten's reign.

The form of Amenhotpe III's praenomen on the sarcophagus fragment is worthy of note. Here, in place of the seated goddess, the word *mꜣʿt* is written out phonetically. The reason for this is clearly Akhenaten's abhorrence of imputing divinity to any human being, animal, or thing apart from his god Aten. The modification of Amenhotpe's praenomen was thus done at Akhenaten's own behest. But did Amenhotpe III on his own monuments ever write *mꜣʿt* phonetically, without the seated goddess? A thorough search by the present writer has failed to turn up a single example of the praenomen of Amenhotpe III[73] known to have been inscribed during that king's lifetime in which the seated goddess  is suppressed in favour of a purely phonetic writing.[74] Even such late texts as the Sinai inscriptions,[75] the Silsileh inscription,[76] the mortuary texts of Kheruef's tomb,[77] and those from Amenhotpe's own tomb in Biban el-Moluk,[78] show  consistently. If there were a coregency approaching a decade or more, is it not a little strange to find no trace of a phonetic writing, especially during the later years of Amenhotpe III's reign? The present phenomenon is part of the wider problem connected

[72] *MIOF* 2 (1954), 198; similarly W. S. Smith, *The Art and Architecture of Ancient Egypt*, 278, n. 37.

[73] I.e. in monumental inscriptions; in hieratic  or  with or without the seated goddess would be quite normal.

[74] , which occurs on the statue of Kamose (Edwards, *Hieroglyphic Texts . . .*, 8, Pl. 13), is an integral part of the name of a regiment, and not the king's praenomen per se. Two other occurrences of the praenomen in the same inscription show the seated goddess. The date of the Petrie offering table from Amarna (*CoA* III, 233ff.) is uncertain, but may come from Akhenaten's reign.

[75] Helck, *MIOF* 2 (1954), Plate.

[76] *Urk.* IV, 1920 (713).

[77] A. Fakhry, *ASAE* 42 (1943), 449ff.

[78] E. Hornung, *MDIAK* 17 (1961), 118, n. 2; the decoration of the tomb was only partly completed, being cut short in all probability by the king's death.

with the complete absence in Amenhotpe III's monuments right up to the end of his reign of any suppression of the old polytheism. Yet, according to the proponents of the coregency, many of these monuments must date from a period when the Amarna revolution was in full swing. Some have attempted to circumvent the difficulty by assuming that Akhenaten set on foot his programme to purge the land of the vestiges of polytheism only after his father had died.[79] But if this is so, then there is every likelihood that Meketaten's sarcophagus was carved during this purge, and thus it could not be used as evidence of a coregency.[80]

6. The evidence next offered by Fairman consists of the lintel scene and jamb-inscriptions of the north door to the first hall in the tomb of Huya, Tell el-Amarna (no. 1).[81] The lintel shows two balanced groups separated by a vertical line. On the left Akhenaten (in blue crown), beneath the many-armed sun-disk, is sitting with Nefertity, both facing left (although the queen's head is turned back toward the king). Behind the king are two cartouches of the Aten (late form), while before the queen are two more cartouches bearing her own name and the praenomen of her husband. Approaching from the left with fans are four of Akhenaten's daughters, to whom Nefertity seems to be gesturing. The group on the right shows the figure of a king, wearing a tight-fitting wig and streamer, and drawn in the

[79] Giles, "The Amarna Period," 75ff.

[80] Aldred in a recent article (*JEA* 47 [1961], 47) suggests that the suppression of 𓁦 in the writing of *mꜣꜥt* occurred not later than Akhenaten's year 12, and perhaps a little earlier. In the same article (45, n. 1) he states "As the praenomen of Amenophis III bears witness, it [i.e. the spelling of *mꜣꜥt* with 𓁦] was out of date before his death." The present writer confesses that this statement baffles him, since, as he has just pointed out, he knows of not a trace of evidence to support it. Aldred himself in the same note admits that the evidence is ambiguous; two pages later, however, he draws an important conclusion from the absence of the seated goddess in the spelling of *mꜣꜥt* on the "coffin of Tiy." That the change to a purely phonetic spelling occurred well on in Akhenaten's reign seems certain—but that Amenhotpe III was still living at the time is not supported by the writing of his praenomen.

[81] Fairman, *CoA* III, 155; Helck, *MIOF* 2 (1954), 197f.; Giles, "The Amarna Period," 37f.; Campbell, *The Chronology of the Amarna Letters* . . ., 10f.; see also Davies, *The Rock Tombs of El-Amarna*, III, Pl. 1 (plan), Pl. 18 (lintel), Pl. 21 (jambs); P–M IV, 210 and 212.

"Amarna" style, sitting on a chair, and facing right; behind him are his obliterated cartouches. On the right, facing the king, Tiy is sitting, and at her knee stands a small girl identified by a vertical column of inscription in front of her as "the king's daughter, of his body, whom he loves, Baketaten."[82] Both Tiy and Baketaten raise their hand towards the king in what *appears* to be a gesture of adoration. The many-armed sun-disk is once more present, and dominates the scene. Between the king and Tiy are a pair of cartouches; the one on the left, though fragmentary, reads *nsw-bit Nb-mꜣ ʿt-rʿdi ʿnḫ,* and is read from the direction in which the king is looking. The cartouche on the right reads *ḥmt-nsw wrt Ti ʿnḫ,ti,* and must be read from the direction in which the queen is looking. The same cartouches appear again behind Tiy, but this time the hieroglyphs face in the same direction as the queen. Four vertical columns behind Tiy and the cartouches contain laudatory epithets of the queen, and underneath them stand three unidentified princesses shouldering fans.

The inscriptions on the jambs fill two vertical columns, and occur twice on the right. The first column gives the cartouches of the Aten (late form), followed by the praenomen of Akhenaten "given life", the praenomen of Amenhotpe III, and the cartouche of Tiy, in that order. The second column is identical, save for the fact that the nomen of Akhenaten occurs in place of his praenomen.

Davies already realized that this scene and juxtaposition of names could be utilized as evidence for a coregency, ". . . even at this late date in Akhenaten's reign." But he rejected such an interpretation, preferring to see in the gesture of adoration by Tiy and Baketaten towards the royal figure evidence that Amenhotpe III was here represented as deceased.[83] Pendlebury did not exercise the same caution as Davies. On two occasions he affirmed that the lintel scene (referred to as on the "façade") showed Amenhotpe III alive.[84] Pendlebury further noted that "inside the tomb" a scene occurs showing Tiy *alone* on "a visit" to Amarna in "the twelfth year of Akhenaten's reign." Since the latter scene was, according to Pendle-

[82] On the proposed identity of Baketaten with a certain king's-daughter Baket-Amun, see Gauthier, *ASAE* 10 (1910), 207f.

[83] *The Rock Tombs of El-Amarna*, III, 16.

[84] *Tell el-Amarna*, 12; *JEA* 22 (1936), 198; followed by Giles in *Aegyptus*, 32 (1952), 299.

bury, carved later than the façade, "surely that seems to imply the death of Amenophis III between the carving of the façade and of the interior, and suggests that Teye's visit was in the nature of a state 'progress' to her son on the occasion of his father's death."[85] Carter affirms that the lintel "not only confirms the coregency of the two kings, but gives reason to suppose that Amen.hetep III continued to live for at least a year or so after the birth of Akhenaten's fourth daughter. . . ."[86] Giles more recently based his argument on the presence of Baketaten in the scene.[87] Both Baketaten's size and the presence of a sidelock prove, according to Giles, that she could not be older than fourteen at the most. On the assumption that Tiy married Amenhotpe III in his second regnal year at the age of sixteen, Tiy would have given birth to Baketaten, if there were no coregency, in the last year or so of her husband, when she was fifty-four. Since it is unlikely that Tiy was as young as sixteen at the time of her marriage, or as old as fifty-four at the birth of Baketaten, the assumption of a coregency of about twelve years is almost obligatory.

There have not been lacking those who have rejected the Huya lintel as evidence for a coregency. Scharff, noting that the name of Amenhotpe III was not followed by *di ʿnḫ*, and that elsewhere in the tomb Tiy was shown alone, attributed the references to Akhenaten's father to mere piety, and refused to admit that Amenhotpe III was here represented as living.[88] Helck believed Huya's personal connexions with Amenhotpe III (presumably through his service to Tiy) fully accounted for the scene and inscriptions and, like Scharff, would not admit them as evidence for a coregency.[89] Another who has not accepted Pendlebury's interpretation is Gardiner. He understands the lintel scene merely as illustrating "the cordial relations existing between the senior and junior branches of the family," and the juxtaposition of the names of Amenhotpe III and Akhenaten as "due mainly to filial piety. . . ."[90] Oddly enough Aldred himself, of

[85] *JEA* 22 (1936), 198.
[86] *The Tomb of Tut.ankh.Amen*, III, 5.
[87] "The Amarna Period," 37ff.
[88] *AfO* 10 (1935), 88.
[89] *MIOF* 2 (1954), 197f.
[90] *JEA* 43 (1957), 14; similarly W. S. Smith, *The Art and Architecture of Ancient Egypt*, 185.

late the foremost advocate of the coregency hypothesis, has joined the above-mentioned scholars in rejecting this evidence: the lintel scene, he says, is

> a posthumous representation of Amenophis III. Otherwise it is almost certain that Egyptian ideas of symmetry, even in the el-Amarna period, would have placed the two pairs of kings and consorts back to back in the middle of the lintel, and confronted them with the figures of daughters and attendants. The fact that Amenophis III is shown alone, and is balanced by Tiy and Beketaten who both raise hands in gestures of adoration quite different from those employed by the royal family among themselves at El-Amarna to express greeting or affection, suggests to the writer that Amenophis III was recently dead and deified, though he could not of course be represented as Osiris in the city of the Aten.[91]

Campbell is struck by the anomaly of the new position adopted by Aldred; apparently the coregency theory is now so strongly supported by other evidence that it does not need the monuments that seem to group the two kings together! He says: "the very evidence which first suggested the existence of a coregency is no longer needed or used for the argument."[92]

Once again the proponents of the coregency have allowed hazy thinking to mar their argument. Giles' position is perhaps most vulnerable. His entirely unwarranted manipulation of numbers and his assumptions regarding Tiy's age at various times in her life do not command the respect of the uncommitted reader. Moreover, his statement to the effect that the sidelock of Baketaten proves her to have been a child at the time is baseless. Grown men could be shown wearing the sidelock, as the processions of princes at Luxor and Medinet Habu bear witness; the sidelock seems to have been merely a sign of sonship.

Pendlebury's argument is based on two misconceptions. The first is his assumption that the lintel and jambs, which he states are on "the façade" of the tomb, were carved earlier than the scenes inside the tomb, which show Tiy alone. This he takes as evidence that Amenhotpe III had died in the interim. Actually Pendlebury's order must be reversed. The lintel and jambs occur in connexion with the doorway leading from the first hall into the second, while the

[91] *JEA* 43 (1957), 116f. The present writer is puzzled as to how these considerations are suggestive of the *recent* demise of Amenhotpe III.

[92] Campbell, *The Chronology of the Amarna Letters* . . ., 29.

scenes showing Tiy alone are in the first hall, *in front* of the doorway.[93] Presumably, if the decoration of the tomb kept pace with its excavation, the scenes in the first hall showing Tiy alone would have been carved *before* the lintel and jambs. Consequently, the absence of Amenhotpe III in these scenes loses the significance Pendlebury attaches to it. Pendlebury further assumes that the scenes in which Tiy is shown commemorate her visit to Amarna in year 12. For this there is not the slightest justification. The scene showing Akhenaten on his way to the reception of foreign tribute[94] is dated year 12, second month of *proyet*, day 8; but in this scene, as in all those on the west wall of the hall connected with the reception of the tribute, Tiy is absent.

Admittedly these considerations do not per se render the evidence from Huya's tomb invalid, even though they tend to lessen the weight of the argument as formulated at present. The presence of Amenhotpe III here in person, and of his cartouches, must find some plausible explanation if the lintel and jambs are to be explained away. The references to Tiy find a fitting explanation, as Scharff, Helck, and Gardiner were quick to point out, in the fact that Huya was her steward; but is this sufficient reason to include a representation of Amenhotpe III?

The "shrine of Tiy"[95] from her so-called tomb in the Valley of the Kings also contains references to Amenhotpe III. The transverse above the door contains on the left the inscription

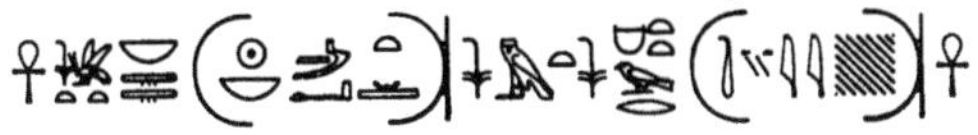

and is balanced on the right by a similar inscription containing the obliterated cartouche (praenomen) of Akhenaten. On the right door-jamb is the inscription

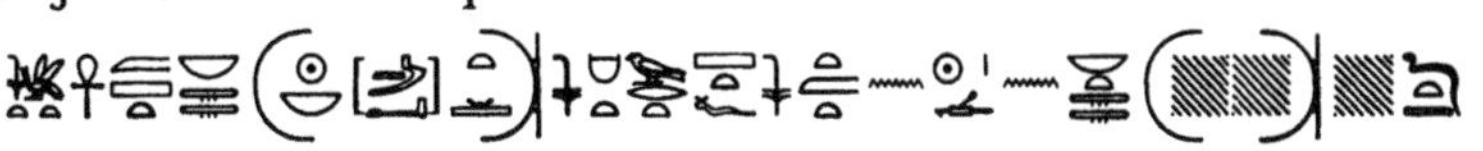

The left jamb also contains a balancing inscription including the cartouches of the Aten (late name), the praenomen of Akhenaten

[93] Davies, *The Rock Tombs of El-Amarna*, III, Pl. 4, 6, and 8; for their distribution see the plan on Pl. 1.
[94] *Ibid.*, Pl. 13.
[95] T. H. Davis, *et al.*, *The Tomb of Queen Tiyi* (London, 1910), Pl. 31 (ro.), p. 13. On the identity of this object see Gardiner, *JEA* 43 (1957), 12ff., and Roeder, *ZÄS* 83 (1958), 69f.

(erased), and the name of Tiy. Finally, on one of the side panels the praenomen of Amenhotpe III occurs again, this time in a vertical column flanking a scene showing Akhenaten and Tiy each making a burnt offering to the sun-disk.[96] The column is on the right and reads

A flanking column on the left may have contained Akhenaten's praenomen, but the cartouche is now obliterated.[97]

That Amenhotpe III was dead when this "shrine" was built is indicated by the fact that it was not he but Akhenaten who provided it for Tiy. We are told so explicitly in an inscription on the object.[98] The "shrine," then, is one object on which Amenhotpe III's name was inscribed after his death; the writing of *mꜣʿt* without the seated goddess and the addition in one instance before the cartouche of the epithet "living on truth" likewise point to a date after Amenhotpe's demise. But why does his name occur here? The reason, the present writer believes, lies in the person and status of Tiy. Tiy was a plebeian by birth. Her only claim to be heiress, in fact her only claim to fame at all, lay in her marriage to Amenhotpe III. The awareness of the awful implications of this marriage seem already to be reflected in the statement on the "marriage"-scarab which says of Tiy, "she is the wife of a mighty king, whose southern border is as far as Karoy, and whose northern as far as Naharin."[99] After her

96 Davis, *The Tomb of Queen Tiyi*, Pl. 29 and 32; the name of the Aten is in its later form.

97 These three cartouches seem to be original. Twice at least, however, the names of Amenhotpe III seem to have been superimposed on other cartouches, presumably those of Akhenaten. Once on the door *Nb-mꜣʿt-rʿ* occurs with [*'Imn*]-*ḥtp ḥqꜣ Wꜣst;* I presume this is in surcharge mainly on account of the epithet "long lived" (*ʿꜣ m ʿḥʿ.f*) following the second cartouche, and must originally have referred to Akhenaten. On the left jamb the praenomen of Akhenaten is replaced by *Nb-mꜣʿt-rʿ* in red ink: Daressy, *apud* Davis, *The Tomb of Queen Tiyi*, 13. A. Weigall (*The Life and Times of Akhenaten Pharaoh of Egypt* [London, 1922], 247) states that it is Amenhotpe III's own name that was replaced by the same king's praenomen; and Gardiner, surprisingly, seems to back Weigall: *JEA* 43 (1957), 13, n. 3. The presence of *ʿnḫ m mꜣʿt* before this cartouche, as well as the fact that Amenhotpe III's praenomen already was to be found on the right jamb, suggests that Daressy was correct.

98 Daressy, *apud* Davis, *The Tomb of Queen Tiyi*, 15; see also Pl. 31 (right).

99 *Urk.* IV, 1741:14–15.

husband's death Tiy's power would continue supreme if it were repeated insistently that she had been Amenhotpe III's queen. This is what seems to have been done; and this, the present writer submits, is the only satisfactory explanation not only for the "shrine" but also for the Huya lintel and the stela published by Griffith.

7. Fragments of a granite bowl found near the desert altars bore an inscription which included the late name of the Aten, the praenomen of Amenhotpe III, and the phrase "in Akhetaten" following a cartouche whose contents are not preserved.[100] Pendlebury at once took this as evidence of a coregency,[101] and Fairman more cautiously followed suit. The latter scholar based himself largely on the presence of the late Aten-name: "Unless all attempts to draw chronological conclusions from the forms of the name of the Aten are useless, it seems difficult to escape the conclusion that Amenhotep III was still alive (and possibly in Amarna) about the ninth year of Akhenaten's reign...."[102]

The *non-sequitur* is apparent: without denying that the forms of the names of the Aten are valid chronological criteria, one is compelled to deny that Fairman's conclusions are difficult to escape from. The presence of Amenhotpe III's praenomen dating from *ca.* the ninth year of his successor no more proves that he was alive at the time than the sporadic occurrences of other kings' names on monuments dating from the reigns of their successors proves that they survived into succeeding reigns. The most these miserable fragments allow is a cautious suggestion, and nothing more, that a cult of Amenhotpe III continued after his death, and this was already suggested by other evidence.

8. The criticism just offered applies equally well to the next item, the offering table from Amarna.[103] This object is actually the fragment of a statue, showing a kneeling human figure holding an offering slab upon his outstretched hands. A band of inscription between the hands gives the later form of the Aten-name followed by the praenomen of Amenhotpe III. The same form of the god's name occurs twice more on the front edge of the table, flanked, on the right side, by the praenomen of Amenhotpe III, on the left by the name of Akhenaten.

[100] *CoA* II, Pl. 47:2–3. [101] *Ibid.*, 102. [102] *Ibid.*, 108.
[103] Fairman, *CoA* III, 155; Helck, *MIOF* 2 (1954), 198; *CoA* III, Pl. 54:4–6.

No one is obliged to interpret these inscriptions as proof that Amenhotpe III was still living when they were written. A priori it is to be expected that cult objects destined for use in offering ceremonies would be inscribed with the names of the recipient(s) of the offerings, i.e. the god(s) or person(s) to whom the cult was dedicated. It is probable that this offering table was used for the offerings dedicated (in part) to Amenhotpe III. But one cannot logically force the evidence to say more. Certainly Engelbach's pronouncement that this statue "definitely shows Amenophis III was alive after Akhenaten's ninth year of reign and coregent with him"[104] is unjustified. In fact, if the present writer's interpretation of the inscriptions is close to the truth, and Amenhotpe III was receiving offerings at Amarna along with the Aten, it is very likely that he was, at the time, defunct.

9. At this point Fairman introduces the evidence presented long ago by Borchardt.[105] Borchardt argued for a coregency on the basis of a scene that occurred in the tomb of Surer at Thebes.[106] The scene in question shows a row of statues being hauled on sledges in a procession. Although none of the statues is identified by inscription, it seems as though the first is Amenhotpe III, and the second and third his queen Tiy. Squeezed into the space between the third statue and the walking figure who brings up the rear is a fourth, smaller statue, depicting a king trampling a Nubian. That this statue is a later insertion, added after the scene had been wholly laid out and at least partly executed, is proved by the fact that its base is on a higher level than the base-line of the others, and overlaps the statue in front and the figure behind. Borchardt concluded from the wholesale destruction evidenced in the tomb that Surer had fallen out of favour towards the close of Amenhotpe III's reign. Since, however, the main theme of the scenes in the tomb is a jubilee, Surer must have survived at least year 30 of Amenhotpe III. Borchardt believed the jubilee in question to have been one of the later ones, either that of year 34 or that of year 36. Since the fourth statue is a later addition, and since Surer surely could not have added a statue of

[104] *ASAE* 40 (1940), 134f.

[105] Fairman, *CoA* III, 155; Helck, *MIOF* 2 (1954), 198.

[106] L. Borchardt, *Allerhand Kleinigkeiten*, 23ff.; T. Säve-Söderbergh, *Four Eighteenh Dynasty Tombs* (Private Tombs at Thebes, I [Oxford, 1957]), Pl. 37.

Amenhotpe III after his fall from favour, Borchardt concluded that this must be a statue of Akhenaten, who, he reasoned, must have become coregent at the time of one of these later jubilees, either in year 34 or 36.[107]

Borchardt's ingenious argument is without foundation. The fourth statue was inserted in the scene before the tomb was given over to destruction, and there is not the remotest difficulty in assuming that this was yet another representation of Amenhotpe III. The statue is, in fact, dressed much like the statue of Amenhotpe III in Kheruef's tomb.[108] There is indeed no evidence at all that Surer was for any length of time a contemporary of Akhenaten.[109] The fact that no inscription is preserved that might assist in identifying the fourth statue justifies the rejection *in toto* of Borchardt's thesis as evidence for a coregency.

10. On the south side of the entrance corridor in the tomb of Kheruef[110] there is a mutilated scene in which Akhenaten is shown offering a libation to two standing (royal) figures, a male and a female. Although, in addition to the damage suffered by the accompanying inscription, the figure of Akhenaten is almost completely destroyed, a fragment of stone fallen from the relief and found near by clearly shows the cartouche of "Amenhotpe, lord of Thebes, of long life."[111] The same fragment bears the cartouches of Amenhotpe III, facing in the opposite direction to that of his son, and thus referring to the male figure whom Akhenaten is worshipping. The female figure standing behind Amenhotpe III is identified by no extant inscription, but the presence of sandals upon her feet indicates that she is a human being and not a goddess.[112] It is more than likely that Tiy is here depicted with her husband, as elsewhere in the same tomb.

The question whether Amenhotpe III is represented as alive in

[107] See also Cornelius, *AfO* 17 (1956), 307.

[108] Campbell, *The Chronology of the Amarna Letters . . .*, 12.

[109] Säve-Söderbergh, *Four Eighteenth Dynasty Tombs*, 35; see further pp. 39f. for criticism of Borchardt's views.

[110] Fairman, *CoA* III, 155f.; Helck, *MIOF* 2 (1954), 199; full references in P–M I², 298.

[111] Entirely within the cartouche; see Habachi, *ASAE* 55 (1958), Pl. 22a.

[112] A. Fakhry, *ASAE* 42 (1943), 463, n. 1.

this scene becomes important in view of the postulated coregency. Davies termed Amenhotpe III "recently deceased," but gave no reasons for this judgment.[113] Helck also holds that the old king is dead, mainly because he is being worshipped as a god: a living coregent would surely not be so portrayed.[114] Habachi's belief that Amenhotpe III is dead in this scene is based partly on the *atef*-crown(?), which he appears to have been wearing, and partly on the epithet "[beloved of] Sokar" recovered from fragments. Fairman, on the other hand, thinks that Amenhotpe III is shown here living and deified: "the dress of the seated Amenophis III is such that it is scarcely possible that we have here either the dead king or a statue of him, and the most probable explanation is that Amenophis IV once more is making offering to his living, deified father. . . ."[115]

Fairman's strong reliance upon the type of costume worn by Amenhotpe III is extremely perilous. The truth is that the costume worn by living kings in formal reliefs and paintings can scarcely be distinguished from that worn by statues and figures of deceased royalty. In the present case Amenhotpe III wears a long, transparent gown over a shorter pleated kilt (probably a *šndyt*), with the customary sash hanging in front. Sewn to the front of the sash is a curious brooch in the shape of a tiny leopard skin. The king's head and shoulders are destroyed, but he probably held his right hand across his breast, perhaps with a flail over his shoulder, His left arm hangs at his side and is caressed by Tiy. There is no pedestal under him, so that this is not the representation of a statue. He seems to have been wearing a head-dress consisting (in part) of two tall feathers, which Habachi calls an "*atef*-crown."[116] With the exception of the leopard-skin ornament, the costume described is identical with one worn sometimes by "Amenhotpe of the town (*pꜣ dmi*)," one of the patron deities of the necropolis workmen.[117] This cult image of Amenhotpe I also wears a long gown, a *šndyt* with sash, and two tall feathers (ornamented with horns and sun-disk).[118] Moreover, in

[113] *JEA* 9 (1923), 135. [114] *MIOF* 2 (1954), 199. [115] Fairman, *CoA* III, 155f.

[116] *ASAE* 55 (1958), 348; Davies (*JEA* 9 [1923], 135) indicates only two feathers with no central white crown. On the distinction between this feathered head-dress and the true *atef*-crown, see H. Jacobsohn, *Die dogmatische Stellung des Königs in der Theologie des alten Ägypter* (Äg. Forsch. 8, 1939), 31.

[117] Černý, *BIFAO* 27 (1927), 166ff.

[118] *Ibid.*, 169, Fig. 6; 171, Figs. 7–8; Pl. 1–3, 5, and 7.

certain cases no pedestal is shown beneath his feet, an indication that the sculptor did not intend the viewer to interpret the figure as a statue. And yet, when the scenes in these Nineteenth and Twentieth Dynasty tombs were painted, Amenhotpe I had been dead for over two centuries.

As pointed out above when the discussion centred upon the Soleb reliefs, it would appear that confusion has arisen over two distinct types of scene, viz. the truly commemorative and the idealized. The former type occurs in this very tomb of Kheruef. In the *ḥb-sd* reliefs we see depicted events that actually happened, and of which the sculptor could easily have been an eye witness. In such scenes we see figures who are certainly to be understood as human and alive, and others who are certainly statues, or deceased, and were so intended to be understood by the artist. In the same tomb also the other type of scene is found. The lintel of the entrance shows Akhenaten and Tiy making an offering to Atum and Re-Harakhty, and on the north side of the recess before the entrance Kheruef is depicted intoning a hymn to the rising sun. These are idealized scenes, taken from a repertoire of stock representations. Their content is timeless: one cannot conclude, for example, just because on the outside of the tomb the owner is shown singing—an activity usually engaged in by a living person—that the scene was executed during the lifetime of the owner. The scene of Akhenaten making a libation to his parents belongs to the category of idealized portrayals. It is not a specific incident that is here being recorded. Nor can one argue that just because Amenhotpe III is shown receiving an offering and about to eat—activities again reserved for the living—he must have been alive when the relief was carved. The scene conveys a truth that is above the mundane and is in no way connected to the temporal: the god Neferkheprure performs the duties of a faithful son for his father, the god Nebmare. The controversy over whether a figure in this type of scene is alive or dead is wholly irrelevant.

It is another matter to argue that this *genre* of scene, viz. a king making an offering to one or more other kings, might be used by a tomb owner under specific historical conditions, say, during a coregency to depict the two coregents. There is no evidence that this was the practice, and it is a priori improbable. For by its very nature the type of scene under discussion would be likely to be used only if the king(s) to whom the offering was being made were deceased at the time. This is true of scenes such as those in the Karnak "hall of ancestors," in which the contemporary monarch makes offering to his forbears. The essence of the offering ritual precludes that the recipient should be a living person. He may be a god—even a god derived, like Nebmare, Lord of Nubia, from a real person—but not the living prototype.

We conclude, therefore, that the scene from Kheruef's tomb is no proof at all for a coregency. The scene merely expresses Akhenaten's piety towards the memory of his father.

Giles has constructed around the scene under discussion and others in the vicinity an entirely different argument in favour of the coregency.[119] He points out that the reliefs carved around the entrance all seem to date from Akhenaten's reign. The scenes deeper within the tomb, on the other hand, are dated to Amenhotpe III's reign by the depiction of the *sd*-festival, and by the dates year 30 and year 36. He further notes that in the usual method of construction of an Egyptian rock-cut tomb, the excavation and decoration of the various parts of the tomb went on simultaneously, the sculptors and painters following closely on the heels of the stone-cutters. It follows then, since the decoration, like the excavation, began at the outside and progressed inward, that scenes on the façade and in the entrance corridor would be earlier in date than those farther inside. In the case of Kheruef's tomb this would mean that the scenes dated to Amenhotpe III's reign, which ostensibly were carved during his lifetime, are later in date than the decoration of the entrance, where Akhenaten appears as king. Giles concludes: "this is further, and the author feels, conclusive evidence that Amenhotep IV–Ikhnaton was co-regent with his father long before the latter's death."[120]

Giles' reasoning is invalid, at least where Kheruef's tomb is concerned. It is true that usually sculptors and stone-cutters worked simultaneously on tombs, but the present tomb seems to have been one of the exceptions. Beyond the short entrance corridor, the tomb consists of an enormous open court lined with colonnades on the east and west, a pillared hall beyond the western colonnade, and finally(?) a long room containing two rows of square piers. This

119 Giles, "The Amarna Period," 48ff.

120 *Ibid.*, 50.

enormous hypogeum displays decoration on only a few walls, and there is good evidence that the work had halted abruptly, perhaps on the fall from favour or the death of Kheruef.[121] If Giles' theory is correct, it ought to be only the innermost reliefs that are unfinished. But this is not so. The wall of the western colonnade on which the *sd*-festival scenes appear was almost completely decorated except for 150 cm. at the north.[122] The work on the eastern colonnade, however, which is closer to the entrance, had barely been begun when the work stopped.[123] Similarly, the sculptured relief in the entrance corridor seems to have been completed, and the scene on the north face in front of the entrance showing the owner singing to the sun is also complete. The opposite (i.e. the south) face of the rock before the entrance had only been marked out with a grid, preparatory to the execution of a relief, when work stopped.[124] If all these stoppages took place at one and the same time, it must be admitted that sculptors were at work in the several parts of the tomb at the same time. In any case the presence of unfinished work around the entrance and on the hither side of the great court proves conclusively that the decoration of the tomb did not follow the usual progression from the outside inward. Giles' criterion is *ipso facto* invalid, and his argument falls.

11. Fairman climaxes his argument by citing a graffito from the pyramid temple of Meidum.[125] It reads: "year 30, under the majesty of the king of Upper and Lower Egypt Nebmare, the son of Amun (*sic*), satisfied ⟨with⟩[126] Truth, Amenhotpe ruler of Thebes, lord of might, ruler of happiness, who loves him(?) who hates falsehood;[127] causing the male to sit down(?) upon the seat of his father, establishing his inheritance [in][128] the land." With reference to the latter part of the inscription, "causing the male . . .," Fairman says: "while

[121] Habachi believes the tomb was left unfinished because of Akhenaten's accession and the religious revolution that followed; see *ASAE* 55 (1958), 347.

[122] Fakhry, *ASAE* 42 (1943), 468.

[123] *Ibid.*, 455 and 467. [124] *Ibid.*, 455.

[125] Fairman, *CoA* III, 156; Helck, *MIOF* 2 (1954), 200; facsimile of the graffito in W. M. F. Petrie, *et al.*, *Medum* (London, 1892), Pl. 36 (18).

[126] Supply *ḥr;* or construe as agential genitive.

[127] A peculiar epithet; one would have expected perhaps *mꜣʿt* after *mr* to make two balanced phrases; see Helck, *MIOF* 2 (1954), 200.

[128] Restoring *m,* which seems to have worn away.

this seems a most unusual way to describe the beginning of a coregency, it is hard to believe it is only a colourless expression; the writing  can surely only refer to the king and not to a commoner, and the infinitive *rdit* must imply that the act actually took place in the 30th year. In spite, therefore, of the unusual mode of expression, I am inclined to believe that the graffito must be accepted as recording the commencement of the coregency in the 30th year of Amenophis III."[129]

Griffith[130] had already noted the importance of this inscription. He saw inherent in it the implication that royal inheritance through the female line could be misused by unscrupulous kings. Since a male heir would be better able to defend his rights, "Amenhotep III may have encouraged male succession as conducive to order." Griffith concedes, however, the possibility that the scribe "refers only to some personal benefit in a suit against a female claimant." This alternative explanation would seem to disregard the divine determinative after *it.f*.

Before Fairman, Carter had adduced this graffito as evidence for a coregency.[131] The reign of thirty years and ten months credited to Amenhotpe III in Manetho constitute, according to Carter, the sole reign of that king. In year 30 a coregency began, involving his son Akhenaten. It is the inception of the coregency that the present text commemorates. In a review of Carter, Scharff[132] registered fundamental disagreement. For Scharff, Griffith's first explanation had been the correct one, viz. that Amenhotpe III was merely ensuring the succession of his male heir. But this, he averred, had nothing whatsoever to do with a coregency of the two.

In his attempt at a rebuttal Helck strangely reverts to something like Griffith's alternative, and less likely, interpretation, viz. that *it.f* refers, not to a royal personage, but to a commoner: "weder wird von 'seinem Sohn' geredet, noch überhaupt von Königtum gesprochen, sondern es ist eine Bemerkung, die sich darauf bezieht, dass der König die Söhne der Beamten das Amt ihrer Väter einnehmen lässt—ein Wunsch dem immer wieder Ausdruck verliehen wird."[33] Helck claims that examples exist of *it.f*, with divine determinative, which

[129] *CoA* III, 156.

[130] *Apud* Petrie, *Medum,* 41.

[131] *The Tomb of Tut.ankh.Amen,* III, 2ff.

[132] *AfO* 10 (1935), 88.

[133] *MIOF* 2 (1954), 200.

clearly refer to non-royalty. This may well be, but the one example he cites is no proof, since the text in question shows a clear  where Helck reads .[134]

Fairman's argument is not compelling. One can agree with his statement that the locution is an unusual way to describe the beginning of a coregency. One can also agree when he says that it is hard to believe the expression is colourless. One can even concur with his conclusion that the use of the infinitive *rdit* implies a specific act that took place in the thirtieth year. But his statement that  "can surely only refer to the king and not to a commoner" is erroneous; for this expression can, and in the present context undoubtedly does, refer to a god as well as the king. The addition after the praenomen of "son of Amun" is especially significant. In formal inscriptions it is Amun who is spoken of as establishing the king on his (i.e. Amun's) throne. Amenhotpe III says: "I repeated monuments for him who begat me, Amun-re, lord of Karnak, who established me upon his throne (*nst.f*),"[135] and the king is said to have "appeared on the throne (*nst*) of Amun, like Re, eternally."[136] Amenhotpe III is further called "eldest son [of the king of] the god[s], the precious egg of Amun."[137] With reference to the establishment of an inheritance in the land, one may compare the allusion to "his (Amenhotpe III's) inheritance, his kingship, his throne,"[138] and the emphatic statement "it is he (Amenhotpe III) who is the heir of Atum,"[139] as well as the epithet "heir of Re," which sometimes occurs in the cartouche containing his praenomen. These expressions, all applied to the king, are stock, and are to be found in the inscriptions of many rulers. But this fact in itself points the way to the correct interpretation of the graffito. The inscription refers entirely to the king; it is he who is called the "male," and it is his own inheritance that is spoken of as being established. "His father" is none other than Amun, the epithet "son of Amun" in the first line

[134] R. Anthes, *Die Felseninschriften von Hatnub* (Leipzig, 1928), Pl. 16 (gr. 16:2), and p. 36. Cf. also K. A. Kitchen, *Suppiluliuma and the Amarna Pharaohs* (Liverpool, 1962), 6, n. 4.

[135] *Urk.* IV, 1652:11 (stela from mortuary temple); cf. also 1682;13, 1686:6, 1690:18, 1697:13, 1701:4, 1711:4, 1667;7-8.

[136] *Ibid.*, 1663:6; cf. 1702:7, 1679:2-3, 1781:4.

[137] *Ibid.*, 1709:3–4; cf. 1689:20, 1726:7.

[138] *Ibid.*, 1761:3; cf. 1688:15–16.

[139] *Ibid.*, 1822:14.

being possibly a semantic antecedent. The infinitive *rdit* in line 3 certainly indicates a specific incident, as Fairman has seen, but this is not the inception of a coregency. The imagery is clearly apropos of only one event, in fact the single most important event of Amenhotpe III's thirtieth year, viz. the first *sd*-festival. The re-establishment of the king on his ancestral throne and the re-confirmation of his inheritance are precisely what the *sd*-festival is concerned with. The present writer believes there can be little doubt that it was this important ceremony the author of the graffito had in mind, and not the beginning of a coregency.

12. The next piece of evidence to be examined was put forward by Cyril Aldred.[140] In many Egyptian tombs of the New Kingdom a type of scene appears in which a number of foreigners, introduced by the tomb owner, make a presentation of tribute to the king.[141] An accompanying inscription usually speaks of the ruler as appearing "as a king (so Aldred) on the great throne" or something similar. Aldred notes that Egyptians as well as foreigners are sometimes present in the ranks of the tribute bearers. If these tribute scenes represent the aftermath of a campaign (the explanation usually given), how are the native Egyptians to be accounted for? To Aldred "it is clear that such scenes have nothing to do with a parade of the spoils of war but represent a public ceremony, following closely on the coronation rites, in which the widespread sovereignty of the new ruler was recognized by his reception of gifts and homage from foreign nations as well as from representatives of his own people."[142] At the same "durbar," the king would have appointed new officials to high offices, or reinstated old ones. This explains the prominence of the tomb owner in this *genre* of scene; hence also the importance of the scene in the *cursus vitae* represented by the court officials in

[140] *JEA* 43 (1957), 114ff.; Campbell, *The Chronology of the Amarna Letters . . .*, 19ff.; E. Hornung, *Untersuchungen zur Chronologie und Geschichte des neuen Reiches* (Wiesbaden, 1964), 73.

[141] Invariably this scene occurs on the back wall of the transverse hall, to the left or right of the doorway leading to the long hall. In this position opposite the entrance, the figure of the king would receive most of what little light filtered into the tomb: N. de G. Davies, *The Tomb of Kenamun at Thebes* (The Metropolitan Museum of Art Egyptian Expedition, 5 [New York, 1930]), I, 17.

[142] *JEA* 43 (1957), 114.

their tombs. Separate scenes are sometimes devoted to the installation of the tomb owner, but these are closely connected to the "coronation-homage" scene in position and iconography. The fact that this scene of coronation tribute is absent from both Theban and Amarna tombs constructed before year 12 of Akhenaten's reign is taken as evidence that Akhenaten had not received such tribute before that time. In two of the latest tombs at Amarna, however (those of Huya and Merire II), the scene is present, and is there specifically dated to Akhenaten's twelfth year. "It is difficult," Aldred concludes, "not to gain the impression that this tribute dated so precisely as the chief event of an *annus mirabilis* was offered to Akhenaten on his accession to sole rule."[143] Aldred finds proof that we are dealing with coronation tribute in the Amarna scenes, in the presence of dancers and wrestlers, who are shown elsewhere in scenes connected with the accession or rejuvenation of a monarch. The lateness of Huya's tomb is ascribed by Aldred to the fact that Huya rose to power comparatively late in the reign, around year 12. Since on Amenhotpe III's death the old king's harem would become the responsibility of Akhenaten, it is not without significance that Huya's chief office was that of steward of Tiy. His appointment to that position, according to Aldred, coincides with the inception of Akhenaten's sole rule.

Aldred's first assumption is that all those tribute scenes that show the tomb owner leading tribute bearers into the presence of the king belong to a single *genre* representing the giving of a special "coronation tribute" at a public ceremony held shortly after the king's coronation. Aldred adduces two facts in support: first (although it is not formally presented as proof), the presence near the king of an inscription recording that the monarch "appears as king . . ."; and, second, the fact that *both* Egyptians *and* foreigners are to be found presenting tribute. Both considerations are quite insufficient to support Aldred's thesis. The bald statement that "king N appeared upon the great throne"[144] is no proof at all that a coronation has taken

[143] *Ibid.*, 116.

[144] Aldred adds "as king." One wonders whether this is his translation of *ḫʿy*, or whether he has the adjunct *m nsw* in mind. I have been unable to locate any example of the present type of scene in which the inscription before the king includes *m nsw*. Most are fragmentary, it is true, but those that can be read do

place in the recent past. The verb *ḫ'y*, as pointed out in Chapter 1, is used of *any* formal appearance of the king, and is by no means confined to his accession, though its use in connexion with that ceremony is well attested. In the context of the type of scene here under discussion, *ḫ'y* merely means that the king has graced the ritual of tribute-bringing by putting in a formal "appearance." The presence of Egyptians in such tribute scenes—if indeed there are examples showing them[145]—is again no proof that the occasion for the celebration was a coronation. The Egyptian concept of kingship represented native Egyptians on the same footing as out-and-out foreigners, in a state of subjection to Pharaoh (compare, for example, the traditional "nine bows" which number Upper and Lower Egypt among themselves). Tribute scenes depicting Egyptians and outlanders would, with more likelihood, be seeking to typify the totality

---

not include any qualifying adverbial element with *ḫ'y*. Cf. Theban tomb 48 (Surer), "appearance of the king on the great throne like his father Re every day" (Säve-Söderbergh, *Four Eighteenth Dynasty Tombs,* Pl. 31); tomb 84 (Amunnedjeh), "appearance of the king on the great throne in the palace of southern Heliopolis . . ." (P–M I², 168; *Urk.* IV, 951); tomb 75 (Amenhotpe), "the king [appeared] ⸢on⸣ the great [throne] . . ." (Davies, *The Tombs of Two Officials of Thutmosis the Fourth* [EES Theban Tomb Series, 3; London, 1923], Pl. 11); tomb 93 (Kenamun), "the king [appeared] on the ⸢great⸣ [throne] on the dais of electrum [ ]" (Davies, *op. cit.,* Pl. 8); the inscription in tomb 226 (Davies, *The Tomb of Menkheperrasonb, Amenmose and Another* [EES Theban Tomb Series, 5; London, 1932], Pl. 41) is too fragmentary for certain reconstruction. Cf. also *Urk.* IV, 140 (Thutmose II's inscription at Aswan): "Lo, his majesty appeared on the dais while the living captives which this army had brought to his majesty were dragged in"; *Urk.* IV, 1345 (Amenhotpe II): "his majesty appeared in the midst of Thebes on a great dias . . . (there follows the reception of tribute)." The inscription accompanying the carrying chair of Akhenaten in Huya's tomb (Davies, *The Rock Tombs of El-Amarna,* III, Pl. 13) states simply that the king and queen "appeared . . . on the great palanquin of electrum to receive the tribute. . . ."

[145] Aldred cites as examples scenes in tomb 95 (*JEA* 43 [1957], 114) and tombs 86 and 93 (*ibid.,* 114, n. 6). In tomb 95 (Mery) I have been unable to locate any tribute scene (for references see P–M I², 195ff.), and the scene in tomb 86 (Menkheperreseneb) contains no Egyptians (cf. Davies, *The Tomb of Menkheperrasonb . . .,* Pl. 4–7; Libyans are present [Pl. 7], whom Davies (p. 4) terms "practically Egyptians"). The "Egyptians" shown in tomb 93 (Kenamun) are merely personifications surmounting name-rings, grouped with other foreign peoples on the base of the king's throne; clearly they have nothing to do with the formal "tribute" scene.

of a king's conquests, not the universal acknowledgement of his recent inheritance.

This *genre* of scene, if taken as the presentation of tribute at the coronation, would be singular in its complete lack of reference to that event in word or artistic motif. Even those tombs that seem to have been decorated early in a reign (e.g. nos. 89 and 226 of the Theban necropolis, both early in Amenhotpe III's reign[146]) yield not a trace of evidence that the tribute scene was to be understood as taking place at the time of the coronation. The scene in no. 89, in fact, is in close proximity with one showing the tomb owner leading a trade delegation to Pwenet.[147] The purpose was doubtless merely to stress the man's instrumentality in procuring goods from foreign lands, whether by trade or exaction. Two tombs cited specifically by Aldred, viz. 75 and 93 (of Amunsiese and Kenamun respectively),[148] do not contain tribute scenes at all, but rather presentations of manufactured goods from Egyptian workshops. And while the significance of the scene in Kenamun's tomb remains obscure,[149] the objects shown in Amunsiese's tomb are designated as gifts to Amun.[150]

146 Davies, *JEA* 26 (1940), 131ff. (89); *idem, The Tomb of Menkheperrasonb* . . ., 37ff. (226).

147 Davies, *The Tomb of Menkheperrasonb* . . ., Pl. 23–4 (presentation of tribute), Pl. 25 (inhabitants of Pwenet).

148 Davies, *The Tombs of Two Officials* . . ., Pl. 11–12 and p. 12 (75); *idem, The Tomb of Kenamun* . . ., Pl. 11, 13 and pp. 22ff. (93).

149 In both the tomb of Kenamun and the mortuary chapel of the Twentieth Dynasty mayor Paser (S. Schott, *Wall Scenes from the Mortuary Chapel of the Mayor Paser at Medinet Habu* [SAOC 30; Chicago, 1957], Pl. 1) the gifts are said to be "brought (by) (*ms*)" the official in question. Davies (*The Tomb of Kenamun* . . ., 24) believes them to be articles manufactured by the royal workshops specifically for the court; cf. the recurrent descriptive phrase in the Paser scenes "bringing a statue (with descriptive qualifications) to the broad halls (*wsḫwt*) of the palace (*pr-nsw*) of Usermare-meryamun (by) the mayor of the city, Paser." One wonders whether the highest officials in the state were charged with the supervision of the production of a certain number of statues, chariots, and other such items, perhaps at their own expense, though the work may have gone on in the royal workshops. On the other hand the statues Paser is shown bringing could just as easily be interpreted as private gifts.

150 Cf. the phrases (Davies, *The Tombs of Two Officials* . . ., Pl. 12, lines 6 to 7) "seeking out excellent things for [his father Amun], adorning his house with electrum."

Likewise the statues of the king Paser is shown presenting to Ramses III on the walls of his mortuary shrine seem to be destined for various temples.[151] There is no reason to believe the artist wished the viewer to infer a connexion between the scene and the coronation of the king. In fact, an inscription accompanying the Kenamun painting makes it clear that the event took place at New Year's, and is thus probably to be understood as an annual occurrence. Three of the presentations Paser makes are dated—to year 2, fourth month, day 10, to year 3, fourth month, day 19, and to year 18, fifth month, day 14, all belonging to the reign of Ramses III.[152] All these dates are within a month of the feast of *nḥb-kꜣw,* which Schott characterizes as "a kind of second New Year's feast at the beginning of winter . . .";[153] and it may well be that the statues depicted are Paser's gifts to his sovereign at this festive season. But again, the ceremonies have nothing to do with the coronation, or the anniversary thereof, which in Ramses III's reign took place on the twenty-sixth day of the ninth month.[154]

Apart from considerations of inherent probability or improbability, there is reliable evidence to show that this type of scene, whatever else it may be, was *not* intended to commemorate tribute received at the time of the king's coronation. The tomb of Huy (no. 40) provides an example of such evidence. On the south wall of the transverse hall to the right (east) of the entrance, Huy is shown receiving his commission as viceroy of Kush from Tutankhamun.[155] There is no evidence that this induction took place at Tutankhamun's coronation, or that Huy wishes us to believe that it did. The royal name is Tutankh*amun, passim,* and a priori it is most likely that Huy was appointed after the return of the court to Thebes from Amarna. To the left of the entrance, again on the south wall, Huy's voyage to Nubia is depicted together with his arrival.[156] He then sets about his duties, *among which* is the collection of tribute.[157] This he piles into boats[158] (still on the south wall), and finally on the north wall (left of

[151] Schott, *Wall Scenes . . .,* Pl. 1.

[152] *Ibid.*

[153] *Ibid.,* 16.

[154] J. Černý, *ZÄS* 72 (1936), 114.

[155] N. de G. Davies and A. H. Gardiner, *The Tomb of Huy* (EES Theban Tomb Series, 4 [London, 1926]), Pl. 4–9.

[156] *Ibid.,* Pl. 10–15.

[157] *Ibid.,* Pl. 16–17.

[158] *Ibid.,* Pl. 18.

door), back in Thebes, he presents it formally to the king.[159] Obviously, this can in no way be construed as "coronation" tribute; the artist is merely depicting his employer pursuing the *normal tasks* connected with the office of Nubian viceroy. Gardiner aptly quotes as illustrative of this scene the model letter in Koller 3, 3–5, 4, which refers (4, 7) to the collection of taxes "each year."[160]

The evidence from other tombs is no less emphatic. In tomb 42 (Amenmose) the owner is shown on the back wall of the transverse hall, left of the door, leading a procession of Syrian tribute-bearers into the presence of a king, who is either Thutmose III or Amenhotpe II.[161] Immediately adjacent to this scene on the left end-wall of the same hall the capture of a Syrian town by Egyptian troops is depicted.[162] The Egyptians lead off captives, among whom is a "chief of Lebanon," and a damaged inscription records a campaign by Amenmose(?) in the district of Negau. Whether this is the record of a specific attack or not, it is clear that the artist intended us to construe it as antecedent to the scene of tribute on the next wall. Here then without a doubt is a representation of the spoils of war, the aftermath of a victorious campaign. Similar scenes in the tombs of Rekhmire and Menkheperreseneb (nos. 100 and 86) likewise presuppose victorious campaigns. The Rekhmire scene[163] refers specifically to the "plunder (*ḥꜣqt*) of all lands," and the Keftiuans[164] (who appear with their tribute) are said to have "heard of his victories over every land." The Syrians present, in fact, bring their tribute "in order to be loyal to his majesty, (for) they have seen his very great victories."[165] In Menkheperreseneb's tomb "the chiefs of every land . . . extol the might of his majesty, their tribute being upon their backs";[166] and an inscription above the tribute bearers refers to the defeat of Mitanni, known to have occurred in the thirty-

159 *Ibid.*, Pl. 22–31.

160 *Ibid.*, 27f.; R. Caminos, *Late Egyptian Miscellanies* (London, 1954), 437ff.

161 Davies, *The Tomb of Menkheperrasonb . . .*, Pl. 33–35.

162 *Ibid.*, Pl. 36.

163 N. de G. Davies, *The Tomb of Rekhmire at Thebes* (The Metropolitan Museum of Art Egyptian Expedition, 11 [New York, 1943]), II, Pl. 16; similarly tomb 90 (Nebamun): Davies, *The Tombs of Two Officials . . .*, Pl. 28.

164 *The Tomb of Rekhmire . . .*, Pl. 18ff.

165 *Ibid.*, Pl. 21ff.

166 Davies, *The Tomb of Menkheperrasonb . . .*, Pl. 4.

third year of Thutmose III: "you (Thutmose III) have destroyed the lands of Mitanni, you have hacked up their towns, their chiefs are in hiding. . . ."[167] Far from being occasioned by the coronation, this presentation of tribute took place during the festival of Djeser-akhet on New Year's day.[168] From Haremhab's destroyed tomb at Memphis there is a block (now lost) describing a reception of tribute.[169] After a summary account of a southern campaign led by Haremhab, the text continues, "lo, his majesty [ ] appeared upon the throne for receiving tribute, when the tribute of south and north was received; the heir apparent (*iry-pʿt*) Haremhab was standing at the side of the th[rone]." Again this is not a question of "coronation" tribute, but of booty from the wars. Moreover, in itself, the fact that Haremhab was already heir apparent militates in favour of placing this incident well along in the reign of the unnamed king.

Aldred is mistaken in his interpretation of this *genre* of scene. The procession of tribute bearers led on by the tomb owner may well represent the plunder from a foreign campaign. On the other hand it may equally well depict the arrival of the yearly tribute imposed by the Egyptians on the provinces of their empire. In either case the purpose seems to have been to show the tomb owner as somehow officially connected with the formal reception of the tribute. The one interpretation, however, that is everywhere excluded is the very one Aldred proposes, viz. that this presentation of tribute took place at the time of, and in honour of, the coronation. The present writer would not wish to deny that a special tribute was demanded by etiquette at the accession of a monarch,[170] but that it was made the theme of a particular type of tomb scene is without proof.

167 *Ibid.*, Pl. 7.

168 *Ibid.*, Pl. 3.

169 Wiedemann, *PSBA* 11 (1889), 423ff.; *Urk.* IV. 2087.

170 Nevertheless evidence is scanty. The inventory of Tushratta's gifts referred to by Aldred (*JEA* 43 [1957], 116, n.2) represents the Mitannian princess's dowry, and has nothing to do with coronation tribute; cf. EA 25, IV, 65. EA 41:7ff. and 33:16 refer to substantial gifts from foreign kings to Akhenaten shortly after his accession, but such gifts were constantly arriving at the Egyptian court, and there is nothing in these contexts that would indicate a special "coronation tribute." The customary present from his peers to a newly crowned monarch is specified in *KBo* 1:14 rev. 6ff. as royal garments and fine oil for anointing.

The second of Aldred's assumptions is that the same scene of "coronation tribute" also records the appointment of the tomb owner to office at the time of the coronation of his sovereign. He admits that upon occasion such scenes could be polite fictions on the part of the owner, that his appointment had been coeval with the king's accession. In either case, however, Aldred's assumption is entirely without proof. Not only is there no inscriptional evidence accompanying these scenes that might support his interpretation, but the foregoing demonstration that the representations of tribute bearers have nothing to do with a "coronation tribute" knocks the base out from under the assumption. Separate scenes showing the owner's induction into office, which Aldred insists "are closely related to the coronation-homage scene in position and iconography," are never at pains to represent the induction as taking place at the time of the coronation. This has already been pointed out in the case of Huy's induction (see above), and is certainly true of the like scene in Ramose's tomb;[171] in fact, as will appear later, the latter is not an "induction scene" at all. In Nebamun's tomb (no. 90), where the induction scene is left of the door, balanced by the tribute scene on the right, the induction itself is dated specifically to year 6 of Thutmose IV.[172] In short, neither artists nor tomb owners show any desire to foster the belief that induction and coronation were contemporary.

Aldred's third assumption is that the "durbar" shown in the tombs of Huya and Merire II at Amarna, and dated to Akhenaten's year 12, belongs to this same type of scene, which he has singled out and labelled "coronation tribute." Since, as has been pointed out, the "coronation tribute scene" is not itself a single *genre* and has nothing to do with the coronation, this assumption requires at least some other basis. The scene in the two Amarna tombs, specifically dated as it is, does not likely commemorate a regular (annual) reception of tribute. More likely, in spite of Aldred's vigorous denial that any other interpretation but his own has captured the real significance of the scene, we have here the captives and booty of a campaign,

171 N. de G. Davies, *The Tomb of the Vizier Ramose* (The Mond Excavations at Thebes, I [London, 1941]), Pl. 33ff.

172 Davies, *The Tombs of Two Officials . . .*, Pl. 26.

or a round-up of vassal kings or specially exacted tribute.[173] Certainly the presence of dancers and "athletes" proves nothing. Evidence is lacking that this motif is confined to, or even usual with, scenes of coronation and jubilee rites. At any festive occasion dancing and fighting would be customary among the lower classes, and might be expected to turn up in an artistic representation.

To sum up, the scene of tribute bearers in many Eighteenth Dynasty tombs has nothing to do with tribute exacted at the time of a king's coronation, or with the appointment of officials. It rather illustrates one of the tomb owner's important functions, and may represent the yearly reception of imposts or the arrival of booty from a campaign. While a comparison of this type of scene with the two examples from Amarna may be justified, this is no reason to believe that Akhenaten's accession to sole rule had recently taken place.

13. In the same article[174] Aldred mentions briefly further evidence for the coregency, arising out of the dates in a group of account papyri from Kahun.[175] W. S. Smith has also noted the potential case to be made out of these dates,[176] and Giles has recently, in a more extensive treatment, formulated an argument based largely upon them.[177]

The papyri in question, which came to light partly through Petrie's excavations and partly through a purchase by Borchardt, are four in number, and concern themselves with the business dealings of a "herdsman (*mniw*)" called Mesia. The earliest transaction (A, 1) is dated to year 27 of Amenhotpe III, eleventh month, day 20. On that date Nebmehy, "being a herdsman of the house of Amenhotpe," received from Mesia a quantity of clothing in exchange for the services of two of Nebmehy's slave girls, Haret and Henut. The deal was concluded in the presence of a number of witnesses. The same papyrus follows the account of this transaction with another

[173] Cf. Frankfort, *CoA* III, 24.

[174] *JEA* 43 (1957), 114.

[175] Published by F. Ll. Griffith, *The Kahun Papyri* (London, 1898), Pl. 39, and A. H. Gardiner, *ZÄS* 43 (1906), 27–47.

[176] *The Art and Architecture of Ancient Egypt*, 278, n. 38.

[177] "The Amarna Period," 50ff.; a good, though brief, summary of the evidence is also found in Campbell, *The Chronology of the Amarna Letters . . .*, 18f.

(A,2) dated to year 2 of Akhenaten, on day 27 of an unknown month of *proyet*. Again Nebmehy comes to Mesia, this time seeking a cow, for which he agrees to pay three acres of land. Once more a number of witnesses are present. Finally, in year 3 (of Akhenaten), on the fourth epagomenal day, a certain At(?), son of the soldier Menkheper, hires out to Mesia the slave girl Henut for two days' service, in exchange for a quantity of goods (A,3). Apparently in the interim At(?) had acquired at least one and probably both girls. The two papyri published in Griffith's *Kahun Papyri* are dated to year 33 of Amenhotpe III, first month, day 5 and day 10 respectively. They are concerned with a similar deal. In the first (B) Mesia purchases the services of the slave girls, Haret for seventeen(?) days and Henut for four days. The owner of the pair is now a woman Piya. In the second document (C) Mesia buys the services of Haret again, this time for six days. Both transactions are witnessed by a "council of judges (*qnbt sğmyw*)" belonging to the town of *Pr-Wsir*. The fourth papyrus (D) is more difficult to interpret. It dates to Akhenaten's year 4 (second month, day 7), and recounts a court case between Mesia and a fellow called Hat, apparently arising out of an agreement similar to those described in the other papyri. Whatever be the interpretation of the details, it is clear that the decision is in favour of Mesia.

Fortunately, no doubt surrounds the dates and the personnel involved. The year numbers are quite clear, as are most of the month- and day-figures; and, while upon occasion the personal names are difficult to read, the identity of the chief characters is unambiguous. All four papyri, if there is no coregency, cover a period of fifteen or sixteen years.

Giles finds a period of fifteen years too long in the light of the contents of the papyri. The compression into a much shorter span,[178] which he feels is necessary, can only be effected by positing a coregency. The considerations necessitating such a compression, he feels, are: (a) the fact that the three contracts of A were written on a single sheet of papyrus; (b) the recurrence of individuals, mentioned in the contract of year 27, in the contracts of years 2 and 3 (that the same persons should have been present over a period of 15 years is

[178] Aldred suggests six years: *JEA* 43 (1957), 114.

unlikely);[179] and (c) the identical wording of the introductions to the first two transactions of Berlin 9784, dated respectively to Amenhotpe III year 27 and Akhenaten year 2. The first begins (1.3–4, after the date

"the day on which Nebmehy . . . came before the herdsman Mesia"; the second (1.15–16) reads

"this day when again Nebmehy came before the herdsman Mesia." After each such introduction follows the petitioner's statement. Giles notes the notion of repetitive action present in the word *wḥm*, and believes that the use of this term indicates that the two contracts were made close together in time. He concludes: "Year 27 of Amenhotep III and year 2 Amenhotep IV–Ikhnaton were so close together in time that a scribe having written up one transaction in the former year would use a construction with the verb of repetitive action in describing a transaction in the latter year."[180]

While this evidence appears to be weightier than what has so far been examined, its actual contribution to the case for the coregency is greatly lessened by a close inspection of the documents themselves. Giles' argument, in so far as it is based on the format alone, is invalid. Gardiner has pointed out that whoever wrote the present text, Berlin 9784, did so at a single sitting, and not over a period of years as Giles apparently assumes. It is clear that what we have here is an abstract from a number of fuller accounts, perhaps drawn up for the purposes of a court case or for someone's official records. The similarity of the constructions does not prove a closeness in time between the two transactions, but rather that the scribe wrote the present account of both at the same sitting and only seconds apart. He uses the verb *wḥm* in A,2 merely because the same man, Nebmehy, is involved, and because the general purpose of his coming is the same as before.

[179] The slave-girl Henut is most noticeable, being involved in the first and third transactions. The herdsman Nen is a witness at all three, and the herdsman Aper and a certain Pen at the first and third. Finally, the scribe who wrote up all three contracts was Tutu.

[180] Giles, "The Amarna Period," 52f.

The recurrence of the same individuals throughout the period covered by the documents is the only reliable evidence on which an argument can be founded; yet even here the foundation is by no means secure. In the first place, it can be argued that fifteen years is not an impossible span in the life of an individual of the Eighteenth Dynasty. A person who was thirty years old when it began would be only forty-five when it ended; he would still be in possession of all his faculties and fully capable of taking part in public life. Even a person who was thirty at the end of such a period would probably have been mature enough fifteen years earlier to be a witness. In the second place it must be pointed out that the three transactions of Berlin 9784 took place in a single town. Communities in ancient times never experienced the rapid change-over of modern towns. In our day a span of fifteen years would be sufficient in many cases for an almost complete replacement of a town's population, but anciently this was not true at all; the majority of families, with their members, who lived in Kahun in Amenhotpe III's twenty-seventh year would probably still be present fifteen years later. In the third place, the four papyri are concerned entirely with the business affairs of a single individual, the herdsman Mesia. Presumably he moved in more or less restricted circles, and it might well be expected that members of his coterie would recur in his transactions over a period of years.

Thus far the present critique has taken the form of a rebuttal. Positive arguments will now be presented, which tend to support the traditional view that the papyri cover fifteen or sixteen years.

There are three considerations. First, during the period covered by these papyri the slave girls Haret and Henut were owned by at least three different masters. In year 27 of Amenhotpe III (A,1) their owner was Nebmehy; in year 3 of Akhenaten (A,3), At(?), son of Menkheper; in year 33 of Akhenaten (B, C), Piya and her son Miny. Although there is not much evidence on how frequently slaves changed hands in Egypt, three owners in six years seems a little too many. *A fortiori* this fact supports a longer period of time for the span of the papyri. Second, two generations seem to be represented by the groups of witnesses attested in Berlin 9784. In the first transaction twelve witnesses are present, none of whom is accompanied by children. In the second transaction six witnesses are present, including two pairs of father and son. In the third there are fourteen witnesses, including a mother and daughter, and a priest, his wife and daughter. Presumably the witnesses to Mesia's business deals were chosen from his associates and acquaintances, who in all probability would be his contemporaries, of his own generation. The fact that in the first transaction none of the witnesses has offspring present, while in the second and third early in the reign of Akhenaten, several sons and daughters are named, again suggests the passage of considerable time. Third, the nature of the deals suggests that they were not of frequent occurrence. Gardiner[181] has noted that the prices paid by Mesia for the services of the slave girls are very high. "A day's service," he writes, "is valued at 2 rings[182] whence it may be calculated that 4 days' hire would have procured the owner of the slave a bull!" This, he concludes, "is hardly thinkable in the matter of a paltry arrangement for a few days' ordinary service." The evidence suggests that we are dealing with a special sort of deal, involving very high sums of money, and sometimes plunging both parties into litigation. It is not inherently impossible that a wealthy man could get involved in such transactions fairly frequently; but it does seem a little astonishing that a common cowherd could have negotiated six such deals in six years. Again the evidence can be satisfied only by positing a longer period of time for the papyri. The present writer is compelled by the facts presented to cling to the traditional period of around sixteen years between Amenhotpe III's twenty-seventh year and Akhenaten's fourth.

14. In an article in the *Journal of Near Eastern Studies* Aldred has argued for a coregency on the basis of the dates of Ramose's tenure of office, and the date of his death.[183] Unlike the evidence already examined, the very bearing of which on the matter of a coregency is often dependent upon subjective interpretation, the facts adduced by Aldred, if correctly understood—and if indeed they are facts—virtually compel acceptance of a twelve-year coregency. Aldred's case is built in part around the person of Simut, the fourth prophet

181 *ZÄS* 43 (1906), 44.

182  : *šʿty*? or *šnʿt;* on the term and its meaning, see Gardiner, *ibid.*, 45ff., J. Černý, *JWH* 1 (1954), 911ff. A recent treatment with references is to be found in J. Vergote, *Joseph en Egypte* (Louvain, 1959), 169ff.

183 C. Aldred, *JNES* 18 (1959), 113–20; Hornung, *Untersuchungen* . . ., 74.

of Amun.[184] In year 20 Simut, already in possession of that office, was outranked by Meryptah, Anen, and Amenemhet, who held the posts of first, second, and third prophets respectively.[185] At his death, however, sometime late in Amenhotpe III's reign, he had advanced to the office of second prophet of Amun, presumably only after the deaths of Amenemhet and Anen. Aldred sets about to pin-point the date of Simut's advancement more closely. He finds among the jar dockets from Malqata a number, probably dating to year 34, which record donations of honey made by the Greatest of Seers, Amenemhet.[186] Identifying the office as that of the local pontificate of Re-Atum at Karnak, Aldred proceeds to equate this Amenemhet with the third prophet of Amun. But one holder of this solar pontificate is already known for Amenhotpe III's reign, and that is Anen.[187] Since presumably Amenemhet could not take over this office until the death of its previous occupant, Anen must have died *not later* than Amenhotpe III's year 34. At the same time the general shuffle of the four highest offices, with Simut advancing one or perhaps two grades, must have occurred.

Aldred next turns his attention to Ramose. He finds this southern vizier attested in texts dating from around year 30, but surprisingly in no later documents. Ramose is absent even from ceremonies and functions taking place in Thebes, his own bailiwick: he is not mentioned in later dockets from Malqata, and in the decree endowing the mortuary temple of Amenhotpe son of Hapu, his northern colleague Amenhotpe is found ostensibly doing duty for him.[188] Aldred can explain this odd silence of the inscriptions in no other way than by assuming that Ramose had died shortly after year 30. Since a scene in the tomb of Ramose shows him, according to Aldred, being appointed vizier by Akhenaten, and since Ramose as vizier is known to have made donations to Amenhotpe III's first jubilee,[189] the conclusion is inescapable that the two kings were coregents for a fairly long time. The capstone of Aldred's argument is provided by the

[184] G. Lefebvre, *L'Histoire des Grands Prêtres d'Amon de Karnak* (Paris, 1929), 24ff.

[185] Statue of Nebnefer: bibliography *ibid.*, 240; *Urk.* IV, 1884f.

[186] Hayes, *JNES* 10 (1951), 94.

[187] *Urk.* IV, 1894.

[188] C. Robichon and A. Varille, *Le Temple du scribe royal Amenhotep, fils de Hapou* (FIFAO XI [Cairo, 1936], I. 6.

[189] Hayes, *JNES* 10 (1951), 100.

scene on the south wall of the first hall in Ramose's tomb.[190] According to Aldred the tomb was finished in haste, and the scene in question (which shows the funeral procession) was one of those abandoned when the work stopped. One of the last groups to be included on the southern wall—it was actually in process of execution when work stopped—comprised the figures of the four prophets of Amun. Only the last in the group, the fourth prophet, is named; and although the name was later partly erased by the Atenists, enough remains to show that it was Simut.[191] When Ramose died, therefore, and the tomb was abandoned, Simut was still fourth prophet of Amun; in other words Ramose could not have died later than year 34. By that time Akhenaten was thus already on the throne, a deduction that supports a coregency dating from Amenhotpe III's twenty-eighth year.

Aldred's argument will be seen to rest primarily on his identification of the "Greatest of Seers" Amenemhet with the third prophet of Amun of the same name. His interpretation of the absence of Ramose's name from inscriptions dated after year 30 contributes unessential, though considerable, support. Without successfully demonstrating the identity of the two Amenemhets, Aldred would not be able to find any support whatsoever for the date he postulates for Simut's promotion, and his entire argument would be invalidated. It behooves the enquirer, therefore, to examine very closely this kingpin of the distinguished scholar's thesis.

The title *wr mꜣꜣw*, "greatest of seers," is well known in the Theban nome during the New Kingdom. "The Greatest of Seers of Re-Atum in Wese" was the title of the chief priest of the solar cult at Karnak.[192] A similar title, "the Greatest of Seers in southern Heliopolis" (Hermonthis?), is also attested.[193] This latter office has occasioned some confusion in time past. Was there a second solar cult at

[190] Davies, *The Tomb of the Vizier Ramose*, Pl. 27.

[191] Actually the sign (or signs) following 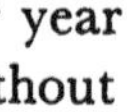 is almost completely destroyed. It is conceivable that what was erased was the *mwt*-bird, but the divine name *'Imn* cannot be ruled out; cf. *Urk.* IV, 1789. An examination of this scene on the spot in May, 1962, failed to convince the present writer that the restoration *mwt* is as certain as Aldred maintains.

[192] See H. Kees, *Orientalia*, 18 (1949), 439.

[193] See *Wb* I, 329:8; for the "Greatest of Seers of Horakhty," the title of the High Priest of Aten at Thebes, see M. Doresse, *Orientalia*, 24 (1955), 125f.

Hermonthis, besides the one at Karnak, or are these merely variant designations of the same priestly office (at Karnak)? Scholars had frequently assumed the existence of a solar cult at Hermonthis independent of that at Karnak, and had conjured up a vague connexion between this apparent fact and the alleged coronation of Akhenaten in that town.[194] The convincing demonstration by Varille[195] that "southern Heliopolis" can, upon occasion, be an epithet of Thebes has brought about a change of view. It was now seen to be a real possibility that but one solar cult existed in the Theban nome, and that at Karnak. As Kees[196] piled up more and more evidence that "southern Heliopolis" could, and frequently did, designate Thebes during the New Kingdom, the view became increasingly attractive that "the Greatest of Seers of Re-Atum in Wese" and the "Greatest of Seers in southern Heliopolis" were one and the same priest.[197]

There is much to be said for this view. Besides the inherent improbability of two important solar cults existing in the same nome, the use of both priestly titles reveals an interesting chronological bifurcation.[198] The title "Greatest of Seers of Re-Atum in Wese" was used from the end of the Eighteenth Dynasty into the Twenty-Second Dynasty, while that of "Greatest of Seers in southern Heliopolis" is confined to the late period from the mid-Twenty-Second Dynasty on. The two do not appear to have been used simultaneously. This suggests that we are dealing, in the case of "the Greatest of Seers of Re-Atum in Wese," with a designation which went out of fashion in the Twenty-Second Dynasty, and was *replaced* by "the Greatest of Seers in southern Heliopolis."

194 Cf. H. Kees, *ZÄS* 53 (1917), 81ff. (in answer to Borchardt in *ZÄS* 44 [1907], 97f.); G. Legrain, *RT* 23 (1901), 62; H. Schaefer, *Religion und Kunst von El Amarna* (Berlin, 1923), 30; L. Borchardt, *MDOG* 17 (1917), 26ff.; A. Scharff, *Ägypten und Vorderasien im Altertum*, 141.

195 *ASAE* 33 (1933), 86f.

196 *Orientalia*, 18 (1949), 434 and 440f.; see also Doresse, *Orientalia*, 24 (1955), 123f. The view is rejected by Otto (*Topographie des thebanischen Gaues* [Untersuchungen 16; Berlin, 1952], 35f.), who clings to the old view that southern Heliopolis is Hermonthis. C. F. Nims (*JNES* 14 [1955], 120) seems undecided.

197 See H. Kees, *Der Götterglaube im alten Ägypten* (Leipzig, 1941), 361; *idem, Das Priestertum im ägyptischen Staat vom neuen Reich bis zur Spätzeit* (Leiden, 1953), 26f.

198 See the list of all known bearers of the titles in Kees, *Orientalia*, 18 (1949), 431ff.

The list of holders of the office compiled by Kees shows that it was the prerogative of one of the high-ranking prophets of Amun. Beginning with Bakenkhonsu (no. 4 of Kees's list), who lived under Ramses II, nine out of sixteen incumbents also held, or passed through, at some time in their careers the rank of third prophet of Amun. This startling proportion might even be increased if more biographical material existed for the others. It would seem, therefore, that except in cases out of the ordinary[199] the office of High Priest of the Re cult at Karnak belonged to the third prophet of Amun. Anen, if indeed his title is to be equated with that of High Priest of Re at Karnak, would doubtless have functioned at some time in his life as third prophet of Amun. He need not have held the office until his death; in fact, if it were as intimately connected with the office of third prophet as the sources indicate, Anen would have relinquished it upon becoming second prophet. This would not, of course, mean that he was obliged henceforth to omit the title *wr mꜣꜣw* from his inscriptions, since strings of titles can represent *all* the offices held during a lifetime even though the writer may have enjoyed only a few of them at the time of writing. It is thus quite unnecessary, if not unjustified, to assume as Aldred does[200] that the title "Greatest of Seers" passed from Anen only at his death.

The burden of the discussion thus far has been to show that, granted the three major assumptions Aldred makes, his conclusions are *non-sequitur*, and his postulated advancement in the upper echelons of the Amun priesthood about year 34 is without support. It is now necessary to look more closely at his assumptions. These are, first, that the jar dockets from Malqata that mention Amenemhet date from year 34; second, that the office held by Anen was that connected with the solar cult at Karnak; and third, that the Amenemhet of the jar dockets is identical with Amenemhet, third prophet of Amun, who functioned as "Greatest of Seers" in Karnak as successor to Anen.

The first assumption, it must be admitted, seems sound. The three dockets mentioning Amenemhet came from honey jars, and

[199] E.g. the deliberate reshuffling of the top offices of the Amun priesthood under Ramses II, when Nebwennef was brought in as High Priest from Denderah: Lefebvre, *L'Histoire des Grands Prêtres d'Amon* . . ., 118.

[200] *JNES* 18 (1959), 116.

were found together with a honey docket dated "year 34," i.e. the year of Amenhotpe III's second jubilee. Although they themselves bear no date, it is quite likely that all the donations of honey came from the same year. Thus it is probable that the "Greatest of Seers" Amenemhet was in that office around year 34.

The other two assumptions, however, are by no means well founded. The evidence at hand casts grave doubts on whether Anen really was High Priest of Re at Karnak. His title, "Greatest of Seers in the house of the prince (*wr mꜣꜣw m ḥwt sr*)," seems to be unique. It is *not* the title of the High Priest of Re at Karnak, which is, as has already been noted, "Greatest of Seers of Re-Atum in Wese." On the other hand, it bears a striking resemblance to another kind of title known from the Eighteenth Dynasty, one in which "Greatest of Seers" is followed by a qualifying phrase containing the name of a building. Rekhmire, for example, is called "*sm*-priest in the *pr-nsr*, Greatest of Seers in the *pr-wr*,"[201] and Khaemhat was "Greatest of Seers in the noble chamber."[202] Senemah bears the title "*sm*-priest, Greatest of Seers in the beautiful house."[203] It is probable that Ramose had a similar title, though all that is left in the fragmentary inscription is "Greatest of Seers [ ]."[204] Kees believes that such titles were connected with the palace or the place of embalmment;[205] but it is exceedingly doubtful whether they bear any relation to the Re cult at Karnak. Moreover, with the exception of Anen, all holders of this High Priesthood belong to the Nineteenth Dynasty or later, and a sizable number of them are now known. The conclusion seems to be that this cult was not established until after the Amarna period, and that Anen had nothing to do with it. The assumption that Amenemhet of the Malqata dockets is not the High Priest of Heliopolis, but the third prophet of Amun at Karnak, is similarly unfounded. Aldred is forced to assume that one of the most prominent officials in the state, bearing the important title of third prophet of Amun, was designated only by one of his lesser offices. The fact that the first prophet of Amun is designated as such in the Malqata dockets[206] is opposed to Aldred's assumption. If the third prophet *had*

201 Davies, *The Tomb of Rekhmire at Thebes*, Pl. 11. 202 *Urk.* IV, 1848.
203 *Urk.* IV, 515. 204 Davies, *The Tomb of the Vizier Ramose*, Pl 3.
205 Kees, *Das Priestertum . . .*, 27, n. 3.
206 Hayes, *JNES* 10 (1951), 111, Fig. 23.

actually donated something to the palace, there can be no reasonable doubt but that he would have been called "third prophet of Amun" on the dockets. The "Greatest of Seers" Amenemhet at Malqata can only be the Heliopolitan high priest. The fact that it is honey that is being given by him *a fortiori* supports this identification, since honey is a product of the Delta, and is frequently mentioned in the Heliopolitan sections of the Harris Papyrus.[207] Nor is a difficulty raised when Aldred points out that the name Amenemhet does not suggest a Heliopolitan origin.[208] The name Amenhotpe does not suggest a Delta origin either, and yet during Amenhotpe III's reign three prominent men bearing this name had connexions with the Delta, one as a native of Athribis, another as steward at Memphis, and a third as northern vizier. Again, the name Ptahmose does not suggest a Theban origin; yet a Ptahmose appears as High Priest of Amun in the same reign. Obviously the ring of a name provides no reliable guide to the background of the individual bearing it.

In sum, Aldred's demonstration fails utterly to remove the possibility that Amenemhet of the Malqata dockets is the High Priest of Re at Heliopolis. Not only does the possibility remain, but it becomes a distinct probability in the light of the facts presented above. There is, thus, from this line of reasoning at least, no means whatsoever of pegging down the date of Simut's promotion to the position of second prophet. The weight of the argument is now thrown on to Ramose and the date of his death.

Aldred makes much of the fact that Ramose disappears from the Malqata dockets and from other dated sources after year 30.[209] At first sight this seems impressive. On closer inspection, however, it appears that not only is Ramose absent from the Malqata dockets after year 30, but so also is *anyone else* holding the vizierate, either in south or north. How is this silence to be explained? Did the office of vizier fall out of use after year 30? It would be absurd so to maintain, but by the same token it is also absurd to infer, as Aldred does, that the silence bespeaks Ramose's death. The *argumentum e silentio* is at best a weak recourse. In the present case it proves nothing. For the last decade of Amenhotpe III's reign there are only *two* dated texts in

207 Harris Papyrus, 39:6–8.

208 *JNES* 18 (1959), 115.

209 *Ibid.*, 117f.

which a vizier is mentioned,[210] and in one of them[211] the word "vizier" is doubtful. How in all seriousness can the statement be made that "the inference to be drawn from these notable silences is that Ramose had died soon after year 30"?[212] The evidence is too meagre for such a possibility to receive even a moment's consideration.

The scene on the rear (west) wall of Ramose's transverse hall is interpreted by Aldred as the induction of Ramose to the office of vizier under Akhenaten.[213] The contents of the scene show that it is nothing of the kind. Akhenaten, together with his wife, depicted in the "Amarna" style, leans out of a window of appearances, and makes a speech to Ramose standing below. The speech is unfortunately shot through with lacunae, but enough remains to show that it is not "an attenuated version of the conventional installation homily."[214] The contents certainly had to do with a royal command, as is clear from such scattered phrases as "the matters with which I have charged you (*mdwt rdi.i m ḥr.k*)," and "I have commanded it," but nowhere in the surviving portion is the matter made explicit. That the command was specific, and concerned the carrying out of certain tasks, is suggested by an adjacent scene in which Ramose transmits the information he has received to his underlings.[215] The inclusion of a scene in which Ramose is decorated with collars shows that the royal appearance was made, at least partly, for the purpose of rewarding Ramose, perhaps for meritorious service. It is, moreover, worthy of note that Ramose, wherever he occurs on this wall (especially beneath the window of appearances), is accompanied by the titles "hereditary prince, sole friend, mayor of the town and vizier." The ceremony thus has nothing to do with the *installation* of a vizier, but rather with a specific decree issued to one who was *already* vizier, and who had functioned in that office long enough to be rewarded for it.

210 Robichon and Varille, *Le Temple du scribe royal* . . ., Pl. 1; G. Legrain, *ASAE* 4 (1904), 197; in both cases the name is "Amenhotpe," and it has been assumed that he was the northern vizier: see Helck, *Verwaltung*, 304f.

211 Legrain, *op. cit.*, 210.

212 Aldred, *JNES* 18 (1959), 118.

213 Davies, *The Tomb of the Vizier Ramose*, Pl. 32ff.; Aldred, *JNES* 18 (1959), 118.

214 *Ibid.*

215 Davies, *The Tomb of the Vizier Ramose*, Pl. 36.

But it can be proved that Aldred's belief that Ramose died late in year 30, or early in year 32,[216] is untenable. On the east wall (south half) in the transverse hall in Ramose's tomb[217] Ramose is twice shown seated before a company of people who are likewise provided with seats. The presence of food-laden tables indicates that a meal is about to commence. But it is not a meal of which the tomb owner partakes: the accompanying text in both scenes stresses the fact that this is an offering to Ramose's father and mother, and to his "brethren who are in the necropolis."[218] The guests depicted are thus deceased relatives of Ramose. Among them Amenhotpe son of Hapu is found[219] along with that other Amenhotpe son of Heby, who was steward at Memphis during much of Amenhotpe III's reign.[220] Amenhotpe the steward was still in office in year 31,[221] and may have survived until year 35.[222] That he died subsequent to the passing of Amenhotpe son of Hapu seems to follow from the fact that for a certain length of time he held the office of scribe of recruits,[223] so intimately connected with Amenhotpe son of Hapu. It is probable that he did not come into possession of that distinction until his more illustrious namesake ceased to hold it. The death of Hapu's son must have occurred not earlier than year 34, for until that date the Malqata dockets show him to have been alive and active.[224] If, however, both Amenhotpes

[216] Rather than his unnecesarily loose "soon after year 30." In order to use as evidence Ramose's absence from the endowment ceremony of Amenhotpe son of Hapu's mortuary temple, Aldred must place Ramose's death before iv, 6 of year 31 (the date of said ceremony). For the following see also *JAOS* 83 (1963), 241, n. 22.

[217] Davies, *The Tomb of the Vizier Ramose*, Pl. 8–12.

[218] *Ibid.*, Pl. 10 and 11; p. 16.

[219] So from his titles 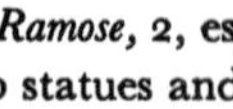 and 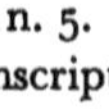 (cf. 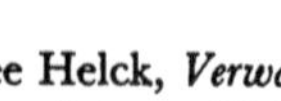 and  : *JEA* 15 [1929], Pl. II, 2), and from the appearance of the figure; see Davies, *The Tomb of the Vizier Ramose*, 2, esp. n. 5.

[220] For references to statues and inscriptions, see Helck, *Verwaltung*, 483f.

[221] Mentioned in a Malqata docket of that date: Hayes, *JNES* 10 (1951), 44, Fig. 4:17.

[222] If the shrine at Silsileh is correctly ascribed to him.

[223] *Sš-nsw nfrw:* Leiden pyramidion, *Urk.* IV, 1812.

[224] He appears at Malqata as "Huy the king's scribe" (Hayes, *JNES* 10 (1951), 100), and once perhaps as "Amenhotpe the king's scribe" (*ibid.*, 105, Fig. 17). That this is, in fact, Amenhotpe son of Hapu is proved (a) by his title "king's scribe"; (b) by his connexion with the estate of Satamun (*ibid.*, 48, Fig. 8:95): cf.

are shown deceased on the east wall of Ramose's hall, year 34 must be the *terminus a quo* for the decoration of that wall. Since the scenes in question are very close to the entrance, they were probably among the earliest in the tomb to be executed. Next in order would come the funeral scenes on the south wall,[225] and finally the royal scenes on the west (rear) wall.[226] That the work was not finished with undue haste is the judgment of Davies,[227] and the excellence of the workmanship in both excavation and decoration is in full agreement. Thus the tomb, begun not earlier than year 34, was in process of construction during the last years of Amenhotpe III. Are we to assume, then, that Ramose had died over two years before a tomb was begun for him? The absurdity of this assumption is all too clear. Ramose must have survived the thirty-fourth year of his sovereign, and in all probability a decade more.

Aldred's argument, in consequence of the above deductions, is invalid. The date for Ramose's death he arrives at is incorrect, and cannot be used to establish a *terminus ad quem* for Akhenaten's accession. Indeed, far from opposing the traditional view that there was no coregency, the evidence from Ramose's tomb actually supports it. For if the earliest decoration in the tomb is known to date from some time after year 34 of Amenhotpe III, the latest, viz. the unfinished relief showing Akhenaten in the Amarna style, is *a fortiori* pushed closer to what opponents of the coregency theory would consider the correct date. And in view of the real possibility that work on the tomb began much later than year 34, and taking into consideration the slowness of execution evidenced by the careful painting and relief, the tomb presents a strong case against any coregency of Amenhotpe III with Akhenaten.

15. From Rowe's excavations of 1938 at Athribis[228] comes a large (52 by 42 by 59 cm.) limestone block, bearing on one side three more

the title of Amenhotpe son of Hapu "steward of the estate of the princess and king's wife Satamun" (*Urk.* IV, 1828); (c) by the fact that all other officials named Huy or Amenhotpe in the dockets are excluded from possible identification by occupation or filiation; (d) by the enormous number of dockets on which his name occurs (86), precisely what one would expect of the most important official in the kingdom.

[225] Davies, *The Tomb of the Vizier Ramose*, Pl. 22ff.

[226] *Ibid.*, Pl. 29ff.

[227] *Ibid.*, 10.

[228] A. Rowe, *ASAE* 38 (1938).

or less obliterated cartouches. The first is completely effaced, but the second can be restored  . The third shows part of the seated goddess *mꜣʿt,* and a *nb*-sign and is to be restored  . Fairman, who has recently utilized this inscription in support of the coregency,[229] confidently assigned the nomen with its epithet *nčr ḥqꜣ Wꜣst* to Amenhotpe IV, restoring the damaged cartouche as his praenomen, *Nfr-ḫprw-rʿ Wʿ-n-rʿ*. Originally, according to Fairman, the block was part of a thick temple wall, and was immediately followed on the right by another block with the nomen of Amenhotpe III. He thus envisages an inscription in which the names of Amenhotpe IV *preceded* those of his father, probably serving as superscription to a scene in which the figures of the kings were depicted. Since the cartouches all face the same direction (left), Amenhotpe IV could not have been shown making an offering to his father, as in Kheruef's tomb. The two must have been side by side, and facing the same direction. Fairman finds it "difficult to escape the conclusion that both kings were alive and reigning together, i.e. that they were coregents." The fact that Amenhotpe IV would have been shown *ahead* of his father must indicate that he was already the "dominant partner."

It should be pointed out first of all that the ascription of the surviving nomen to Amenhotpe IV is not beyond doubt. The epithet *nčr ḥqꜣ Wꜣst* does occur *passim* in the nomen of Amenhotpe IV, it is true, but it is not entirely unknown with the nomen of Amenhotpe III. In the Berlin papyrus discussed above, under no. 13, Amenhotpe III's nomen is written, like his son's in the same papyrus, with the addition of *nčr ḥqꜣ Wꜣst.* Since, as Gardiner has shown, the papyrus was a résumé of earlier contracts, and was written at one sitting, and since the latest date mentioned is Akhenaten's year 4, the papyrus clearly cannot have originated earlier than that year. One may pose the question whether the scribe copied the titulary of Amenhotpe III exactly as he found it in his source, which was presumably drawn up when Amenhotpe III was still alive, or whether he wrote the earlier king's name from memory. In view of the fact that the epithet *nčr ḥqꜣ Wꜣst* is usual only with Akhenaten's nomen, there is a strong

229 *JEA* 46 (1960), 80ff.; Kitchen, *Suppiluliuma and the Amarna Pharaohs*, 8; Hornung, *Untersuchungen*, 75.

likelihood that the scribe was influenced by the reigning king's titulary. The same influence of Akhenaten's nomen on the form of his father's could easily account for Fairman's block, if the latter came from a temple which was erected early in Akhenaten's reign. Why such a temple, dedicated in whole or in part to the worship of Amenhotpe III, should have been built at Athribis is surely not difficult to imagine, in the light of the connexions of Athribis with that monarch through the person of her illustrious son, Amenhotpe son of Hapu.

Nevertheless, the prima facie probability of Fairman's reconstruction of the cartouches cannot be gainsaid. If he is right, we have in this inscription a piece of evidence which, in contrast to much of the evidence examined heretofore, is wholly relevant to a discussion of the hypothetical coregency.

Fairman does not, however, found his case on the cartouches alone. It is the scene in which the cartouches occur that provides the main force of his argument. It must be stressed that the scene itself is a pure reconstruction. The block contains, both in its original condition and in its present state, such a small amount of text that Fairman's elaborate reconstruction becomes uncertain. Why must it necessarily be the superscription to a relief scene? Why not a decorative border (frieze or dado) of alternating cartouches?[230] The even spacing between the three surviving cartouches would be in favour of such a reconstruction.

But the chief weakness of the evidence is its ambiguity. Once again it is the specific interpretation one places on the inscription that gives it weight. A single example of the names of two kings side by side cannot possibly be accepted as evidence of anything without the presence of further suggestive details. This kind of bald juxtaposition carries little weight unless, and only unless, it is found frequently. And even then an inference has to be made on the part of the observer. In the present case it is the first and only occurrence of such formal juxtaposition of names, the vast numbers of inscriptions otherwise known from both reigns providing not a single comparable example.

[230] Such borders are fairly common; cf. U. Hölscher, *The Excavations of Medinet Habu*, 5 (Chicago, 1954), Pl. 276a and c; Pl. 335ff.; J. Leclant, *MDIAK* 15 (1957), Pl. 23:2; *HSE*, 341, Fig. 215.

16. In a recent article in the *Journal of Egyptian Archaeology* Aldred makes the following statement about one of the tablets in the Amarna cache:[231] "... a letter which clearly from its context must have been one of the first written by Tushratta to Akhenaten, is ... dated by a hieratic docket to year 12." The letter in question, EA 27, is by virtue of its docket one of the most important, but at the same time the most controversial, in the entire series. Since the docket, as its contents plainly indicate, records the date when the letter was received in Egypt, the regnal year date, if complete, could have precluded the voluminous debate on the coregency. Alas, such is not the case, and the fragmentary state of the text precludes instead even the least hazardous of opinions.

The hieratic docket, first published by Erman,[232] reads as follows: "[year–(?)] 2, first month of *proyet*, [day ...], when one was in the southern city, in the castle (*bḫn*) of *Ḫʿ-m-ꜣḫt*; copy of the Naharin letter which the messenger Pirizzi and the messenger [Pupri][233] brought." The regnal year figure was restored by Erman to read [1]2, on the assumption that there was enough room for a "10"-sign before the "2." Knudtzon, however,[234] followed by Mercer,[235] expressed doubts about Erman's reading and preferred to read "[year] 2." Of late Gardiner[236] has thrown the weight of his scholarly opinion behind Knudtzon, declaring that "the facsimile in Schroeder ... makes it clear that year 2 was written, not year [1]2, as Erman at one time thought possible." Actually, on the evidence of the traces alone, both readings can be maintained. There is certainly enough room between what was once the edge of the tablet and the beginning of the extant writing for the insertion of both 𓆳𓏏𓇳 and 𓎆; yet, as Campbell has pointed out,[237] the usual shape of an Amarna tablet precludes the possibility that the scribe would have been able to begin the line at the very edge. The tiny trace of ink ahead of the "2" could conceivably have been part of the arm of a "10"; but it could just as easily, and perhaps more likely, have belonged to the

[231] *JEA* 43 (1957), 38. [232] *ZÄS* 27 (1889), 63.

[233] Restored from lines 89 and 100 of the letter itself.

[234] *EAT*, 240, n. *b*.

[235] S. A. B. Mercer, *The Tell el-Amarna Tablets* (Toronto, 1939), I, 160.

[236] *JEA* 43 (1957), 14, n. 1; cf. *Egypt of the Pharoahs*, 213.

[237] *The Chronology of the Amarna Letters ...*, 32.

circular *sp*-sign, since the left side of the trace (the original edge of the stroke) seems to be curved.

If the date of the docket cannot be used effectively either for or against the coregency, the nature and purpose of the docket can. The phrase "when one was in the southern city . . ." has been interpreted by Hayes as a reference to a special visit to Thebes by Akhenaten on the occasion of his father's death, "the only event important enough to require his deserting Akhetaten for the purlieus of the ancient capital."[238] Hayes is virtually forced to adopt this interpretation, since he accepts the restoration "year 12"; and by that date in his reign, of course, Akhenaten had long since moved to his new capital at Amarna. Leaving aside, however, the reading of the regnal year, the present writer cannot help but feel that Hayes is resorting to a far less likely interpretation than the one that must at first glance suggest itself to every observer. For *iw.tw m niwt rsyt* surely in the present context refers to permanent residence, rather than a fleeting visit. We have here, then, an allusion to that period of recent history when the king and his court resided at Thebes, i.e. the five or so years of Akhenaten's reign immediately preceding the move to Amarna. The same locution is used in EA 23, which was written to Amenhotpe III, where it refers not to a *visit* of Amenhotpe III to Thebes—that city after all was his main residence—but to the period when the court lived there. The most reasonable explanation of these dockets[239] is that they were written by the king's secretaries at Amarna to distinguish those tablets that had been brought along when the court moved to Amarna from those that later came directly to the new capital. On this basis alone a restoration of the date as "[year 1]2" seems suspect.

Any further discussion of the docket would be fruitless at this point, especially since it will come up again for consideration when we examine the evidence of the Amarna letters as a whole (see below, pp. 151ff.). One fact should, however, be noted before moving on. The letter to which this docket is appended, EA 27, was written shortly

[238] *JNES* 10 (1951), 180.

[239] There are not many (see Erman, *ZÄS* 27 [1889], 63). The reason is probably to be sought in the fact that the edges of a good number of tablets have been worn away rather than in the assumption that only a few letters ever bore dockets (see Giles, "The Amarna Period," 86, n. 53).

after Amenhotpe III's death. Tushratta reminisces *passim* about the friendship he enjoyed with the addressee's father, and expresses the hope that the young man will himself entertain friendly relations with the Mitannian king. Consequently the letter is rightly understood to be the first written by Tushratta to Akhenaten after the latter's entry upon sole rule. The allusion to "the great feast for mourning (*isinu rabû ana kimri*)"[240] shows that the funeral rites for Amenhotpe III were either still in progress, or had just been concluded. Now there are but two possible restorations of the date, year 2 or year 12. No other number will suit the traces. If year 2 is restored, only a very short coregency amounting to but a few months at the most is possible. If year 12 is restored, a coregency of not less than eleven years is as good as proved. The docket of EA 27 thus effectively disposes of any suggested coregencies longer than a few months and shorter than eleven years.

17. P. van der Meer has pointed out[241] that at least three names of buildings or estates compounded with Amenhotpe III's praenomen occur in dockets, jar sealings, and inscriptions from Amarna. The names in question are "the castle of Nebmare," "the house of Nebmare," and "the house of Nebmare-in-the-barque."[242] Following Fairman, van der Meer finds an epithet of Amenhotpe III in the name "the house of Aten-Gleams (*pr Čḥn-'Itn*)." Since he sees no reason to connect these foundations with any like-named ones elsewhere in Egypt, he locates them with some confidence at Amarna. He concludes: "hence it follows that it is likely Amenophis III lived at Akhetaten."[243]

Van der Meer's conclusion is *non-sequitur*. To the contrary, there is no reason at all for thinking that Amenhotpe III ever lived at Amarna. In the first place, there is a distinction between living in a

[240] EA 27:100. [241] *Ex Oriente Lux*, 15 (1957–58), 78.

[242] For discussion and references, see Fairman, *CoA* III, 199f.

[243] *Ex Oriente Lux*, 15 (1957–58), 78. It is interesting to note that in cases where these names occur in well-preserved dockets, the date is mostly later than year 12: cf. *TA*, Pl. 22:4 (yr. 15); *CoA* II, Pl. 58:15 (yr. 14); *CoA* III, Pl. 85;17 (yr. 17) and 20 (yr. 13). Thus they cannot be elicited as proof that Amenhotpe III was living at Amarna at the time the dockets were written. They can suggest nothing more than the possibility that he had *at one time* lived in the new city or had founded estates there.

town and owning estates in it. Amenhotpe III undoubtedly had residences all over Egypt in which he rarely if ever set foot. In the second place, there is not the slightest grounds for believing that at a given site all the dockets and sealings mention only buildings located on that site. Dockets from the Ramesseum and Malqata conclusively disprove this.[244] In the present case the "castle of Nebmare" cannot be separated from the like-named building that is mentioned four times at Malqata.[245] Both clearly refer to the mortuary foundation of Amenhotpe III at Memphis. Mention of the "house of Nebmare" occurs no less than sixty-five times at Malqata,[246] and if figures alone are any guide, this institution—whatever it was—must have been located at Thebes. Mention of the "house of Nebmare-in-the barque" is found twice at Amarna,[247] and possibly once at Malqata;[248] nothing can be said regarding its location. The "house of Aten-Gleams" is mentioned fifteen times at Malqata.[249] Borchardt[250] believed it to be identical with the Malqata palace, but Fairman[251] thinks this unlikely on the slim grounds that the name "the house of Rejoicing" is attached to at least part of that palace. Yet even if the identification with the Malqata palace is given up, there is no evidence for locating it at Amarna.

There is an interesting fact regarding the occurrence of these names in the jar dockets which van der Meer seems to have overlooked. The position of the name in the dockets (immediately following the date and the commodity) shows clearly that it was the source of supply of the contents of the jar.[252] Now in some cases such sources of supply, be they estates or other agencies, would be located or have their headquarters in the city where the jars were brought, but by no means was this necessarily the case. There must have been many institutions all over the land that were required to supply Akhetaten, and specifically the Aten temple, with food-stuffs. *Pr*, "house," in these expressions is to be taken only in the broad sense of

[244] The reader is referred to the discussions of Hayes in *JNES* 10 (1951), 96f., and W. Spiegelberg, *ZÄS* 58 (1923), 25ff.

[245] Hayes, *JNES* 10 (1951), 97.

[246] *Ibid.*, 96, c and d.

[247] *CoA* III, Pl. 85:16 and one unpublished occurrence: *ibid.*, 200.

[248] Hayes, *JNES* 10 (1951), Fig. 1:1; see also p. 181.

[249] *Ibid.*, 96(g).

[250] *MDOG* 57 (1916), 25; cf. W. Wolf, *ZÄS* 59 (1924), 110f.; Hayes, *JNES* 10 (1951), 97f.

[251] *CoA* III, 200.

[252] Hayes, *JNES* 10 (1951) 82.

"properties," "ownings"; and the most that can be squeezed out of these miserable graffiti is the mere possibility that the estates in question owned property in or near Amarna. But it would be as illogical to conclude from mere dockets and sealings that Amenhotpe III had lived at Amarna as it would be to conclude that he was at one time living near the Sphinx simply because Kamal found there a sizable number of similar sealings.[253]

The above seventeen items comprise the sum total of evidence upon which the various hypotheses of a coregency have been founded. Most of the arguments depend for their validity largely upon the particular interpretation the authors place upon whatever of this evidence they adduce in support. One of the results of the examination we have attempted is the proof that much, if not all, of the evidence cannot support these interpretations, and that the arguments formulated in pursuance thereof are thus invalid.

There is another difficulty in accepting this mass of heterogeneous material as evidence.[254] For any theory that lacks compelling or decisive proof, the value of the circumstantial evidence that can be called up lies in its cumulative weight. Unfortunately, the coregency theories do not enjoy this kind of support. To the contrary, much of the evidence examined above is mutually exclusive. A scholar who seeks support for a coregency lasting up to four or five years may make use of items numbered 2, 9, 10, and 15, but all the rest, with the exception of 1 and 13, will not only be unusable but will prove an embarrassment to him. A theory of a coregency of eight or nine years will find support in 11, but not in all those texts that mention Amenhotpe III in the same context as the later Aten name, viz. 3, 4, 6, 7, and 8, or in most of the others. Proponents of a ten-year coregency will find opposition in 11, 5, and 16, and will find it hard to elicit support from 2, 6, 9, 12, 14, and 15. Those who plump for twelve years as the length of the coregency will indeed find little opposition apart from 11, but will really not be able to use 2, 9, 10, or 15. This curious conflict within the body of evidence itself, coupled with the necessity of interpreting the material in the same improb-

[253] A. Kamal, *ASAE* 10 (1910), 145ff.

[254] Already pointed out by Campbell, *The Chronology of the Amarna Letters . . .*, 26ff.

able way as the proponents of the theory, explains why so many scholars have refused even to take cognizance of the theory. Nor is it any longer, in some cases, a matter of choosing one of a number of possible interpretations of the evidence: the above discussion has tried to show that nos. 2, 4, 10, 12, and 14 do not admit of the interpretation the supporters of the coregency have adopted, and in consequence are irrelevant in the present investigation.

Up to this point we have been concerned with a rebuttal of the alleged evidence. That there are formidable obstacles, besides a lack of evidence, to the hypothetical coregency, has long been known. The remainder of the present chapter will be concerned with a delineation of these obstacles.[255]

Perhaps the most serious difficulty in accepting the fact of a coregency is the requisite overlapping of the last decade or so of Amenhotpe III's reign with the first of Akhenaten's. The embarrassment becomes most acute if the longest coregency, twelve years (which enjoys the support of the most "evidence"), is posited. The proponents of the theory must then reckon with the contemporaneity for five or six years of two cults that were anathema to each other; they must reckon with the complete absence in contemporary texts of any suggestion that this situation obtained. They must also explain why it is that two separate and distinct dating systems are *never* co-ordinated in inscriptions, although, on the hypothesis, both were in use simultaneously and throughout Egypt. Finally, the proponents of the coregency hypothesis must explain how two separate bureaucracies could have managed the country, each ostensibly reaching to the limits of the land, without conflicting with each other, or, what is more remarkable, without leaving some trace of the other's presence in contemporary inscriptions. "A careful examination of all the published dockets from Hayes [the dockets from the Malqata complex] and from the COA series reveals that *in no case* does one find the same officers in the same position in the same place in dockets coming from both palaces."[256]

[255] For earlier discussions of the positive objections to the coregency, see Helck, *MIOF* 2 (1954), 196ff.; Gardiner, *JEA* 43 (1957), 13f.; Campbell, *The Chronology of the Amarna Letters* . . ., 26ff.

[256] Campbell, *ibid.*, 22f.; the italics are the author's.

A few examples drawn from what is known about some of the more prominent officials of the period will suffice. It has been demonstrated above that Ramose was still in office as vizier when Amenhotpe III died, and later served under Akhenaten. Yet at Amarna Nakht-pa-Aten is vizier,[257] and that at a time which would correspond to Amenhotpe III's last years if there were a coregency. It is not possible to resort to the expediency of assuming that there was a northern and a southern vizier, since neither Ramose nor Nakht-pa-Aten would qualify as vizier of the Delta, both of necessity having to be "southern" viziers. For the last two decades of Amenhotpe III's reign we possess monuments of a family who held the office of treasury overseer during that span. The first member, Nakht-sebek, who was steward of Amun, is mentioned in the statue inscription of Nebnefer dated to year 20.[258] His son, Sebekmose, later held the office of treasury overseer,[259] and later still (probably after the tenure of Meryptah)[260] his grandson Sebekhotpe.[261] The latter probably remained in office until the death of Amenhotpe III or beyond; at least he was still around in that king's thirty-sixth year.[262] From the Amarna period there is evidence of two treasury overseers, Huy and Suta,[263] of whom the former at least seems to have held office early in Akhenaten's reign. Although there seems to have been at times a bifurcation in the Egyptian treasury,[264] it is strange not to find mention of Suta or Huy in texts from Amenhotpe III's reign. It is even more puzzling that the names of Sebekmose and Sebekhotpe should be missing from Amarna inscriptions. The difficulty for the coregency in the two examples just cited, though arresting, is not insurmountable. This cannot, however, be said of the next piece of evidence. Amenhotpe son of Heby and steward in Memphis is

257 Helck, *Verwaltung*, 305.

258 *Urk.* IV, 1886.

259 Helck, *Verwaltung*, 403ff.

260 *Ibid.*, 404.

261 *Ibid.*, 403f.

262 A. H. Gardiner and J. Černý, *The Inscriptions of Sinai* (EES Memoir 45 [London, 1952]), no. 211; Helck, *MIOF* 2 (1954), 189ff.; *Urk.* IV, 1891.

263 Helck, *Verwaltung*, 405.

264 *Ibid.*, 187; note, however, that from the end of the reign of Amenhotpe III there is evidence of a centralized command in the treasury; cf. *imy-r pr ḥḏ wr* in Davies, *The Tomb of the Vizier Ramose*, Pl. 27. The family of Sebekhotpe, moreover, seems to have exercised authority all over Egypt, a fact that might suggest the unity of the office of *imy-r pr ḥḏ*.

attested on jar dockets dated to years 30 and 31 from Malqata.[265] It may be he who dedicated the shrines at Silsileh, which are dated in Amenhotpe III's thirty-fifth year, and which mention a much-titled Amenhotpe, formerly supposed to be the northern vizier of that name.[266] That he survived into Amenhotpe III's thirty-fifth year at least has been demonstrated above in connexion with the discussion regarding Ramose's tomb. Exactly when he died is not known, but when the east wall of Ramose's columned hall was carved, late in Amenhotpe III's reign, he was already deceased. Thus his tenure of office extended at least up to Amenhotpe III's thirty-fifth year, and conceivably a little beyond that date. His son Apy succeeded him as steward of the king in Memphis sometime before year 5 of Akhenaten. The only dated text in which Apy is mentioned comes from that year, and indicates clearly that he was then holding his father's position.[267] Since the assumption of a joint tenure of office by both father and son not only lacks evidence, but also runs counter to what little we possess,[268] it is safe to say that Apy took over as steward when his father died. It follows, therefore, that Akhenaten's fifth year postdates Amenhotpe III's thirty-fifth year. But according to the hypothesis of a twelve-year coregency, year 5 should *precede* it, and should, in fact, be coeval with year 31 or 32. There is no other alternative but to declare, on this evidence alone, a twelve-year coregency quite impossible.

It is exceedingly strange that none of those who hold to a twelve-year coregency have shown any real inclination to examine what

[265] Hayes, *JNES* 10 (1951), 100.

[266] G. Legrain, *ASAE* 4 (1904), 210f.

[267] Griffith, *The Kahun Papyri*, Pl. 38.

[268] Contrary to the statements of Hayes (*JEA* 24[1938], 24) and Helck (*Verwaltung*, 370), there is no evidence that Amenhotpe and his son Apy ever held the office of chief steward at Memphis jointly. The stela to which Hayes refers as proof (his "E," *Urk.* IV, 1807f.) was erected after Amenhotpe had died, as is shown by the concluding phrase: "it is his son who causes his name to live . . .." Helck adduces a stela published by Petrie (*The Palace of Apries: Memphis*, II [London, 1909], Pl. 25), but Amenhotpe is not shown thereon, his name occurring only in the filiation of Apy. And the title *imy-r pr*, which Helck asserts is applied to Apy, is his own restoration. At Malqata, where the names of both Amenhotpe and Apy occur in dockets, the latter is called only *sš-nsw* (Hayes, *JNES* 10 [1951], Fig. 15. no. 240).

support the Amarna letters might offer their position. Surely this most important source of historical information for the period under discussion must shed some light on the problem. One would think, indeed, that the Amarna correspondence would be the first testing ground for any coregency hypothesis formulated on the basis of other evidence. Yet neither Fairman, Pendlebury, nor Aldred has thus tested his theory; and Giles, who is possibly more at home in this body of texts than the other three, has approached the letters with the presupposition that the twelve-year coregency is a fact.[269]

It is true that the Amarna letters present problems to the chronologer. One need only refer to the widely differing estimates on the length of time covered by the archive to demonstrate that fact. At one end of the scale are the estimates of fifty or sixty years by Bilabel[270] and de Koning;[271] at the other the brief fifteen years assigned by Giles.[272] There are no regnal year dates in the body of the letters themselves, and only a very few dated hieratic dockets in ink, supplied by Egyptian scribes, are extant. Moreover, the writers of the letters refer only rarely to spans of time that can be assigned a *terminus a quo* at some point earlier in the correspondence. Without such means for relative or absolute dating, scholars can perhaps be excused for holding widely divergent opinions about the particular period in Amenhotpe III's or Akhenaten's reign when a given letter was dispatched. The relative order of the letters is another problem that has not found a solution. The wealth of content in the Amarna archive held out hope, and still does for those embarking on a study of it, that it might well be possible to arrange the letters in a definite chronological order. The attempts made in the past fifty years have effectively dashed such hopes. For the substantially different arrangements of the letters offered by such scholars as

[269] "The Amarna Period," 56.

[270] F. Bilabel, *Geschichte*, 298ff. He maintains that one letter (EA 51) was written to Thutmose IV (p. 299).

[271] J. de Koning, *Studiën over de El-Amarnabrieven en het Oude-Testament inzonderheid uit historisch oogpunt* (Amsterdam, 1940), 116ff., 430ff.

[272] "The Amarna Period," 276. For other estimates and discussions, see Albright, *JEA* 23 (1937), 191ff.; *idem, JNES* 6 (1947), 58f.; Meyer, *Geschichte*, I, 2, 334ff.; E. O. Forrer, *PEFQ* 1937, 101; Helck, *Beziehungen*, 174; Hornung, *Untersuchungen* . . ., 65.

Knudtzon,[273] Riedel,[274] Sturm,[275] de Koning,[276] and Campbell[277] have, if nothing else, pointed up the limitations of the data at our disposal. Many of the letters are simply ambiguous, a characteristic that is, unfortunately, shared by correspondence of any age. The writers were well aware of what they were talking about, and so were the addressees; there was no reason, from their standpoint, to be specific or to go into unnecessary detail.

One of the circumstances that has bedevilled Amarna studies from the outset is the nature of the initial discovery of the letters. There might have been some hope, had the tablets been uncovered by scientific excavation, of detecting some order in the storage of the documents. Tell el-Amarna was not, after all, abandoned hurriedly as were some Asiatic towns, and there is no reason for thinking that the letters *in situ* lay strewn about the floor as though dropped in flight.[278] The clandestine discovery of the archive, however, and its early dispersal among dealers and private individuals prevent any statement of worth on this important point. Even the subsequent tablet finds at the site can shed little light on how the cuneiform texts were kept.[279]

But the above considerations, sobering though they may appear, should not blind one to the possibilities offered by a study of the Amarna letters. For one thing, the archive does contain a number of more or less complete "dossiers," which can provide a chronological backbone. The Rib-addi correspondence comes first to mind (EA 68–138), but the letters from Tushratta and Alashia are also helpful in this regard. Although, as pointed out above, an absolute order is

273 Knudtzon, *BA* 4 (1902), 279ff.

274 W. Riedel, *Untersuchungen zu den Tell el-Amarna-Briefen.*

275 J. Sturm, *Klio* 26 (1933), 1ff.

276 *Studiën over de El-Amarnabrieven . . .*, 116ff.

277 *The Chronology of the Amarna Letters . . .*, 31ff.

278 Which was the case, for example, at Alalakh: Sir L. Woolley, *A Forgotten Kingdom* (Baltimore, 1953), 122f.

279 Petrie (*TA*, 23f.) describes that quarter of the records office where he was sure the natives had earlier discovered the tablets, but there is no statement from him as to how they might have been stored, save that a few fragments were unearthed in a rubbish pit *under* the building. The later expedition apparently found some fragments in the same area, and one (no. 371) in a nearby scribe's house: C. Gordon, *JEA* 20 (1934), 137; *idem, Orientalia,* 16 (1947), 1ff.; *CoA* III, 130.

difficult to achieve, the letters of these dossiers naturally fall into groups that can be fitted into a chronological scheme with certainty; thus the general sequence of events is not as open to conjecture as might first appear. Secondly, the point in the dossiers when the change of reign, from Amenhotpe III to Akhenaten, occurs can be discerned with surprising clarity. This is true not only of the dossiers in which the royal names are mentioned, but also of those where they are absent. And, thirdly, the number of historical texts that have come to light and are coming to light in Syria and Asia Minor[280] is providing an increasing number of checks upon the Amarna data. There is thus every reason to believe that repeated hammering at the problems will not only crack them to the satisfaction of all scholarship, but will result in the dovetailing of our disparate data and a true picture of the succession of events in the Amarna age.

A study of the Amarna letters also holds out hope of a solution to the coregency problem. Those who engage in such a study with this as their objective will be seeking the answers to several questions: Is there express mention of a coregency in the letters? When does the Amarna archive close, or better, what is the date of the last extant letter? How long did Akhenaten continue to receive letters after his assumption of sole rule? The answer to the last question will correspond to the length of time that elapsed between Amenhotpe III's death and Akhenaten's death, unless the archive closed before the latter event. I believe specific answers are forthcoming for all three questions; but before entering into a discussion of them, one ought to point out what answers the proponents of a twelve-year coregency are bound to expect. First, clear indication of a coregency should appear in at least one of the following forms: (a) letters addressed to both kings jointly; (b) a clear bifurcation in the letters

[280] Primarily at the sites of Boğaz Köy and Ras Shamra: for the Boğaz Köy material (consisting mainly of treaties and annalistic writings), see E. Weidner, *Politische Dokumente aus Kleinasien* (Leipzig, 1923); E. Cavaignac, *REA* (1931), 228ff.; H. G. Güterbock, *JCS* 10 (1956), 41ff., 75ff., 107ff.; for the Ras Shamra texts, see J. Nougayrol, *Le Palais royal d'Ugarit*, III: *Textes accadiens et hourrites des archives est, ouest, et centrale* (Mission de Ras Shamra, VI [Paris, 1955]); *idem*, *Le Palais royal d'Ugarit*, IV: *Textes accadiens des archives sud* (Mission de Ras Shamra, IX [Paris, 1956]. For an attempt to integrate some of this material with the Amarna letters, see the Appendix to the present work.

as to the addressees, if the coregents divided the burdensome foreign correspondence between them, or mention of one coregent in letters specifically addressed to the other. Second, the period during which Akhenaten was receiving letters as sole ruler should not exceed five or six years.[281]

The answer to the first question is in no way equivocal. There is no letter among the 340-odd addressed to both kings as coregents; the addressee is either specifically named (*Nimmuaria* or *Napkhururiya*) or the letter is addressed simply to the "king, my lord." Nor is there any evident bifurcation in the correspondence. It might be assumed, for instance, although the artificiality of this assumption is apparent, that Amenhotpe III took care of correspondence with kings of equal rank (i.e. "great kings"), while Akhenaten handled the vassal correspondence during the hypothetical coregency. Yet Amenhotpe III is known to have received letters both from equals and from vassals long after the coregency is supposed to have started;[282] and, as Campbell has pointed out,[283] the earliest letters to Akhenaten as sole ruler presuppose a complete ignorance on his part of foreign affairs, such as would be inexplicable if he had indeed been his father's partner.[284] Moreover, the very presence of letters addressed to Amenhotpe III at Amarna would be hard to explain, if there were a coregency, especially since the old king was resident at Thebes during the last decade of his life. The only reasonable explanation of

[281] I.e. if his reign terminated in his seventeenth year.

[282] EA 23, from Tushratta, Amenhotpe's "brother" and a "great king," dates from year 36: C. Bezold and E. A. W. Budge, *The Tell el-Amarna Tablets in the British Museum* (London, 1892), Pl. 42; EA 254 from a vassal, Labaya of Shechem, probably dates from year 32: Albright, *JNES* 6 (1947), 59; H. Winckler and L. Abel, *Der Thontafelfund von El-Amarna* (Berlin, 1889), 112; Campbell, *The Chronology of the Amarna Letters* . . ., 69f. Although the reading of the numeral is not beyond doubt, Labaya and his generation belong early in the period covered by the letters; certainly Meyer's reading of the date as "year 12" (*scil.* of Akhenaten, see *Geschichte*, II, 1, 336) is out of the question. Part of Rib-addi's correspondence was directed to Amenhotpe III (cf. EA 132:12ff.); and EA 369 (to use Gordon's numbering in *Orientalia*, 16 [1947], 2) was written by Amenhotpe III to his vassal Milkili of Gezer: G. Dossin, *RA* 31 (1934), 125ff. (esp. 129).

[283] *The Chronology of the Amarna Letters* . . ., 138.

[284] Especially illuminating in this regard are EA 26 and 27 from Tushratta to Tiy and Amenhotpe IV respectively, and EA 41 from Suppiluliumas to Akhenaten.

the presence of letters addressed to him at Amarna is that such letters were retained in the royal archives, undoubtedly for reference purposes, when Akhenaten moved to his new capital. But then letters such as EA 23, dated specifically to Amenhotpe III's year 35, would necessarily *antedate* the move to Amarna. Finally, there is no reference to another living coregent in any of the letters: mention of Akhenaten is never made in his father's letters, and whenever Amenhotpe III is mentioned in the correspondence of his son, it is clear either that he is deceased or that the deed for which he is being cited is in the past.[285] Thus from the content, at least, of the Amarna letters, there is no support forthcoming for a twelve-year coregency, or for that matter for a coregency of any other length.

An answer to the second question is necessary before the third can be attempted. And the answer to the second in turn depends upon the date when Tell el-Amarna was abandoned or, better, when the court left the site. There can be little doubt that the latter event occurred during Tutankhamun's reign. It is known that at some point in his reign Tutankhamun was living in Memphis;[286] and, as is well known, he was buried at Thebes. Thus for an undetermined period terminating with his death, Tutankhamun lived away from Amarna. The evidence from the site itself bears out this conclusion. Tutankhamun's is the latest royal name found in sufficiently numerous inscriptions to warrant the belief that the bearer actually occupied the city.[287] In fact in some districts objects inscribed with his cartouches are as numerous as those of Akhenaten himself. There is thus a strong suggestion that the latest occupation of the site is to be dated to his reign,[288] since debris for a given occupational period on any site tends to heap up towards the close of the period. Some of Tutankhamun's objects bear the later form of his name (i.e. Tutankh*amun* in place

[285] The following is a selection of such passages referring directly or indirectly to Amenhotpe III in letters to Akhenaten: EA 16:22f., 27 *passim;* 28:46; 29:6ff., 21ff., 40ff.; 41:7ff.; 117:21ff.; 131:32ff.; 132:12ff.

[286] J. Bennett, *JEA* 25 (1939), 12.

[287] *CoA* III, 3.

[288] In the north palace, inscriptions naming Tutankhamun, Ankhesenpaaten, and Nefertity occur frequently, but not so those of Akhenaten: Pendlebury, *JEA* 17 (1931), 243; the workmen's village likewise shows many occurrences of Tutankhamun's cartouches: L. Woolley, *JEA* 8 (1922), 60. Objects bearing Tutankhamun's name from the north suburb are equal in number (62) to those of Akhenaten from the same district: *CoA* II, 2.

of the earlier Tutankh*aten*).[289] This fact need not be taken to mean that the change of name was effected while he was still resident at Amarna, but only that the site continued to be occupied to some extent after the king recanted. The wine-jar dockets from Amarna and from Tutankhamun's tomb assist in establishing more closely the date of the abandonment of the ill-fated city. Dockets from Amarna are dated from year 1 to year 17. There can be no doubt that the majority of these come from Akhenaten's reign. Those of the lower year dates, however (specifically years 1 to 4), are probably not to be assigned to him. For the reign of any ruler one should expect a priori an upward progression in the number of dockets from year to year, year 1 being represented by fewest, and the latest years by considerably more. But such is not the case here. From the central city there are more dockets of year 1 (thirty-eight) than any other year.[290] The number of dockets dated in year 2 is almost as many (thirty-seven), but thereafter in years 3 and 4 there is a sharp decrease (nine and six respectively). Year 5 shows a sudden rise (sixteen), and from this point on dockets are relatively plenteous right up to year 17. Dockets from the north suburb display a similar numerical decline after year 2, with a rise after year 6.[291] The conclusion seems probable that years 1 to 3 are to be placed at the end rather than at the beginning of the series, and thus do not come from Akhenaten's reign at all. Rather they date to the reign of Akhenaten's successor, and illustrate graphically the move away from Amarna, which must finally have been abandoned by the court at the end of year 2 or the beginning of year 3.[292] The dockets from Tutankhamun's tomb seem to corroborate this conclusion. There are eighteen legible dockets[293] provided with dates, and of these the earliest is year 4 (five examples). The wine bottled during Tutankhamun's first three years had presumably been

[289] Frankfort, *JEA* 13 (1927), 217; *idem*, *JEA* 15 (1929), 145, n. 2.

[290] See Fairman, *CoA* III, 159; Petrie's figures (*TA*, 32) are added in the total.

[291] Fairman, *CoA* II, 104; note that years 3, 4, and 5 are not represented at all by dockets from this area.

[292] So already Griffith, *apud TA*, 32 (he attributes years 1 and 2 to Smenkhkare); also Fairman, *CoA* III, 160. The problem of where Smenkhkare's reign is to be fitted in will be discussed in the next chapter.

[293] So Engelbach, *ASAE* 40 (1940), 163; Carter (*The Tomb of Tut.ankh.Amen*, III, 147f.) mentions three dozen wine jars, and states further that "each . . . bears a docket written in hieratic, which gives the date, place and vintage of the wine. . . ."

shipped to Amarna while the court was still in residence then. It was only beginning with year 4 that the vintagers of the northern estates began sending their wine to Thebes once again; and when, later, provisions were being sought for Tutankhamun's burial, wine of year 4 was the oldest available.

The oft-repeated statement that Amarna was abandoned around year 3 of Tutankhamun's reign is thus well founded.[294] None of the letters found at Amarna can postdate the end of the first third of Tutankhamun's reign. On the other hand, very few are probably to be dated to his first three years, since it is most likely that letters of importance received during that time would have been taken along for reference when the court moved to other quarters. Once more the Amarna archive is in full accord: only two extant letters are addressed specifically to *Nipḫururiya* (transcription of Tutankhamun's praenomen, *Nb-ḫprw-rʿ*?), and even in these cases the reading is not above dispute.[295] To all intents and purposes then, the Amarna letters come to a close with the beginning of Tutankhamun's reign.

Before proceeding we must deal with one apparent recalcitrant piece of evidence. EA 170 tells of the advance into the regions of Amki and Nukhashshe of nine thousand Hittite troops under the command of Lupakku and Zitana. The writer of the letter, one Baaluya,[296] states that he is going to send a certain Batti-ilu "into his (Zitana's) presence," i.e. to receive them.[297] The incident, news of which is here being reported as it happens, is recounted as history in the annals of Suppiluliumas, compiled by his son and second successor Mursilis II (I quote Goetze's translation):[298] "While my

[294] There is nothing in favour of Cavaignac's view (*Kêmi*, 3 [1930], 37) that Amarna continued to be occupied down to the beginning of Haremhab's reign. although squatter settlement in certain parts of the town may be attested.

[295] EA 9 and 210 (fragmentary); on this subject see Sturm, *Klio*, 26 (1933), 12; E. Edel, *JNES* 7 (1948), 114f.; W. von Soden, *Orientalia*, 21 (1952), 431; P. van der Meer, *Ex Oriente Lux*, 15 (1957–58), 96; Campbell, *The Chronology of the Amarna Letters . . .*, 53f. I can see no support for Hornung's view that the Amarna archive closed shortly after Akhenaten's twelfth year: *Untersuchungen*, 66.

[296] Probably the brother of Aziru: cf. Campbell, *The Chronology of the Amarna Letters . . .*, 60.

[297] So S. Smith, *Halil Edhem Hatira Kitabi* (Ankara, 1947), 40; not "against him" as Mercer, *The Tell el-Amarna Tablets*, 541.

[298] *Apud* J. B. Pritchard, *ANET*², 319.

father was down in the country Karkamis he dispatched Lupakkis and Tessub-zalmas to the country of Amka. They proceeded to attack the country of Amka and brought deportees, cattle (and) sheep home before my father. When the people of the land of Egypt heard about the attack on Amka, they became afraid. Because, to make matters worse, their lord Bibkhururiyas had just died, the Egyptian queen who had become a *widow*, sent an envoy to my father and wrote him as follows. . . ." There follows the famous letter, requesting that the Hittite king send one of his sons to marry the writer. The transcription of the Egyptian name offers the hope of pinning down the event to a specific date. When the document first came to light, opinions were divided as to the Egyptian *Vorlage* of Bibkhururiyas. Some scholars maintained that it could only be *Nb-ḫprw-rʿ*, the praenomen of Tutankhamun, since the first vowel of the name, *i*, corresponded to the vowel of the word *nb*, which was pronounced **nib* (cf. *Nimmuaria*).[299] Others, largely on the basis of historical considerations, opined that Bibkhururiyas was a garbled form of *Nfr-ḫprw-rʿ*, Akhenaten's praenomen (Amarna *Napkhururiya*).[300] A recently discovered parallel text of the annals, however, gives in place of Bibkhururiyas the variant Nibkhururiyas;[301] and most scholars are now agreed that it is the praenomen of Tutankhamun.[302]

[299] C. F. A. Schaeffer, *MDOG* 56 (1915), 15; Meyer, *ibid.*, 15; E. O. Forrer, *MDOG* 61 (1921), 32; A. H. Sayce, *Ancient Egypt*, 1922, 66f.; 1927, 33f.; *JEA* 12 (1926), 168f.; F. Bilabel, *Geschichte*, 148 and 283f.; H. Zimmern, *ZA* NF 1 (1924), 37; A. Goetze, *AO* 27 (1927), 30; H. Carter, *The Tomb of Tut.ankh.Amen*, I, 57f.; J. Sturm, *RHA* 13 (1933), 161ff. For a number of years Cavaignac has maintained that Bibkhururiyas is really the praenomen of Ay, *Ḫpr-ḫprw-rʿ*: *Kêmi*, 3 (1930), 33f.; *RHA* 3 (1931), 61; *ibid.* 40 (1940), 215ff. But he has not gained a following.

[300] Goetze, *Klio*, 19 (1925), 347, n. 1; J. Friedrich, *AO* 24 (1925), 12, n. 10; 13, n. 1; Meyer, *Geschichte*, II, 1, 338; W. Wolf, *ZÄS* 65 (1930), 101, n. 7; Albright, *JEA* 23 (1937), 194; Smith, *Halil Edhem* . . ., 41.

[301] *KUB* 34, 24:4.

[302] E. Edel, *ZIS* 60 (1949), 83, n. 2; Friedrich, *Bib. Or.* 5 (1948), 50; Goetze, *JAOS* 71 (1951), 79; *idem, apud* Pritchard, *ANET*², 319, n. 3; O. R. Gurney, *The Hittites* (Harmondsworth, 1952), 31 and 217; A. Malamat, *VT* 4 (1955), 6, n. 4; H. Güterbock, *JCS* 10 (1956), 94, n. *e*; Campbell, *The Chronology of the Amarna Letters* . . ., 59; H. Kees, *Ancient Egypt: A Cultural Topography* (London, 1961), 305; Gardiner, *Egypt of the Pharaohs*, 241; Edel, *JNES* 16 (1957), 69; F. Cornelius, *AfO* 17 (1956), 307; J. Vergote, *Toutankhamon dans les archives hittites* (Istanbul, 1961), *passim*.

But if the events recorded in this section of the annals took place around the time of the death of Tutankhamun, how could EA 170 ever have found its way into the Amarna archive, which closed in that king's third year? There are two possibilities: either EA 170 does not refer to the same event as the Hittite annals, or Nibkhururiyas in the Hittite text is a mistake.[303] As S. Smith has demonstrated well,[304] the identity of the Amka campaign of EA 170 with that of the Hittite annals cannot be gainsaid. The personal names as well as the locale put it almost beyond doubt; and the allusion in the letter to nine thousand troops shows that, like the campaign in the annals, it was no trivial affair. It is true that Tessub-zalmas is not mentioned in the letter, but after all the latter is, in contrast to the annals, only a brief and contemporary account. (Rommel in the winter of 1942–43 might well have written to his wife that "Montgomery is forcing us to retreat"; but the official history of the British army, written decades later, in describing the same campaign, would undoubtedly have included the name of Alexander.) It is to be expected that in letters only a selection of facts should be included.

We are thus left with the alternative that Nibkhururiyas is an error. Although to postulate an outright mistake seems like taking the line of least resistance, in the present case it is the most plausible solution. *KBo* V, 6 and *KUB* XXXIV, 24, as already noted, form part of the annals of Suppiluliumas, compiled by Mursilis well on in his reign. Perhaps more than twenty-five or thirty years separate the account from the event. It is not especially difficult to imagine an original Napkhururiyas being mistaken for Nipkhururiyas, perhaps through a *Hörfehler*, or perhaps through a genuine confusion of historical personages.[305] It is interesting to note that in EA 41, one of the few Hittite letters in the Amarna cache, Suppiluliumas addresses Akhenaten as *Ḫuriya*. This is a hypocoristic form in which

[303] A third possibility, viz. that Mursilis misplaced the two Amki campaigns in his account, is not likely. Names may easily be confused in ancient historical texts, but less likely events.

[304] *Halil Edhem* . . ., 33f.; *contra* Sturm, *RHA* 13 (1933), 164f.

[305] Cf. Albright, *JEA* 23 (1937), 194. Mursilis says specifically that he was only a child when the Egyptian king died, and so had no first-hand knowledge of the events of that time: *KUB* 31, 121; see now Güterbock, *RHA* 66 (1960), 57ff., especially 60f.

nfr (Akkadian *nap-*) has been elided. If this reflects a common, or even occasional, shortening of Egyptian praenomens involving the elements *ḫprw* and *rʿ*, we may have the clue to the confusion surrounding Bibkhururiyas in the annals. If Mursilis or his scribes, in recalling from memory the events of former days, or even in consulting written records, encountered the shortened form *Ḫuriya*, they would have no means of telling whether they were dealing with Akhenaten or Tutankhamun. For the praenomens of these two kings, *Nfr-ḫprw-rʿ* and *Nb-ḫprw-rʿ* respectively, when stripped of the first element, would both be pronounced *Ḫuriya* (or *Ḫururiya*).[306] A Hittite scribe might well be forgiven if, in attempting to reconstruct the full name from the ambiguous hypocorism, he wrote *nib-* where he should have written *nap-*. By the time of inscripturation the garbled events of two generations previous had undoubtedly become so hazy that the confusion of two foreign kings of like-sounding name, whose reigns had been successive, was the most natural mistake a scribe could make.

The conclusion that it is Akhenaten's death to which the Hittite annalist refers has the following argument in its favour. Egyptian kings, and especially those of the New Kingdom, sought to begin their reigns in grandiose fashion by embarking on a military campaign. Those kings who we are reasonably certain undertook wars by their third years are Kamose, Thutmose I, Thutmose II, Thutmose III (reckoning from his assumption of independent rule), Amenhotpe II, Sety I, Ramses II, and perhaps Merneptah and Ramses III. It is probable that other kings for whom evidence is lacking also campaigned soon after their accessions. Now if we identify the late pharaoh of *KBo* V, 6 with Akhenaten, his death must fall six years before the end of Suppiluliumas's reign.[307] The latter's death will have occurred in the sixth year of Tutankhamun, and, allowing one year

[306] *Ḫuriya*, from *Ḫururiya*. For philological discussions of the form see H. Ranke, *ZÄS* 56 (1920), 74 and n. 3; Vergote, *Toutankhamon dans les archives hittites*, 12ff.; *idem*, *Bib. Or.* 18 (1961), 212; Edel, *Bib. Or.* 20 (1963), 35f. On the possible equation of *Ḫuriya* with the Manethonian "Horos," see Sethe, *ZÄS* 41 (1904), 50; Helck, *Untersuchungen zu Manetho*, 40, n. 1.

[307] On the crucial datum of *KUB* 19, 9, see Cavaignac, *REA* (1931), 232; Goetze, *KlF* 1 (1930), 117f.; Nougayrol, *Le Palais royal d'Ugarit*, IV, 33 (with references).

at most for Arnuwandas,[308] we may place Tutankhamun's decease in the second year of Mursilis. Ay's four years will correspond to years 3 to 6 inclusive of Mursilis, and the latter's seventh year will mark the first and perhaps part of the second regnal year of Haremhab. I do not think it fortuitous that year 7 in Mursilis' annals is signalized by the first mention (in the annals) of an Egyptian campaign in Syria.[309] Mursilis implies that the campaign reached as far north as the states of Nukhashshe, and significant it is that the one topographical list which without question is to be assigned to Haremhab's reign mentions only north Syrian sites.[310]

There is, the present writer feels, adequate justification for reading Napkhururiyas for Nibkhururiyas in *KUB* XXXIV, 24:4.[311] The presence of EA 170 in the Amarna cache thus poses no real problem, and the unanimity of the evidence in favour of the abandonment of Amarna in Tutankhamun's third year is unimpaired.

Since the Amarna archive, as we have it, came to a close shortly after Akhenaten's death, all but a few of the later letters will have been written to him. The period during which Akhenaten was in receipt of correspondence will extend, in terms of letters, from the point at which his father died down to virtually the end of the archive. This period, as pointed out above, corresponds to Akhenaten's sole rule. If the twelve-year coregency is a fact, it will amount to five or possibly six years in length. The task at hand now is to examine very closely this part of the correspondence to see whether it can be fitted into so short a span.

Tushratta's correspondence with Akhenaten totals three letters (EA 27, 28, and 29). Since the content indicates that Akhenaten refused to answer the Mitannian king's letters, it is quite possible that no more were written after the third. The first, EA 27, was carried by the messengers Pupri and Pirizzi, and bears the controversial hieratic docket discussed above (cf. pp. 144ff.). The third, EA 29,

308 Goetze, *MVAG* 38 (1932), 11.

309 *Ibid.*, 82ff.

310 J. Simons, *Handbook for the Study of Egyptian Topographical Lists Relating to Western Asia* (Leiden, 1937), 50ff., 134ff.

311 The present writer consequently takes the widowed Egyptian queen who wrote to Suppiluliumas to be Nefertity. Her name is not mentioned in the Hittite annals, but her title "king's wife" appears in the form *Daḫamunzu (tꜣ ḥmt-nsw)*: W. Federn, *JCS* 14 (1960), 33.

gives in line 113 the information that Akhenaten had kept Pupri and Pirizzi at the Egyptian court for four years. Those who hold to a twelve-year coregency are forced to date EA 29 at least as late as year 16, and perhaps year 17 (since we do not know when the letter was actually sent, or how long it took to get into Akhenaten's hands). Thus at the very end of Akhenaten's reign, on the assumption of a twelve-year coregency, Tushratta would still be reigning unchallenged over Mitanni and its empire. A challenge to his right to rule came eventually, however, and that from his archfoe, Suppiluliumas of Khatte. In the latter's great Syrian campaign, recounted in the preamble to the treaty between Suppiluliumas and Tushratta's son Mattiwaza,[312] Tushratta is seen in utter defeat, fleeing from his capital city (which fell into Hittite hands), later to be assassinated by a faithless son. That the three letters from him to Akhenaten predated this defeat will not be questioned: with his land ravaged, his city devastated, his empire seized by the enemy, and the routes to Egypt cut off, he will not have wasted his time writing to an unfriendly son-in-law who was slow to answer. Since the "Great Syrian" campaign therefore marks the beginning of the end for Tushratta and, more importantly, a *terminus ad quem* for his letters, its date must be fixed as accurately as possible. Now if the personal names of certain Syrian rulers mentioned in the preamble to the Mattiwaza treaty are compared with those of rulers of the same principalities in the later Amarna letters (see table on next page), an important chronological fact will emerge.

The only possible conclusion is that the later Amarna letters represent the period of the next generation after that of the preamble to the Mattiwaza treaty. But on the hypothesis of a twelve-year coregency Tushratta is still in command of things and writing letters at the very end of Akhenaten's reign. The "Great Syrian" campaign could thus not be dated before the early years of Tutankhamun, in which case the generation of Syrian rulers who wrote the later Amarna letters would be thrust into an even later position, partly contemporary with Tutankhamun and partly with Ay and Haremhab. Since Amarna was abandoned around Tutankhamun's third year, this downward dating of the generation in question is not possible. But the alternative is to raise the date of the "Great Syrian"

[312] *KBo* I, 1, 7ff.; E. Weidner, *Politische Dokumente*, 6ff.

campaign well into the reign of Akhenaten. This in turn necessitates a like raising of the date of Tushratta's letters to Akhenaten, with the result that EA29 will be placed a good deal earlier than Akhenaten's sixteenth year. More important, EA 27, the relative date of which is fixed four years earlier than EA 29, will be pushed back *earlier* than year 12, an eventuality clearly incompatible with the reading of the hieratic docket "year [1]2." The only other possible reading is "year 2," but this excludes any coregency (cf. p. 146).

The king of Alashia wrote seven letters to Akhenaten (EA 33 to 39 inclusive). In the earliest of the series, EA 33, he congratulates Akhenaten on his accession, and expresses the wish that they write

	Mentioned in:	
King of	*The Preamble to the Treaty with Mattiwaza*	*The Later Amarna Letters*
Kadesh	Sutatarra[313] (son, Etakama)	Etakama[314]
Abina/Upi (Damascus)	Ariwanakhi[315]	Biryawaza[316]
Niya	Takuwa[317] (brother Aki-teshup)	Aki-teshup(?)[318]
Nukhashshe	(Sarrupsi)[319] Takib-sar	Addu-nirari[320]

[313] *KBo* I, 1, vo. 40.

[314] Known from many references in the Amarna letters; see Weber, *EAT*, 1560. It was Etakama who wrote EA 189.

[315] *KBo* I, 1, vo. 43.

[316] Many references in *EAT*, 1559 and 1565; on the reading *Biryawaza* for the older *Nam*yawaza, see F. Thureau-Dangin, *RA* 37 (1940), 171.

[317] *KBo* I, 1, vo. 30.

[318] Perhaps the same as EA 59:15, 18? At any rate Aki-teshup, Takuwa's brother, must be identical with the Aki-teshup king of Niya at the time of the insurrection against Suppiluliumas attested by RS 17.132, RS 17.227, and RS 17.340 (see *PRU* IV, 35ff.). That this incident postdates the campaign described in the preamble to the Mattiwaza treaty is proved (a) by the different personal names, (b) by the disparity of the two accounts, and (c) by the fact that the Syrian kings in the Ras Shamra texts are spoken of as having renounced "the treaty and the peace with the Hittite land" (RS 17.132 ro. 23f.); they were thus already Hittite vassals, a vassalage that was imposed first during the Great Syrian campaign recounted in *KBo* I, 1. See further below, in the Appendix.

[319] *KBo* I, 1, vo. 38f.

[320] EA 51, written probably just before or during the north Syrian insurrection against the Hittites, of which Addu-nirari was one of the prime movers.

regularly to each other, in fact *each year*.[321] There is, however, evidence that both parties were prone to delay answering by return messenger. Thus in EA 35:26 it is stated that the Egyptian messenger (who brought Akhenaten's last letter?) has been detained three years in Alashia. In EA 36:18 it seems that the Alashian ruler is accusing Akhenaten of detaining his messenger in Egypt, this time for two years. The impression one gains from such passages is that more often than not a longer period elapsed between letters than the optimum one year. The very lowest number of years that could be assigned to the correspondence is, therefore, seven, but if the delays pointed out above are taken into account. the number would be ten or more. Now in the first of the series, Amenhotpe III is already dead, and Akhenaten has entered upon his sole reign.[322] Thus seven letters, covering not less than seven and perhaps ten years or more, must be fitted into the span of Akhenaten's sole rule, a quite impossible feat if that span occupied only five or six years.[323]

The king of Babylon wrote at least four letters to Akhenaten (EA 7, 8, 10, and 11). This number could be augmented to six if we could be sure that Nibkhuriruya of EA 9 were Akhenaten and not Tutankhamun,[324] and if the lost name of the addressee of EA 6 were that of Akhenaten as well.[325] As in the case of the letters from Alashia, so also in the case of those from Babylon there is evidence to suggest that they were sent at infrequent intervals. It seems to have been a procedure tacitly accepted by kings of the time that the letter-bearing messengers should be kept waiting at the foreign court months or even years for a reply. Tushratta represents himself as being prompt in his reply if he sends the messenger back within six months,[326] or even within the same year.[327] When he wishes to

[321] EA 23:37ff.

[322] Cf. EA 33:9–11 *u ištêmi anāku [an]uma aṣbata êli [ku]ssī bît abīka*, "and I have heard that you sit on the throne of your father's house," an unusual locution if the father were still living.

[323] See Campbell, *The Chronology of the Amarna Letters . . .*, 56ff.

[324] Admittedly the form appears to be a rendering of *Nb-ḫprw-rʿ*; cf., however, Campbell, *ibid.*, 64.

[325] There is no compelling reason to read the traces of the name [Ni-ib-mu-a-ri]-a (see now van der Meer, *Ex Oriente Lux*, 15 [1957–58], 94); [Na-ap-ḫu-ru-ri]-a would suit just as well.

[326] EA 27:83.

[327] EA 20:23.

exaggerate greatly about his practice in bygone days, he boasts that he dispatched a certain messenger to Egypt "in three months in great haste."[328] If this refers to a round-trip, we should probably be too low in estimating that a rapid round-trip from Babylon to Thebes and back to Babylon took between four and five months. Without a doubt the fastest courier of the day would be hard pressed to bring back a reply within six months. That such dispatch never attended the trips of the royal messengers is the oft-repeated testimony of the Amarna letters. Amenhotpe III kept Babylonian messengers waiting on one occasion for six years,[329] and Akhenaten on another for over two years.[330] Add to this the frequent request to speed the envoy on his way, and one feels that a single year between letters on an average is too little. Allowing, however, one year for each Babylonian letter, and taking into account the two-year delay presupposed by EA 7:49, we arrive at a minimum of five years for four letters, or seven years if EA 6 and 9 were actually written to Akhenaten. With difficulty then the Babylonian correspondence can be fitted into a sole reign beginning with year 12. But although this is barely possible, in the light of the above considerations it must be admitted that probability lies elsewhere.

Rib-addi, the king of Byblos, wrote over sixty of the Amarna letters. The earlier ones, in which he mentions as his adversary a certain Abdi-Ashirta, were written to Amenhotpe III (although the latter is nowhere named). At just what point in the letters Amenhotpe III's death is to be put is not as clear as one might wish, but EA 108 seems definitely to be dated to Akhenaten. EA 106 probably also comes from Akhenaten's reign, if the tenor of the letter and the seeming ignorance of the addressee are any criterion. Both of these letters fall very early in that portion of Rib-addi's correspondence that is concerned with the depredations of Aziru of Amurru, his sworn enemy.[331] This means that over thirty letters which can definitely be dated to the "Aziru"-period (i.e. EA 108–138 and some others) must fall in Akhenaten's reign. It is not known how often Akhenaten wrote to Rib-addi, or how long his messengers took to

[328] EA 29:26.

[329] EA 3:14.

[330] EA 7:49. For the reading, see W. von Soden, *Orientalia*, 21 (1951), 429.

[331] In EA 108 only the "sons of Abdi-ashirta" are mentioned (of whom Aziru was one), suggesting that Aziru had not yet distinguished himself.

make the round-trip to Egypt and back, but a very fast round-trip is represented by Rib-addi as two months.[332] If two months is taken as an average—and in reality a longer span must be closer to the truth—the last thirty-odd letters of Rib-addi would cover around five years. Since the last letter, EA 138, seems to have been written after a twelve month silence,[333] the figure may have to be raised to six. This span could with difficulty be squeezed into a sole reign beginning with year 12, in which case Rib-addi would have died around the time Akhenaten passed away, or shortly after. But such a coincidence is excluded by the fact that between Rib-addi's last letter and the end of Akhenaten's reign must be inserted a large proportion of the other Amarna letters. The Abi-milki correspondence (ten letters) falls in this category,[334] as does EA 162 from Akhenaten to Aziru, and many of the latter's letters. EA 162:42ff. presupposes the passage of one year, and the numerous postponements of his trip to Egypt reflected in the letters of Aziru bespeak months or even years.[335] Furthermore, the entire career of the villain Etakama of Kadesh falls after the last letter of Rib-addi; nowhere does the latter mention him, and during Abi-milki's floruit he is just beginning to appear on the scene.[336] Thus one is forced to postulate a span of several years' duration between the end of the Rib-addi correspondence and the death of Akhenaten. This in turn results in the forcing back of Rib-addi's death towards or before the middle of Akhenaten's reign, an expedient quite opposed to the hypothesis of a twelve-year coregency.

The dockets examined in the preceding paragraphs are unanimous in the evidence they provide. Each presupposes a much longer span of time for Akhenaten's sole rule than the five or six years a coregency

[332] EA 81:29, 82:42.

[333] Lines 20–21.

[334] EA 146–155; Albright, *JEA* 23 (1937), 190ff.

[335] Cf. EA 163–168 *passim.*

[336] Etakama occurs twice(?) in letters from Abi-milki, whose correspondence comes at the end of the period covered by the letters (Albright, *JEA* 23 [1937], 191f.), and in the letter of Ilurabikh, which follows not only the death of Rib-addi, but also probably the visit of Aziru to Egypt; cf. EA 140:22 *amur arnama yipuš Aziru ina urrubišu ana muḫḫika arnu ana muḫḫinu,* "behold Aziru has committed a crime in (?) his having had an audience with you, a crime against us." Etakama is mentioned once more in Akizi's letters (EA 53–54), where he is clearly at the height of his power.

of twelve years can allow. But to postulate that Akhenaten was receiving letters before his father died is, as pointed out above (p. 155), directly opposed to the explicit testimony of the Alashian and Mitannian letters. There is, then, no alternative but to conclude that Amenhotpe III died well before Akhenaten's twelfth year, a necessity that renders the hypothesis of a twelve-year coregency impossible to maintain.

To sum up, the questions posed earlier regarding the bearing of the Amarna letters on the hypothetical coregency have found answers. The Amarna letters do not make direct allusion to a coregency between Amenhotpe III and Akhenaten, although they of all our sources might be expected to do so. Whenever mentioned in the letters of his son, Amenhotpe III appears to be deceased. Since it can be shown that the Amarna archive closes early in the reign of Tutankhamun, most of the letters not otherwise known to have been written to Amenhotpe III must have been sent to Akhenaten. Of four letter-dossiers which belong to Akhenaten's reign, those from Mitanni and Alashia did not commence until after the death of Amenhotpe III. While three of the dossiers could conceivably be compressed into a period of six years, that from Alashia requires at least seven years, and probably over ten. For historical reasons the last letters from Mitanni and Byblos cannot possibly have been written at the end of Akhenaten's reign, but must be elevated by several years. But in so doing, one is obliged likewise to elevate sometime well before year 12 of Akhenaten the first correspondence of these series, thus excluding the possibility of a twelve-year coregency.

If the hypothesis of a coregency of a dozen years is thus invalidated, so also are all other hypotheses that have proposed coregencies of shorter length. For since the hieratic docket of EA 27 will have to be read "year 2," even Borchardt's postulate of a three-year coregency must be given up. It might be argued that EA 27 leaves the door open for a coregency of a few months, but there is no mention of this in contemporary documents. Also such an argument would be spurious. Between the death of Amenhotpe III and the writing of EA 27 there occurred a short but well-attested exchange of letters between Tushratta and Tiy, of which EA 26 is an example.[337] In the light of the length of time taken by messengers travelling back and forth

[337] EA 26:19ff. presupposes at least one earlier letter from Tiy.

between the two courts, this correspondence undoubtedly occupied at least one year. Thus a coregency amounting to months or even weeks is effectually disproved.

The burden of the present chapter has taken the form of an extended rebuttal; no connected attempt has been made otherwise to "explain away" the facts that first led scholars to postulate a coregency. This, perhaps, is as it should be in a discussion concerned primarily with chronology. We have, however, frequently suggested what appear to be plausible explanations of the occurrences of Amenhotpe III's names during the Amarna period. It has been pointed out that some objects bearing his names had a cultic use, and that other inscriptions were from the hands of private individuals who had enjoyed some special relationship with, or had accomplished an important task under, Amenhotpe III. Still others attest the close family loyalty of the house of the great king, coupled with a desire to transfer some of the glory of his floruit to the present revolutionary venture. It must always be remembered, when Amarna is the topic of discussion that one is here dealing with a unique phenomenon in ancient Egypt: a town abandoned relatively quickly and therefore capable of reconstruction to a given period of history. If it were possible to examine the remains of any other of the great royal residences of Egypt at a specific period in history, we should undoubtedly find that the two royal personages most frequently attested by inscriptions there would also be the reigning king and his immediate predecessor.

6

The Coregency of Akhenaten and Smenkhkare

The parentage of Smenkhkare is wholly unknown. No monument known today gives any evidence as to the identity of his father. Smenkhkare has been made out to be the offspring of an "unofficial marriage" of Akhenaten,[1] the son of Amenhotpe III by his union with his daughter Satamun,[2] and the grandson of Amenhotpe III and the king-to-be Ay through the intermediary of an unknown couple.[3] None of these suggestions has any concrete evidence in its favour; the last, in fact, rests solely on the as yet unproved assumption that Smenkhkare and Tutankhamun were brothers.[4] One of these suggested filiations may well prove to be correct, but until such time as it does, wisdom dictates the exercise of extreme caution.

Smenkhkare comes suddenly into view at Amarna. On many small objects his name appears enclosed within a cartouche, which shows that he was already making a claim on the kingly office. The same aspirations are indicated by his assumption of a titulary. This, however, is known to us only in part, his Horus-name and *nbty*-name appearing on no monument extant today. His praenomen, *ʿnḫ-ḫprw-rʿ*,

1 H. Carter, *The Tomb of Tut.ankh.Amen* (London, 1923–33). II, 181f.; III, 18; R. Engelbach, *ASAE* 31 (1931), 106.

2 R. Engelbach, *ASAE* 40 (1940), 160; *HSE* II, 297; G. Roeder, *ZÄS* 83 (1958), 45.

3 K. Seele, *JNES* 14 (1955), 178f.

4 D. E. Derry, *ASAE* 31 (1931), 118f.

probably means "*Ḫprw-rʿ* lives/is living," the transliterated element being the hypocorism of Akhenaten.[5] His nomen, to which the epithet *ḏsr-ḫprw*, "holy of forms," is appended, shows either his birth-name, "Smenkhkare,"[6] or "Nefer-neferu-aten," the same appelative so often borne by Nefertity.[7] Two epithets, "beloved of Nefer-kheperu-re" and "beloved of Wa-en-re," are frequently included after the praenomen.[8]

It is clear from his names alone that Smenkhkare enjoyed a particularly close relationship with Akhenaten. He was, of course, Akhenaten's son-in-law through his marriage to Meretaten, but there seems to be something more. Engelbach has noted[9] that the practice exemplified by the use of the epithet *mri Wʿ-n-rʿ* (or *Nfr-ḫprw-rʿ*), viz. the occurrence of a royal name where in other cartouches a *god's* name would have appeared, is unique,[10] and that here Akhenaten is treated like a god. That the relationship was intimate, in fact bordering on homosexuality, has been inferred from such Amarna remains as the group dubbed "the kissing king,"[11] in which a king, presumably Akhenaten, is shown fondling a second figure supposed to be Smenkhkare.[12]

More important for chronological purposes, it may legitimately be inferred from such evidence that Akhenaten and Smenkhkare were for a time coregents. Roeder has collected all the evidence consisting of the juxtaposition of the names or figures, and his list is quite complete.[13] His judgment, however, seems to be less reliable. Can we honestly admit as evidence for a coregency trial pieces and such

[5] See above, pp. 160f.

[6] On the reading of the name, long mistaken for Seakare *(Sʿꜣ-kꜣ-rʿ)*, or Senakhtkare, see the discussion of H. Gauthier in *Livre*, II, 362, n. 4, and the definitive treatment by P. E. Newberry in *JEA* 14 (1928), 3f.

[7] Gauthier, *Livre*, II, 356ff. The two names seem to alternate promiscuously: there is no distinction of place or time in their employment. Cf. W. Wolf, *ZÄS* 65 (1930), 100, n. 3.

[8] Cf. Petrie, *History*, II, 234, Fig. 145.

[9] *ASAE* 31 (1931), 105.

[10] As Engelbach also notes, however *(ibid.)*, the same epithet occurs on the coffin from the so-called "tomb of Tiy," an object which it is now conceded was made for a woman: C. Aldred, *JEA* 47 (1961), 41ff., esp. 53; cf. K. Seele, *JNES* 14 (1955), 173, n. 40.

[11] Roeder, *ZÄS* 83 (1958), Pl. VIIc.

[12] Newberry, *JEA* 14 (1928), 7f.

[13] *ZÄS* 83 (1958), 43ff.

which show two royal heads side by side, one of which differs slightly from the other in very minor details?[14] When a sculptor or painter is merely practising, any material at hand will do, and the technique to be perfected will be repeated as often as space allows. Another stricture on Roeder's work is his altogether unjustified assignation of a large number of heads and figures to Smenkhkare merely on the basis of what he considers to be Smenkhkare's peculiar physiognomy. When dealing with Egyptian art of any period one is most unwise to resort to such a criterion. In Amarna art in particular the artists strove to make every male resemble Akhenaten, and it is very doubtful whether individual traits were allowed to show through in royal portraiture. When the host of doubtful pieces are removed, however, there does remain a small but substantial number of objects on which the intended juxtaposition of two kings or their cartouches is undeniable.[15] The question now arises: Is juxtaposition[16] in art alone enough to warrant postulating a coregency?

Perhaps a more important question from the standpoint of the chronologist would be: Did Smenkhkare ever rule alone? The highest —indeed the only—date attested for his reign is year 3; and this occurs, strangely, at Thebes in the tomb of Pere, in a graffito of one Pawah.[17] The date makes no mention of Akhenaten, and a priori we should have to conclude that he was dead. Was Smenkhkare, then, ruling alone in his third year and, if so, for how long had he enjoyed this status of sole monarch?

Before attempting to answer these two questions, the meagre evidence bearing upon political events towards the close of Akhenaten's

[14] Cf. *ibid.*, Pl. Vc; *CoA* III, Pl. 59:1.

[15] E.g. *CoA* III, Pl. 107. 2–3 (Roeder, *ZÄS* 83 [1958], 47 [C III, 2]); Newberry, *JEA* 14 (1928), Pl. 4:1 (Roeder, *ZÄS* 83 [1958], 48 [C III, 4]); Roeder, *ibid.*, 48, Fig. 1 (C III, 5); *ibid.*, Pl. Va (p. 50 [C IV, 4]); Roeder, *MDIAK* 14 (1956), Pl. XI:1 (*ZÄS* 83 [1958], 50 [C IV, 5]); Newberry, *JEA* 14 (1928), 9, Fig. 4 (Roeder, *ZÄS* 83 [1958], 46 [C II]); Newberry, *JEA* 14 (1928), 5f.

[16] Note that the juxtaposition is of a wholly different order from the juxtaposition of the names of Amenhotpe III and Akhenaten. The argument of Fairman (*CoA* III, 156) that the evidence of juxtaposition ought to be taken as equally valid in either case is answered effectively by E. F. Campbell, *The Chronology of the Amarna Letters with Special Reference to the Hypothetical Coregency of Amenophis III and Akhenaten* (Baltimore, 1964), 19.

[17] See P–M I², 253 for references; also Roeder, *ZÄS* 83 (1958), 63f.

reign must be examined. The facts are these. At Akhenaten's death Nefertity was opposed by forces inimical enough to impel her to request a marriage outside Egypt, and then to cause the murder of her prospective husband before he even set foot in the country.[18] The conclusion is justified that at that time Egypt was torn by at least two factions, one of which centred around Nefertity and the other of which *inter alia* controlled the approaches to Egypt. The evidence from Amarna is in perfect accord. Here in the southern complex called "Maru-aten"[19] the British excavators found the name and figure of Nefertity consistently replaced in the latest reliefs by the name and figure of her eldest daughter, Meretaten.[20] The replacement was even carried out in texts that served only to indicate the identity of Meretaten's mother.[21] In the northern part of the city in the "north palace," which seems to have been built around the time of the estrangement of the royal couple, Akhenaten's name is found fairly often accompanied by those of Smenkhkare and Meretaten, while Nefertity is mentioned not at all.[22] In one case Meretaten's name appears "palimpsest," presumably over her mother's.[23] Yet from the north palace come a large number of wine-jar dockets with Nefertity's name to the exclusion of Akhenaten's;[22] and generally throughout the northern part of the city her name, sometimes with those of Tutankhamun and Ankhesenpaaten (but never with Smenkhkare), occurs frequently.[24] The conclusion must be that late in his reign Akhenaten became estranged from his wife, elevated his eldest daughter, and presumably her husband Smenkhkare, to the foremost position in the state, and expunged Nefertity's name *everywhere* in the capital.[25] After her husband's death Nefertity returned

[18] Cf. Mursilis's Plague Prayer: translated by A. Goetze in *ANET*², 395.

[19] "The Seeing-place (?) of Aten"; cf. A. Badawy, *JEA* 42 (1956), 58.

[20] B. Gunn, *CoA* I, 151ff.; Woolley, *JEA* 8 (1922), 81f.

[21] Cf. J. Pendlebury, *JEA* 19 (1933), 116f.; *CoA* III, 18.

[22] *Idem, JEA* 18 (1932), 144.

[23] T. Whittemore, *JEA* 12 (1926), 4.

[24] J. Pendlebury, *JEA* 17 (1931), 243.

[25] So most scholars in the wake of J. Pendlebury, *Tell el-Amarna* (London, 1935), 28f.; *JEA* 18 (1932), 144; *HSE* II, 296; A. H. Gardiner, *Egypt of the Pharaohs* (London, 1961), 233; J. A. Wilson, *The Burden of Egypt* (Chicago, 1951), 232f.; Engelbach, *ASAE* 40 (1940), 135; Drioton-Vandier, *L'Egypte*⁴, 346f.; *CoA* I, 155; H. Brunner, *Hist. Zeitschr.* 174 (1953), 553; *idem, Universitas,* 5 (1962), 264.

to Amarna,[26] or at least took up residence in the northern part of the city, and there championed the cause of Tutankhamun and Ankhesenpaaten.[27] When Nefertity died we have no way of knowing with certainty, but she probably did not survive Tutankhamun's abandonment of Amarna.[28]

We shall now attempt to answer the question whether Smenkhkare enjoyed a sole reign, and if so of what length. The conclusions reached in the preceding paragraph unmistakably support the hypothesis of a sole reign. The murder of Nefertity's prospective husband suggests that he who opposed the queen-mother held great power both in and outside of Egypt. Such a description would *a fortiori* be applicable to a king; and the evidenced hostility between Nefertity on the one hand, and Akhenaten, Smenkhkare, and Meretaten on the other, seems to go far towards shedding light on the circumstances of the despicable deed. In short, the opposition to Nefertity after Akhenaten's death finds its best explanation in the continued presence of Smenkhkare as king.

There is other evidence for a sole reign. No double-dated inscription is known from the later years of Akhenaten's reign, although dated hieratic dockets from Amarna are plentiful. The Theban graffito dated in Smenkhkare's third year likewise bears no secondary date according to Akhenaten's regnal year system; the very existence

[26] After a short exile to some other residence? This would explain her apparent absence from Amarna prior to the beginning of Tutankhamun's reign, when even the north palace shows a decoration hostile to her memory.

[27] Cf. Pendlebury, *JEA* 17 (1931), 243.

[28] The suggestion that Nefertity died *before* her husband has sometimes been mooted; cf. Carter, *The Tomb of Tut.ankh.Amen*, III, 19; Gunn, *CoA* I, 155, 166, n. 9; F. Giles, "The Amarna Period" (unpublished doctoral dissertation, University of London, 1958), 103. This possibility would be ruled out, however, if the Egyptian queen who wrote to Suppiluliumas could be shown to be Nefertity (see above, p. 162). Moreover, the Amarna dockets continue to mention an estate of the "king's-wife" from year 14 through 17 (*CoA* III, Pl. 92: 208, Pl. 94:245, Pl. 93:218; I, Pl. 63 [G–K]). This must be Nefertity and not Meretaten (*pace* E. Hornung, *Untersuchungen zur Chronologie und Geschichte des neuen Reiches* [Wiesbaden 1964], 85f.), since the latter continues to appear in the dockets as "king's-daughter" (*CoA* III, Pl. 86:39). If reference must be found to Meretaten in her exalted status of wife of the coregent, one should probably turn to the docket transcribed in *CoA* II, Pl. 58:16 (year 16), where the "estate of the Favorite *(špst)*" is mentioned.

of this text indeed is prima facie evidence for an independent reign. Some reliefs exist, it is true, on which Smenkhkare is depicted in company with Akhenaten, but these could be dismissed as representations of a living king with his deceased predecessor—a fanciful motif that seems to have been popular in Amarna art.[29] Moreover, there is a much larger number of inscriptions—admittedly on small objects—in which Smenkhkare's name appears alone.[30] Again we find prima facie evidence in the painting of Smenkhkare and Meretaten, as king and queen, in the tomb of Meryre II at Amarna.[31] This is one of the latest of the Amarna tombs.[32] On the south (hither) wall of the main hall Akhenaten is shown with Nefertity and five daughters rewarding Meryre;[33] on the east (right-hand) wall is the grand scene showing the reception of tribute in year 12.[34] On the back (north) wall is a hastily executed scene, in quite a different style,[35] which shows Smenkhkare and Meretaten again rewarding the tomb owner Meryre. The royal couple are quite alone, and the cartouches, though now erased, once showed their names clearly.[36] A reasonable inference would be that, as decoration and excavation of the tomb proceeded simultaneously from front to back, Akhenaten died, the latest scene to be executed while he yet lived being that of year 12 on the east wall.

None of the pieces of evidence cited above is compelling, one must admit. Moreover, there are certain arguments in favour of denying *any* independent reign to Smenkhkare, and a good number of modern

[29] Cf. the explanations of scenes showing Amenhotpe III in the company of Akhenaten, put forward above, pp. 92ff.

[30] Cf., for example, the list of objects from the north suburb in *CoA* II, 21.

[31] N. de G. Davies, *The Rock Tombs of El-Amarna* (EEF Archaeological Survey of Egypt 14 [London, 1904], II, Pl. 41.

[32] All six of Akhenaten's daughters are present in the tomb scenes: Petrie, *History*, II, 234.

[33] Davies, *The Rock Tombs of El-Amarna*, II, Pl. 33ff.

[34] *Ibid.*, Pl. 37ff.

[35] *Ibid.*, 43f.

[36] *LD* III, 99a. There is no reason to believe the names have been changed from those of Akhenaten and Nefertity (see Gardiner, *Egypt of the Pharaohs*, 233). I understand Davies' wording "replaced by . . ." (*The Rock Tombs of El-Amarna*, II, 43) as referring, not to superimposition, but to the occurrence of Smenkhkare's name where in many another similar scene Akhenaten's would have been found.

scholars have accepted this line of reasoning.[37] These arguments, together with suggested rebuttals, will now be presented.

First, there is no mention of Smenkhkare in the Amarna letters. His wife Meretaten is mentioned in at least three letters,[38] but in one[39] she is referred to as DUMU.SAL-ka, "your daughter," and a second is clearly addressed to Akhenaten.[40] The third, it is true, mentions no king by name, and could be assigned either to Akhenaten or to Smenkhkare. However, the letter itself betrays no "greenness" on the part of the recipient, and strongly suggests that he has been in control of affairs of state for a long time.[41] Thus all three seem to have been written to Akhenaten, not to Smenkhkare. If the latter were already married to Meretaten, and in possession of the tokens of kingship,[42] this would be good evidence that part of his reign at least was coincident with Akhenaten's.[43]

One may point out in rebuttal of this argument that the Amarna file is by no means complete as it exists today. The few letters that might have been sent to Smenkhkare could have been lost, or could have been taken along with the court when the town was abandoned.

A second piece of evidence against any independent reign for Smenkhkare consists of the reference to "houses" of his in Amarna dockets dated to year 1 of an unnamed king. A "house of Smenkhkare justified (?)"[44] and a "house of Ankh-kheperu-re [ ]"[45] are both mentioned. If the reading *mꜣʿ-ḫrw* in the first is correct, then it is

[37] Engelbach, *ASAE* 40 (1940), 137; Wilson, *The Burden of Egypt*, 233; Drioton-Vandier, *L'Egypte*[4], 347; K. Seele, *When Egypt Ruled the East* (2nd ed., Chicago, 1957), 222; Carter, *The Tomb of Tut.ankh.Amen*, I, 76f., III, 16; Seele, *JNES* 14 (1955), 174.

[38] EA 10:41; 11: (rev.) 26 (W. von Soden, *Orientalia*, 21 [1952], 431f.); EA 155 *assim* (W. F. Albright, *JEA* 23 [1937], 191ff.; *idem*, *JBL* 61 [1942], 304).

[39] EA 10:41.

[40] EA 11: (obv.) 1.

[41] Cf. especially EA 155: 11f., 43ff., 58f.

[42] Note the high regard in which Meretaten is held in EA 155; also her title *bêlti bîtika*, "mistress of your (Akhenaten's) house" in EA 11:25. Already, it would seem, she had replaced her mother as first lady and had presumably been married to Smenkhkare.

[43] Campbell has argued (*The Chronology of the Amarna Letters* . . ., 68ff.) that the order of the Babylonian letters favours placing Smenkhkare's coregency as early in Akhenaten's reign as possible, perhaps even to year 14, thus depriving him of any independent floruit.

[44] *CoA* III, Pl. 86:35.

[45] *Ibid.*, Pl. 86:36.

most likely that Smenkhkare was dead when the docket was written. But even if the reading is not certain, it seems more than probable that these two institutions are mortuary establishments. Thus "year 1" would probably pertain to Tutankhamun's reign. But "year 1" is known to have followed "year 17" (of Akhenaten) very closely: a hieratic docket inscribed in year 17 of Akhenaten was subsequently changed to "year 1",[46] a modification suggesting that the death of Akhenaten followed so closely upon the sealing of the jar that the scribe felt it advisable on second thought to date the contents to the first year of Akhenaten's successor, i.e. Tutankhamun. But if Smenkhkare was already dead in Tutankhamun's first year, and if that year followed immediately upon Akhenaten's seventeenth, Smenkhkare can have had no independent reign at all.[47]

A rebuttal might take the following form. The establishments mentioned in the two dockets need not be mortuary, and *mꜣʿ-ḫrw,* if present, could be as meaningless as *ʿnḫ, wḏꜣ, snb* was throughout the New Kingdom. Smenkhkare himself could thus be equated with the king whose year 1 replaces year 17 in the above docket. And even if year 1 should prove to belong to Tutankhamun, it need not have followed Akhenaten's seventeenth immediately; some few months could have intervened, during which Smenkhkare reigned alone, before the docket was changed.

Third, the epithets indicative of the affection Akhenaten had for Smenkhkare[48] are used by the latter in all his inscriptions, and are even found in the graffito of year 3. This might be accepted as proof that Akhenaten was living throughout the entire span of Smenkhkare's floruit. But the use of such epithets, one could argue, does not prove that Akhenaten was still alive. The epithets in question, as has been pointed out above, are clearly comparable to those describing the royal individual as "beloved of Amun" or of some other god. Thus this locution merely reflects the dogma that Akhenaten himself was a god, on a par with Re or Aten, and cannot be expected to shed light on whether he was alive or dead.

46 *Ibid.,* Pl. 95:279.

47 Cf. Fairman, *CoA* III, 157.

48 "Beloved of Nefer-kheperu-re" and "beloved of Wa-en-re"; note that the praenomen of Smenkhkare, Ankh-kheperu-re, i.e. "Kheperu-re lives," may indicate that at the time it was formulated Akhenaten was still living.

A fourth consideration against any independent reign whatsoever has been set forth by Fairman in *The City of Akhenaten,* Vol. III.[49] He reasons that, since by his third year Smenkhkare had built a temple to Amun at Thebes, he must by that time have renounced the worship of Aten and abandoned Amarna. It is scarcely likely that Tutankhamun, a mere child when he came to the throne, would have been able to reverse the restoration that had already begun, return to Amarna, and champion the Aten for two or three years before finally capitulating. Smenkhkare must, therefore, have been coregent with his father-in-law, and Tutankhamun must have succeeded Akhenaten directly.

The fallacy here lies in assuming that the existence of an Amun temple in Thebes built by Smenkhkare proved (a) that he had left Amarna for residence in Thebes and (b) that he had wholly renounced the worship of Aten. For the first alleged implication there is no proof at all. The heretic kings of the Amarna age, though they resided mainly in Amarna, still moved freely about Egypt, and temples were constructed everywhere.[50] The mere fact that a temple, albeit to Amun, stood in Thebes and was constructed by Smenkhkare is no proof that he resided there. Even if he spent part of the year in Thebes there is no reason for the belief that he had given up the Amarna seat. The second alleged implication, viz. that dedication (of at least part) of the temple to Amun proves that Smenkhkare had renounced Atenism, is baseless. Even if this denotes a partial weakening, we have no reason to think that Tutankhamun's accession is tantamount to a reversion to a "hard line" stand. Why not postulate a gradual and progressive weakening through the last years of Akhenaten, the reign of Smenkhkare, and into the first part of Tutankhamun's floruit? And could not Tutankhamun, with the support of Nefertity and Ay, have maintained himself at Amarna in spite of what Smenkhkare had done? To argue a priori, as Fairman is doing, about motives and personal capabilities in such a confused and little-known period of history is patently absurd.

In this connexion there is something informative about the location of Pawah's graffito, viz. the left jamb of a door in the furthest recesses of an abandoned tomb.[51] The graffito, a prayer to Amun

[49] P. 158.

[50] See Giles, "The Amarna Period," 86f.

[51] P–M I², plan on p. 248 at (5).

that the writer may regain his sight, is one of the earliest examples of a *genre* of penitential psalm that becomes quite common in the Nineteenth and Twentieth Dynasties.[52] But such prayers were intended to be inscribed on stelae and set up near the god they invoked. Why scribble a plea to a god and secrete it in an abandoned tomb? The obvious answer is that Pawah did not wish others to read his prayer. Why? The only reason I can think of is that the deity called upon is Amun. At the time Pawah wrote his supplication, then, the worship of Amun was still something that it was advisable to carry on in secret. In other words, if Smenkhkare had undertaken "some measure of restoration of the old religion," by his third year it had either petered out or still had not acquired much momentum.

The hieratic docket cited above[53] in which year 17 is replaced by year 1 narrows the possibilities for the placement of Smenkhkare's reign vis-à-vis those of his predecessor and successor. Only three solutions are possible: (1) Smenkhkare was until his death the co-regent of his father-in-law. Tutankhamun came to the throne on the death of Akhenaten, and "year 1" at Amarna is his. (2) Smenkhkare was taken into coregency in Akhenaten's fifteenth year, and survived his partner's death by only a few months. The graffito of year 3 in this case would have been written during the brief span that elapsed between Akhenaten's death and Tutankhamun's accession, when Smenkhkare was ruling alone. "Year 1" at Amarna would still belong to Tutankhamun.[54] (3) Smenkhkare, although coregent during an undetermined period at the close of Akhenaten's reign, did not begin to number his own years until Akhenaten died. In this case years 1, 2, and perhaps 3 at Amarna would belong to Smenkhkare.

[52] Cf. A. Erman, *SBAW* (1911), 1088ff.; another early example comes from the reign of Tutankhamun: A. Rowe, *ASAE* 40 (1940). 47ff. (Pl. 9—Huy, viceroy of Kush).

[53] Note 46.

[54] Some few dockets might go to Smenkhkare, who would not have lived to complete his first regnal year. In this case we should have to explain the graffito of year 3 by assuming either (a) a blind loyalty on the part of Pawah, who refused to recognize Tutankhamun and continued to date by the regnal years of the now defunct Smenkhkare, or, more probably, (b) a confusion on the part of the Theban populace as to whether Smenkhkare was going to date his reign from the beginning of his coregency or from his father-in-law's death.

If solution 3 is adopted, we have to ask ourselves whether Tutankhamun is represented at Amarna by any dated dockets. A priori it seems likely that Tutankhamun was in residence in the city for a period of years, since the number of objects bearing his name is by no means negligible.[55] The relatively large batch of dockets dated to years 1 and 2[56] might be taken as indicating that both Smenkhkare and Tutankhamun passed their first two regnal years at Amarna; in other words, that dockets dated to years 1 and 2 are to be divided between two reigns. We should thus have Smenkhkare succeeding after Akhenaten's death in year 17, ruling alone for two years and part of a third, and then being succeeded in turn by Tutankhamun, who ruled two years in Amarna and abandoned the site before his third year was far spent. The attractiveness of this reconstruction is lessened considerably by the fact that fully three-quarters of the dockets from year 2 were found in a single cache,[57] a fact that suggests that the contents of the jars were used at one time, and thus belong to a single regnal year. It is always possible to argue, of course, that Tutankhamun spent only one regnal year at Amarna, in which case only the dockets of year 1 would have to be divided between two reigns. But the large number of objects with Tutankhamun's name is against this. It seems inherently more probable that the dockets of years 1 and 2 belong to one reign, not two. If, however, that reign belongs to Smenkhkare, what becomes of Tutankhamun's stay in the city? It could be assumed that Tutankhamun, refusing to acknowledge the legitimacy of Smenkhkare, antedated his own reign from Akhenaten's death, thus incorporating the reign of Smenkhkare by a blatant fiction into his own. This anathematizing of Smenkhkare would have taken place immediately after his death, and would have been followed in turn by Tutankhamun's abandonment of the site.

[55] Sixty-two objects from the north suburb, as opposed to forty-three for Smenkhkare from the same part of town: *CoA* II, 2.

[56] Forty-three and forty respectively. These figures are the result of totalling the numbers given in *TA*, 32; *CoA* II, 104; and *CoA* III, 159.

[57] In one of the small halls adjacent to the so-called coronation hall, allegedly constructed by Smenkhkare (below, n. 59): *TA*, 7. Petrie takes this as indicating that by year 2 this part of the palace was falling into disuse. Does such an argument support allotting "year 2" to Tutankhamun rather than to Smenkhkare?

Thus year 3 of Tutankhamun would follow immediately year 2 of Smenkhkare. Again this reconstruction founders on the sizable number of objects bearing Tutankhamun's name. Tutankhamun *must* have occupied the city for a not inconsiderable period *as king;* there is no escape from this conclusion.

Beyond the impression that solution 3 is improbable, it seems difficult to get closer to the truth. The present writer would opt for no. 2, but freely admits that the reason he does so is the as yet unproved assertion that Smenkhkare was alive and actively opposing Nefertity shortly after Akhenaten's death.

Whether solution 1 or 2 is adopted, however, an obstacle remains in the inscription of Smenkhkare's year 3. As pointed out above, this inscription is prima facie evidence for an independent reign. A question that naturally comes to mind is: When did the reign, of which this graffito attests the third year, begin? If solution 3 is rejected, as seems wise, one must answer that it began at the inception of Smenkhkare's coregency with Akhenaten. The next question is: Why, if this is so, do we not find double-dated inscriptions from the years of the coregency? On the basis of solution 1, I cannot think of a reasonable answer, but solution 2 brings one to mind at once. Smenkhkare began his coregency in year 15 of Akhenaten, and did not at first intend to number his years from that event. Thus it is that in years 16 and 17 of Akhenaten dockets continued to be dated according to the old system. After Akhenaten's death, however, Smenkhkare for some reason decided to number his regnal years from the inception of his coregency two years earlier, in which case his first year alone in the kingship would be his third regnal year. It was at this time that Pawah scribbled his graffito in Pere's tomb.[58]

In conclusion, a brief summary of the order of events at the close of the Amarna period may be attempted, in the full awareness that we are now passing from the realm of concrete knowledge into the ethereal domain of speculation. Around the close of his year 15, or the beginning of 16, Akhenaten elevated his eldest daughter's

[58] Hornung has attempted to show, on the basis of the twelve years Manetho gives to Akencheres, that Smenkhkare's coregency began in Akhenaten's thirteenth year: *Untersuchungen* . . ., 37f., 84f.

husband, Smenkhkare, to the status of coregent at Amarna.[59] Either prior to this event, or in consequence of it, Nefertity broke with her husband and probably left the city. For the next two years Smenkhkare and Meretaten took first place in Akhenaten's affections; indeed the locution is well chosen, since Smenkhkare appears more as a mascot than as a legitimate partner in the kingship during the coregency. Upon Akhenaten's death in year 17 Nefertity saw an opportunity to regain her lost power. She wrote to the Hittite king Suppiluliumas requesting a son of his in marriage, and promising that he would be king of Egypt. But Smenkhkare, finding himself temporarily sole monarch, was not inclined to accept a rival claimant of his own race, much less one of foreign blood. When the Hittite prince approached the frontiers of Egypt he was murdered by unspecified assailants;[60] but it does not require much imagination to conjure up the Machiavellian hand of Smenkhkare in the bloody deed. It was probably Smenkhkare's last move; he and Meretaten disappear so swiftly that one cannot help but wonder whether the enraged Nefertity effected their downfall more cunningly than they had plotted the murder of her fiancé.[61] At any rate Nefertity reappears at Amarna, champions the claim to the throne of the hitherto obscure Tutankhamun, marries him to her third daughter Ankhesenpaaten, and, in conjunction with Ay, manages to carry on a semblance of ordered rule at Amarna for about two years. It may well be that the event that precipitated Tutankhamun's capitulation and withdrawal from the city early in his third year was her death.

[59] Whether the vast hall on the south side of the palace at Amarna was specially constructed for ceremonies connected with the inception of the coregency is quite unknown, although it does seem to have been one of the latest buildings erected at the site; cf. *CoA* III, 80.

[60] Cf. H. Güterbock, *JCS* 10 (1956), 107f.

[61] With this reconstruction Smenkhkare's sole reign would have lasted only a few months, probably not more than six. This seems quite sufficient for Nefertity's correspondence with Suppiluliumas, late in the fall, and the dispatch of the Hittite prince to Egypt the next spring; cf. *ibid.*, 96.

7

The Date of the End of the Eighteenth Dynasty

Fixing the absolute date for the close of the Eighteenth Dynasty involves the choice and confirmation of a fixed point in Egyptian history from which to reckon. The point that immediately comes to mind is the accession of Ramses II. Several considerations justify this choice. First, the exact length of Ramses' reign is known. Second, the historical milieu in which his reign is situated is well documented. Third, the direct contacts between the Egyptians on the one hand and the Hittites and their dependencies on the other during this reign can be dated fairly certainly. Through the Hittites the Egyptian history of the period comes into indirect contact with that of Assyria and Babylonia, and therefore with a reliable chronology. Fourth, the accession is situated close to the end of the Eighteenth Dynasty, thus necessitating a minimum of reckoning (only the length of Sety 'Is reign need be ascertained) before a *terminus ad quem* can be established.

The points of contact between Egypt and Asia during the reign of Ramses II number three, and all are with the Hittites. The first is the battle of Kadesh in the fifth year of Ramses II, the second is the treaty between Egypt and Hatte in the twenty-first year, and the third is the marriage of the Hittite princess to Ramses in the thirty-fourth year. Between the first and second occurred the death of the Hittite king Muwatallis, the reign of his son Urhi-teshup, and the accession of Hattusilis. If any of these events can be dated in terms of Assyrian kings, an admirable control would be thereby extended over the chronology of contemporary Egypt. Nor is this too much to hope for, since documents from the Hittite capital link Hittite history with Ashur and Babylon. There are two important Hittite letters to the Assyrian king Adad-nirari I, viz. *KBo* I, 14 and *KUB* 23, 102, and one, *KBo* I, 10, written by Hattusilis to Kadashman-Enlil, the king of Babylon. This last letter harks back to a time when Kadashman-Enlil's father, Kadashman-turgu, had entertained friendly relations with Hatte in the face of impending hostility with Egypt. Clearly, this was before the treaty of year 21; but whether the letter itself was sent before that date is hotly debated. The date of Kadashman-turgu's death and the date of *KBo* I, 10 thus become crucial for the chronology of the period.

A good deal of work has been done since the Second World War on the date of Ramses II's accession. The scholar responsible for the best of this work is M. B. Rowton. In 1948 Rowton published an article in which he sought to prove that the Manethonian date for Ramses II's accession, which he computed at 1290 B.C., was trustworthy.[1] He appealed for support to Babylonian chronology, where he found evidence to indicate that Kadashman-turgu died in 1270 B.C. The corresponding regnal year of Ramses II is unknown. On historical considerations alone Rowton had to set a margin of six years: Kadashman-turgu's death could not fall before Ramses' sixteenth year or later than the twenty-eighth. On the choice of the mean, viz, the twenty-second year, the fifty-second year of the Egyptian king would have fallen in 1240 B.C. Now it was in year 52 that the lunar observations of the Leiden Papyrus 350 were made. On the allowance of the same six-year margin of error, the limits for the fifty-second year are 1246 and 1234, and it is in this range that the solution of the Leiden observation is to be sought. Given these temporal limitations, the Leiden Papyrus yields but one solution, viz. 1239 B.C. Thus year 1 of Ramses II would have

[1] *JEA* 34 (1948), 57ff.

fallen in 1290, in perfect accord with the computed Manethonian date.

Later work seemed to confirm Rowton's results. Parker showed[2] that even if we extend Rowton's margin of error to sixteen years instead of six, only three possibilities for Ramses II's accession emerge, viz. 1304, 1290, and 1279. Of these, the first and third seemed, to Parker, excluded on historical grounds. In a study of a part of *KBo* I, 10 Edel concluded[3] that this letter presupposed a state of hostility between Egypt and the Hittites such as could only have existed before the treaty of year 21. Since this letter was sent to Kadashman-Enlil, Kadashman-turgu must have already died. Consequently year 21 of Ramses II cannot have antedated 1270 B.C. The upper limit indicated by Parker for Ramses' accession, viz. 1304, thus becomes untenable, while 1902 remains nicely accommodated.

In spite of the scholarly swing in favour of 1290 as the date for Ramses II's accession, Rowton courageously voiced his misgivings when a re-examination of the evidence seemed to show him that his earlier stand had been wrong.[4] Evidence from the Babylonian King List, so he declared, indicated that his former date for Kadashman-turgu's death was nine years too low. His new date was 1278 B.C. But if the conclusion was valid that Kadashman-turgu had died before the twenty-first year of Ramses' reign, 1290 could not be the accession year of the Egyptian king. The only one of the three possible years that would suit was 1304.

Most of the computations described above are based on the assumed accuracy of the Mesopotamian chronology used. The first task must be to scrutinize this chronology and see how accurate it really is. It is hoped that upon completion of this examination a definite answer will be found to the question: When did Kadashman-turgu die?

BABYLONIAN CHRONOLOGY FROM KADASHMAN-TURGU TO MARDUK-NADIN-AKHKHE

The backbone of Babylonian chronology for the thirteenth century B.C. is the Babylonian King List A.[5] Drawn up in the Neo-Babylonian

[2] *JNES* 16 (1957), 42f.

[3] *JCS* 12 (1958), 130ff.

[4] *JNES* 19 (1960), 15ff.

[5] CT 36, Pl. 24–5.

period, the text purports to give a list of the kings who reigned over Babylon from the First Dynasty of Babylon down to an unknown king of the Chaldean house of Nabopolassar. Since the amount of chronological material other than King List A is negligible, this document has taken on an enormous importance; and the simple result of the unfortunate lacunae—the tablet is broken off at both top and bottom—has been to hamstring all attempts to reconstruct Babylonian chronology prior to the eighth century. Most serious of all are the lacunae at the bottom of column III and the top of column IV. Here sixteen names of kings who ruled between the dynasty of Bazu (*ca.* tenth century) and Nabonassar (746–733) have been lost. In consequence it has proved impossible by dead reckoning to arrive at absolute dates for the Kassite kings of Babylon.

The loss of five kings of the second dynasty of Isin in the lacuna at the top of column III is no longer as serious as it once was. A tablet of unknown provenience and now in the possession of Professor G. Cameron[6] provides us with the names and lengths of reign for the first seven kings of this dynasty (King List C). Thus we can with some assurance construct a relative chronology from Kurigalzu II of the Kassites (mid fourteenth century) down to the end of the Bazu dynasty (tenth century).

Since dead reckoning back from Nabonassar is impossible, an absolute chronology for Babylon must take its rise from a synchronization of contemporary Babylonian history with that of Assyria. Those contacts pertinent to the present investigation, viz. from Ashur-uballit I to Ashur-bêl-kala in terms of Assyrian kings,[7] are set forth in the table on the following page together with the source for each.[8]

[6] Published by A. Poebel, *The Second Dynasty of Isin According to a New Kinglist Tablet* (AS 15 [Chicago, 1955]).

[7] Tabulated by Rowton in *JCS* 13 (1959), 7; for texts of the Babylonian kings, see K. Jaritz, *MIOF* 6 (1958), 187ff.

[8] The following abbreviations not found in the List of Abbreviations are used: SH—Synchronistic History, CT 34, Pl. 38–43; P—Chronicle P, T. G. Pinches, *JRAS* 1894, 807ff. and F. Delitzsch, *Die babylonische Chronik* (Leipzig, 1906), 41ff.

	Synchronism	*Source*
A.	Ashur-uballit I *temp.* Kurigalzu II	SH I, 13ff.; P I, 11ff.
B.	Enlil-nirari *temp.* Kurigalzu II	SH I, 18ff.; P III, 20ff.[9]
C.	Adad-nirari *temp.* Nazimaruttash	SH I, 24ff.; P III, 23ff.
D.	Tukulti-ninurta *temp.* Kashtiliash IV	SH (Sm 2106, ro. 9–10: CT 34, Pl. 42); P IV, 1ff.; BM 98730 ro. 33 (Lambert, *AfO* 18 [1957], 43)
E.	Tukulti-ninurta *temp.* Adad-shuma-usur	P IV, 9ff.
F.	Ashur-nirari III *temp.* Adad-shuma-usur	E. Weidner, *AfO Beiheft,* 12, no. 42
G.	Enlil kudurri-usur *temp.* Ad[ad-shuma-usur][10]	SH II, 3ff.
H.	Ninurta-apil-ekur *temp.* Adad-shuma-usur[11]	SH II, 3ff.
I.	Ashur-dan I *temp.* Zababa-shuma-iddina	Sh II, 9ff.
J.	Ashur-resha-ishi *temp.* Ninurta-nadin-shumi	SKL II, 14; *AfO* 4 (1927), 213ff.
K.	Ashur-resha-ishi *temp.* Nabu-kudurri-usur	SH II (vo.), 1ff.
L.	Tiglath-pileser I *temp.* Marduk-nadin-akhkhe	SH II (ro.), 14ff.
M.	Tiglath-pileser I *temp.* Marduk-shapik-zeri	Weidner, *AfO* 17 (1956), 384; H. Tadmor, *JNES* 17 (1958), 133
N.	Ashur-bêl-kala *temp.* Marduk-shapik-zeri	SH II (ro.), 25ff.
O.	Ashur-bêl-kala *temp.* Adad-apla-iddina	SH II (ro.), 31

According to a chronicle fragment[12] the end of the reign of Marduk-nadin-akhkhe[13] occurred before the end of the reign of Tiglath-pileser. In fact the length of time separating these two events can be set at not less than two years, since in the year following the disappearance of the Babylonian king, Tiglath-pileser is still alive. Consequently Tiglath-pileser must have died not earlier than the

[9] P gives in place of Enlil-nirari, Adad-nirari, but according to the minimal Babylonian chronology VAT 10453 enables us to reconstruct, Adad-nirari (*regnabat* 1304–1273) could never have been Kurigalzu's contemporary (minimal date of death 1312).

[10] This can only be restored Adad-shuma-usur since his successor was Melishihu and since he himself was a contemporary of Enlil-kudurriusur's predecessor, Ashur-nirari III.

[11] This synchronism is not specifically attested in the texts, but it follows from the strong probability that Adad-shuma-usur survived the battle in which Enlil-kudurri-usur was slain; see H. Tadmor, *JNES* 17 (1958), 131f.

[12] VAT 10453; see E. Weidner, *AfO* 17 (1956), 384.

[13] Not necessarily his death; for *šadâ emēdu,* see *CAD* 4, 140.

year after this. Since the AKL indicates that he died in 1076 B.C.,[14] Marduk-nadin-akhkhe cannot have ended his reign later than 1078 B.C. This information enables us to draw up the following table of minimal dates for the Babylonian kings from Kurigalzu II to the end of Isin II.

[14] A. Poebel, *JNES* 2 (1943), 88. Doubt has sometimes been cast upon the accuracy of the Assyrian King List: A. Alt, *Welt als Geschichte*, 8 (1942), 127; A. Goetze, *JCS* 6 (1952), 157; *idem*, *BASOR* 127 (1952), 26; H. Lewy, *Festschrift Isadore Levy* (Brussels, 1955), 259ff.; F. R. Kraus, *WZKM* 52 (1953–55), 238ff.; B. Landsberger, *JCS* 8 (1954), 106f. For the period following Shamshi-adad I at least six kings have been cited as having been passed over in silence by the King List. These are Mut-ashkur, Rimush (?), and Asinu between AKL 40 and 41 (Landsberger, *ibid.*, 31f.), Puzur-sin somewhere between AKL 40 and 69 (*ibid.*; Weidner, *AfO* 15 [1945–], 96f.), Ber-nadin-akhkhe *temp.* AKL 69 and 70 (Lewy, *Festschrift Isadore Levy*, 282), and Enlil-nirari between AKL 72 and 73 (*ibid.*, 279). It should be pointed out, however, that the evidence apropos of the last two is tenuous. Both bear the title **uklum*, "chief," and on the assumption that during the Middle Assyrian period this title was borne only by the king, it is maintained that both men at one time or another must have held the throne of Assyria (*ibid.*, 279, n. 2). Ber-nadinakhkhe, however, in the one contemporary inscription in which he is named (*KAJ* 174, rs. 10), does not bear this title. It is only two generations after his death, in the genealogy of his grandson, that **uklum* appears after his name (*KAJ* 8, 26). As for Enlil-nirari, it is more probable that he is to be identified with Enlil-nirari, the successor of Ashur-uballiṭ (cf. H. A. Fine, *Studies in Middle Assyrian Chronology and Religion* [Cincinnati, 1955], 28). The first four names are probably to be placed around the time of AKL 41ff. That this was a troubled epoch of Assyrian history is shown by the number of usurpers AKL names at this point (nos. 41–7). Undoubtedly the confusion in the King List is to be accounted for by the fact that several rival families were fighting for the crown.

An important distinction should be made between an inadvertent omission on the part of a scribe and a deliberate one. While the former is beyond our ability to control, it is unlikely that such an error would have gone undetected for long. A deliberate omission, on the other hand, may very well have been perpetrated, for two reasons. First, when faced with the names of two rival claimants to the throne who ruled contemporaneously, the scribe would have been forced to omit one, or run the risk of a conflation. Second, at a given period in the compilation of the King List, it is certain that some kings of earlier periods would have been anathematized, and their names would consequently have been omitted as a matter of course. Thus we might reasonably expect the odd gap in the list of personal names on one side of each column in AKL. But would corresponding gaps occur on the other side of the column, where the years are recorded? The tacit assumption of all scholars sceptical of the value of AKL has been that a deficiency

continued on next page

King	*No. of Regnal Years*	*Dates*
Kurigalzu II	22	1338–1316
Nazimaruttash	26	1315–1290
Kadashman-turgu	18	1289–1272
Kadashman-enlil II	15[15]	1271–1257
Kudur-enlil	9[16]	1256–1248
Shagarakti-shuriash	18[17]	1247–1230
Kashtiliash IV	8	1229–1222
Enlil-nadin-shumi } Kadashman-kharbe }	1	1221
Adad-shuma-iddina	6	1220–1215
Adad-shuma-usur	30	1214–1185
Melishihu	15	1184–1170
Marduk-apla-iddina I	13	1169–1157
Zababa-shuma-iddina	1	1157
Enlil-nadin-akhkhe	3	1156–1154
Marduk-kabit-akhkheshu	18	1153–1136
Itti-marduk-balatu	8	1135–1128
Ninurta-nadin-shumi	6	1127–1122
Nabu-kudurri-usur I	22	1121–1100
Enlil-nadin-apli	4	1099–1096
Marduk-nadin-akhkhe	18	1095–1078
Marduk-shapik-zeri	13	1077–1065
Adad-apla-iddina	22	1064–1043

[15] Rowton, *JCS* 13 (1959), 5, n. 24; *UET* VI, 48. I am indebted to Professor A. K. Grayson for the latter reference.

[16] Rowton, *JCS* 13 (1959), 5, n. 25.

[17] Cf. Jaritz, *JSS* 2 (1957), 325ff.; *idem*, *MIOF* 6 (1958), 200.

---

continuation of note 14

in the list of names implies a like deficiency in the computable total of years. However, such an assumption not only is without support, but also is opposed by the evidence. The essential purpose of a king list must lie in the presence of the tabulation of the lengths of reign. And it is surely not too daring to submit that the aim of the compilers was to supply reliable chronological information. But to provide such information the scribes could not afford to leave a single year unaccounted for, though the dropping of names would have less serious consequences. If a king's name were omitted, it would be essential that his reign be added on somewhere else in the list. That this was common practice in the Near East needs no stressing. There is evidence (see below) that in Babylonian lists, while the names of foreign rulers were sometimes suppressed, their reigns were carefully recorded as part of the floruit of a native king. When for some reason such subterfuge was

continued on next page

The synchronisms indicated by the Synchronistic History provide certain checks on these results. If we compare the dates for the Assyrian kings[18] with the minimal Babylonian dates, we shall find no clashes with respect to known synchronisms. No Assyrian king died before the accession of his Babylonian contemporary and, conversely, no Babylonian king died before the accession of his Assyrian contemporary. The synchronism that furnishes the smallest possible range, viz. H, also provides the means for reckoning the maximum dates for the Babylonian kings of the period. The passage in the Synchronistic History that records this synchronism makes it clear that in the last year of Enlil-kudurri-usur (i.e. the accession year of his successor Ninurta-apil-ekur) the Babylonian king Adad-shuma-usur was still alive. Thus the death of Adad-shuma-usur, for which the minimal date is 1185, cannot have taken place before the last year of his Assyrian contemporary Enlil-kudurri-usur, which is 1192. Thus the maximum dates for Babylonian chronology during the Kassite period are seven years higher than the minimal.[19]

Rowton has recently suggested[20] that the period from Tukulti-ninurta's seizure of Babylon, i.e. the end of Kashtiliash IV's reign, to the beginning of the reign of Adad-shuma-usur amounted to over sixteen years. His argument, outlined briefly at the beginning of this

[18] Poebel, *JNES* 2 (1943), 88.

[19] These calculations are based upon the Nassouhi list, which gives thirteen years to Ninurta-apil-ekur (*AfO* 4 [1927], 1ff.). The Khorsabad version gives this king three years, which would bring him to the throne in 1187, a date that would not satisfy synchronism H.

[20] *JNES* 19 (1960), 19.

---

continuation of note 14

not possible, the necessity of naming the foreigner was again obviated by describing his reign as an interregnum (cf. the passage in Ptolemy referring to the rule of Tiglath-pileser III and Sennacherib over Babylon as ἀβασίλευτα ἔτη: F. Schmidtke, *Der Aufbau der babylonischen Chronologie* [Münster, 1952], 41). Assyrian scribes undoubtedly employed the same tricks. Indeed, it has been suggested (F. Cornelius, *JCS* 12 [1958], 101) that, although the names of Mut-ashkur, Rimush (?), and Asinu do not occur in AKL, their reigns were dutifully added on to the reign of Ishme-dagan I, who was then credited with forty years. Thus the objection that certain royal names have been dropped from AKL does not once and for all damn the list as useless. To the contrary, the a priori likelihood that the numerical total is *not* deficient throws the burden of proof entirely on the sceptic.

chapter, must now be examined in more detail. The period delimited above is called by Rowton the "Intermediate Period." According to Rowton, King List A comprised the following names:

Enlil-nadin-shumi		$1\frac{1}{2}$ years
Kadashman-kharbe		$1\frac{1}{2}$ years
Adad-shuma-iddina		6 years
	Total	9 years[21]

According to chronicle P, however, from the end of Kashtiliash's reign to the beginning of Adad-shuma-usur's only seven years elapsed, during which time Tukulti-ninurta ruled as king of Babylonia by means of his own governors. Often in the past it has been assumed that the three names mentioned above are actually those of the Assyrian governors whom Tukulti-ninurta appointed, and that it was only in the late Babylonian tradition that they were made out to have been kings. Rowton points out that such attempts at harmonization are wrong-headed, since we now have documents of this period to prove that at least Kadashman-kharbe and Adad-shuma-iddin were bona fide kings of Babylon.[22] Consequently their floruit cannot possibly have been contemporary with Tukultininurta's rule over Babylon. The seven-year period of Assyrian rule mentioned in Chronicle P, he concludes, must be different from the nine years of King List A. Far from being coeval, the two periods must have been in fact consecutive, the nine years following the seven. Thus the intermediate period lasted sixteen years at least.

There are obvious difficulties to this view. First, it is not at all unlikely that a Babylonian rebel might bear the title "king of Babylon" and perhaps even hold that city at the same time that a foreign conqueror was claiming the same title. The mere fact that

[21] So Rowton and all earlier scholars. J. Brinkman, however, in an unpublished doctoral dissertation, has now shown the error of this total. The figure used with both Enlil-nadin-shumi and Kadashman-kharbe, viz. "one year, six months," is a means of indicating that, although in actual fact the reign amounted to only six months, the king was credited with a "year 1" by virtue of the fact that his *floruit* spanned the change in calendar year. Thus the total for the three kings in king list A is seven years, not nine, in full agreement with Chronicle P. The prima facie probability of Rowton's inflation of the Intermediate Period has thus vanished. I am again indebted to Professor Grayson for this information.

[22] *JNES* 19 (1960), 19, n. 13.

both Tukultininurta I and the three individuals of King List A were each at one time or another called "king of Babylon" does not automatically preclude their contemporaneity. Second, if Tukulti-ninurta had held the legitimate kingship in the south, why does his name not appear in King List A? The same query may be raised with respect to Tadmor's belief that we must insert the reign of the Elamite conqueror Kutir-nakhunte at the end of the Kassite dynasty.[23] The mere fact that neither name appears in the king list does not mean that allowance must be made in the chronology for two interregna. There is no reason to suppose that the Babylonian scribe omitted the reigns of Tukulti-ninurta and Kutir-nakhunte from the lists merely because they were foreigners. Mar-biti-apli-usur, the sole ruler of the seventh dynasty, was an Elamite usurper; yet he found a place in the king list.[24] So also did the late Assyrian kings who had ruled Babylon, Tiglath-pileser III (Pulu), Shalmaneser V (Ululai), Sargon, and Sennacherib. If the names of foreigners *are* omitted, it is altogether likely, as demonstrated earlier for other king lists, that the lengths of their rule were included in the figures given for their successors. In the case of Kutir-nakhunte, for instance, a Babylonian stela (K2660)[25] shows clearly that this is precisely what has taken place. The stela (ro. 12ff.) states that the last Kassite king, Enlil-nadin-akhkhe, was taken off to Elam where, as a captive, he continued to reside. It is not unreasonable to assume that in loyal Babylon documents continued to be dated by him, and that his reign continued to be acknowledged and was duly entered by the king list scribe as three years. But in lines 2f. of the obverse of K2660 we are told that upon the dethronement of his predecessor Zababa-shuma-iddina by the Elamites, Kutir-nakhunte was *immediately* invested with the rule. Enlil-nadin-akhkhe, the rightful heir, who is at once attacked, defeated, and deported (11. 6ff.), obviously did not enjoy an independent reign. The three years credited to him in King List A were in reality occupied by the rule of the Elamite Kutir-nakhunte.[26] I

[23] Tadmor, *JNES* 17 (1958), 137ff.

[24] King List A, vs. (rt): 14; CT 36, Pl. 25.

[25] Tadmor, *JNES* 17 (1958), 137ff.

[26] *Contra* A. Ungnad, *Orientalia*, 13 (1940), 81; G. Cameron, *History of Early Iran* (Chicago, 1936), 109f.; cf. E. Hornung, *Untersuchungen zur Chronologie und Geschichte des neuen Reiches* (Wiesbaden, 1964), 48, n. 43.

see no reason to doubt that the absence of Tukulti-ninurta's name is to be explained in much the same way.

A third difficulty lies in a statement of chronicle P that seems to say that the seven-year period came to a close with the elevation to power of Adad-shuma-usur in Babylon. The passage in question reads as follows: "In Karduniash he (Tukulti-ninurta) appointed governors of his. For seven years Tukulti-ninurta ruled (*uma'ir*)[27] Karduniash. Afterward, the nobles of Akkad (and?) of Karduniash rebelled, and set Adad-shuma-usur upon his father's throne. As for Tukulti-ninurta, who had lifted his hand evilly against Babylon, Ashur-nasir-pal his son and the nobles of Ashur rebelled against him, and removed him from his throne. They confined him in a house in Kar-Tukulti-ninurta, and then killed him."[28] Rowton, however, circumvents the difficulty by translating as follows: "(Later) after the noblemen of Akkad (that is), of Karduniash had revolted, and had seated Adad-shuma-usur on his father's throne, Ashurnasirapli his son and the noblemen of the land of Ashur revolted against Tukulti-ninurta . . ."[29] Rowton's translation reduces the clause beginning *arki,* "afterwards," to subordinate temporal meaning. Then with the bracketed insertion of "(later)" heading the whole, he is released from the necessity of assuming that the events to be narrated brought the seven-year period to a close. With his translation they could as easily have happened many years later.

I should like to make the following objections to Rowton's rendering: (a) In any document of a chronicle type, in which events are set forth in more or less orderly fashion, the scribe is obliged to give equal weight to each important event he has to relate. This would mean a separate paragraph, or at least a separate sentence, for each. But if Rowton has translated correctly, such momentous events as the rebellion in Babylon and Adad-shuma-usur's accession are not even mentioned in the narrative; they are relegated to a subordinate temporal clause, and serve merely to date a later incident, which, from a Babylonian's point of view, could scarcely be as important. Rowton's translation demands that the statement of the rebellion should have been set forth in a preceding independent sentence. But this is not the case. (b) The mention of the exact period of time during

[27] See Rowton, *JNES* 19 (1960), 19.

[28] P, IV, 6ff.

[29] *JNES* 19 (1960), 20.

which Babylon was under foreign rule suggests that the scribe knew, or rather thought he knew, the historical events opening and closing that period. He gives us the account of the events that led to Babylon's fall and the beginning of the Assyrian domination, describes that domination, and tells us how long it continued. Then, according to Rowton's rendering, he relates an event of much later date, returning to his consecutive narrative only with his account of Enlil-nadin-shumi's reign. This, I submit, is absurd. The tenor of the account makes it imperative that, following the statement regarding the exact length of Assyrian rule, we understand the clause commencing with *arki* as telling *what happened next*, i.e. the events that brought the seven years to a close.

Quite apart from the problem of how long the Intermediate Period lasted, a datum is available by means of which the dates of the Babylonian kings may be established. This is the passage in Chronicle P[30] which states that Marduk (Bel) remained in Assyria for [ ]+6 years until the time of ⟨Ninurta⟩-tukulti-Ashur. Now it is a certainty that Marduk's deportation occurred at the same time as the Assyrian conquest, and the end of the reign of Kashtiliash.[31] Consequently, the broken figure constitutes the number of years that elapsed between the end of the reign of Kashtiliash and some point in the reign of Ninurta-tukulti-Ashur. Since the latter ruled for but a part of one year (1133),[32] the lower limit is fixed. Using the minimal dates assigned to the Babylonian chronology of the period, ninety years elapsed from Kashtiliash to Ninurta-apil-ekur; consequently, a restoration of the broken figure as [8]6 is impossible.[33] With the maximum dates this period lasted ninety-seven years, and in consequence a restoration [10]6 is likewise impossible. The restrictive limitations of the minimal and maximum chronologies allows only one restoration, viz. [9]6.[34] Since this is six years higher than the minimal figure for

[30] IV, 12.

[31] Chronicle P (IV, 1–6) states that as soon as Kashtiliash was defeated and carried off to Ashur, Tukulti-ninurta returned and removed Marduk. If Lambert's reconstruction of the Tukulti-ninurta epic is correct (*AfO* 18 [1957], 40), Marduk is depicted forsaking his city before the final overthrow of the Kassite king (*ibid.*, 42).

[32] Poebel, *JNES* 2 (1943), 70; Rowton, *JNES* 18 (1959), 218, n. 20.

[33] Thus Weidner, *AfO* 4 (1927), 13.

[34] It was accepted at one time by Weidner, *MVAG* 20 (1915), 4, 79.

the period, the absolute dates for the Babylonian kings listed above (pp. 187–89) will be uniformly six years higher than the minimal.

The date of Kadashman-turgu's death may now be computed at 1278 B.C. On the basis of the three possible accession years of Ramses II, 1273 would correspond to (a) the twenty-seventh year of the Egyptian king (accession, 1304), (b) the thirteenth (accession 1290), or (c) the second (accession 1279). It is clear that the last correspondence cannot be valid. The Hittite king in Ramses II's fifth year was Muwatallis. His son, Urhi-teshup, ruled at least seven years. Even if Muwatallis died in Ramses' sixth year, Hattusilis could not have come to the throne before the twelfth year of the Egyptian king. But if Kadashman-turgu had died in the second year, he and Hattusilis could never have been contemporaries as the Hittite text *KBo* 1, 10 shows they were. Hence Kadashman-turgu's death must have occurred later than Ramses II's second year, and 1279 is ruled out as a possible accession year of Ramses II.

But of the other two possible dates no choice can be made simply on the basis of the new absolute date for Kadashman-turgu. Historical considerations allow a span of twenty-five years (Ramses II's year 12 to year 37) in which the Babylonian king's death may be placed, but solutions on the basis of 1290 or 1304 can both be accommodated within this broad time-range.

KBo I, 10 offers a possible means of choosing between 1304 and 1290. If it can be shown that this letter was written before the treaty in year 21, then Kadashman-turgu's death is also to be dated before the treaty. Consequently, the twenty-first year of Ramses II must fall after 1278, and 1304 as the year of accession could not be considered. The letter *KBo* I, 10 concerns *inter alia* an objection that had been raised by Kadashman-Enlil II, the addressee, concerning Hittite interference with an Egyptian messenger who had presumably been sent to Babylon.[35] In order to explain his action Hattusilis, the writer, described how, before he and the king of Egypt first became enemies, he had concluded a treaty with Kadashman-turgu.[36] The latter, on the outbreak of hostilities, not only offered troops to

[35] 11:55ff.; for the most recent translation, see Edel, *JCS* 12 (1958), 131f.

[36] This treaty has not turned up in the Hittite archives, but a letter from Kadashman-turgu to Hattusilis (*KUB* 3, 71) proves that this synchronism is not illusory.

Hattusilis, but also cut off diplomatic relations with Egypt. When Kadashman-Enlil succeeded his father, however, he resumed the interchange of messengers with Ramses II, and restored normal relations between the two countries. As Edel has pointed out, Hattusilis seems displeased by this resumption of friendly relations.[37] He protests in what appears to be a rhetorical question that he would never interfere with one of Kadashman-Enlil's own messengers, but the implication seems to be that the dispatch of an Egyptian messenger is a different matter. Edel could only conclude, therefore, that at the time the letter was written Hattusilis was still on inimical terms with Egypt, a conclusion to which the necessary corollary is that the letter dates prior to the treaty of year 21.

Rowton has vigorously contested Edel's dating of the letter.[38] He argues that there are too many events to be crowded into the period between Hattusilis' accession and the writing of *KBo* I, 10 to allow the latter to have been written before year 21. The period in question he divides into the following component intervals:

1. From the accession of Hattusilis to the treaty with Kadashman-turgu.
2. From 1 to the outbreak of the crisis with Egypt.
3. From 2 to Kadashman-turgu's death.
4. From 3 to the writing of *KBo* I, 10, during which Kadashman-Enlil grew from childhood to adolescence.
5. From 4 to the treaty in year 21.

These intervals together with the remainder of Muwatallis' reign after the fifth year of Ramses II total only nine years, and about one half of this total would have to be allotted to interval 4. With the comment "the extreme improbability of this sort of chronological compression hardly needs elaboration," Rowton proceeds to a second objection. *KBo* I, 10, he claims, contains nothing that would necessitate dating it prior to year 21. The concern shown by Hattusilis over the resumption of diplomatic relations between Egypt and Babylon could have other causes besides current antipathy between Egypt and Hatte. In fact, the implication on the part of Hattusilis that he will not hinder Kadashman-Enlil's messengers to Egypt could be taken to indicate that a state of peace existed between Egypt and

[37] Edel, *JCS* 12 (1958), 133.

[38] *JNES* 19 (1960), 16f.

the Hittites, and this could only be after the treaty of the twenty-first year.

Neither the arguments for a date before the treaty, nor those against it, are foolproof. No statement of *KBo* I, 10 is explicit with regard to date, though the balance of probability seems to reside with those who put it before year 21. Rowton's objection on the basis of the component intervals that would have to be squeezed into the nine or so years preceding the treaty is especially weak. We have no means of telling how long any of these intervals was likely to have been; but it is within the realm of possibility that nos. 1–3 together occupied scarcely two years.

A fact that has apparently been overlooked detracts from the effectiveness of Rowton's argument. He begins interval 1 in regnal year $12+x$ of Ramses II; that is to say, according to him, Hattusilis' acession to the throne followed the seven-year reign of Urhi-teshup. Now this may be historically correct; but it is not the way Hattusilis represented his career. *KBo* I, 10 was written well on in Hattusilis' reign, a considerable time after Urhi-teshup was expelled from his homeland. By that time Hattusilis had begun to elaborate his own version of his early history. The historical fact was this: when Muwatallis died, his brother Hattusilis and his son Urhi-teshup divided the Hittite land between them, only the latter, however, taking the title of "Great King." In Hattusilis' Apology the initiative is claimed by Hattusilis: "I took Urhi-teshup, the son of a secondary wife, put him in control of the Hatte-land, and placed all the army under his charge. In the Hatte-land he was the Great King, but I was king in Hakpis" (III, 41–5). In other historical texts from Hattusilis' reign, Urhi-teshup's seven-year floruit has, by a common device in Near Eastern historiography, been retrospectively absorbed in Hattusilis' reign. Thus in the historical preamble to treaties Urhi-teshup's reign is not mentioned; Hattusilis is represented as succeeding directly to the throne after his brother Muwatallis dies.[39] *KBo* I, 10 was written with this reinterpretation of history in mind. It was written in an atmosphere of vituperative debate to a young man who was not alive when these events were taking place, in an effort to convince him of a particular point of view. Urhi-teshup is not

[39] E. Weidner, *Politische Dokumente aus Kleinasien* (Leipzig, 1923), II, 127; *ANET*², 199.

mentioned. Hattusilis figures as the sole wielder of power. The only historical facts that we can distil from these writings of Hattusilis are the following: (a) Hattusilis became king when Muwatallis died; (b) at some point between this event and year 21 of Ramses II Hattusilis contracted a mutual assistance pact with Kadashman-turgu of Babylon. Thus, interval 1 must begin with Muwatallis' death, from which time Hattusilis could claim to have possessed the royal dignity. Consequently, the total of the interval and the remainder of the reign of Muwatallis after the fifth year of Ramses II will be a maximum of sixteen years, not nine, since Urhi-teshup's seven years must be included. The "chronological compression" upon which Rowton placed great weight is in reality not necessary.

There is one consideration that might lend support to a date after year 21 for the composition of *KBo* I, 10. Another passage in the letter mentions that Benteshinna of Amurru was already on his throne and under treaty to Hattusilis. A copy of this treaty is extant (*KBo* I, 8), and in the historical preamble the usual résumé of previous relations between suzerain and vassal is set forth. Benteshinna, it seems, had already occupied the throne of his patrimony under Muwatallis, but the latter had removed him. When Hattusilis came to the throne of Hatte, he reinstated Benteshinna in Amurru, and gave him his daughter as wife. Presumably, following Ramses II's defeat at Kadesh, Amurru was lost by the Egyptians. But by year 8 they had recovered it,[40] and in the following years the battlefront is in Naharin around Tunip.[41] Since Hattusilis cannot have come to the throne before the twelfth year of Ramses, it is highly doubtful (unless Amurru was recovered by Hatte sometime between years 12 and 21, for which there is no evidence) that the reinstatement of Benteshinna could have taken place before the restoration of peace in year 21. Not until then, at the earliest, does it appear that Amurru passed again into Hittite hands.[42] It would thus follow that *KBo* I, 10, since it presupposes Benteshinna's return to his former vassal state, must follow year 21.

[40] W. Wreszinski, *Atlas zur altägyptischen Kulturgeschichte*, II (Leipzig, 1935) Pl. 90.

[41] Cf. the Tunip inscription from Luxor and the Ramesseum: K. Sethe, *ZÄS* 44 (1906), 37f.

[42] Cf. A. Malamat, *JNES* 13 (1954), 239.

But this argument too is not above suspicion. So little is known about the course of the Egypto-Hittite war in the second decade of Ramses II's reign that the picture might be altered radically by new evidence. Amurru may have changed hands long before year 21, and the Egyptian campaigns around Tunip may be nothing more than exceptional incursions into territory that was considered Hittite by both sides. In other words, we cannot set any *terminus a quo* for the reinstatement of Benteshinna: there is really no evidence to prove that it could not have taken place before the treaty.

Without the assurance that *KBo* I, 10 antedates the treaty, we cannot be certain that Kadashman-turgu's death also antedated it. Consequently, it is impossible to state whether Ramses II's twenty-first year fell before or after 1278.

In the light of the ambiguous results from *KBo* I, 10, it would seem that the investigation should follow a different path. As noted at the beginning of this chapter, the country whose contacts with Egypt during Ramses II's reign are tied closest to Egyptian relative chronology is Hatte. Unfortunately Hittite chronology is far less certain than that of Assyria or Babylonia; but a study of it does enjoy the availability of a sizable documentation linking Hatte with the other states of the ancient Near East. The next three sections will be concerned with an investigation of Hittite chronology during the reigns of Muwatallis, Urhi-teshup, and Hattusilis, the three Hittite kings whose reigns overlapped the first half of Ramses II's reign.

THE DATE OF HATTUSILIS' ACCESSION

The date limits of the reign of Hattusilis depend largely on Assyrian chronology, and, *ipso facto*, on the much-discussed letter *KBo* I, 14.[43] This letter, written by Hattusilis[44] to the king of Assyria, his contemporary,[45] is very probably the first communication addressed to

[43] For a translation see A. Goetze, *Kizzuwatna and the Problem of Hittite Geography* (New Haven, 1940), 27ff.

[44] Cf. the reference to Urhi-teshup in vo. 15, and the clear implication that he was the predecessor of the writer.

[45] Weidner (*MDOG* 58 [1917], 77f.) originally thought that the addressee was Ramses II, and he was followed by B. Meissner (*ZDMG* 72 [1918], 44 and 61), Bilabel (*Geschichte*, 317), and most recently H. Schmoekel (*Geschichte des alten*

the latter after Hattusilis' accession to sole rule. Proof is provided by the reference to the coronation of the writer (vo. 4f.), and by the implication that Urhi-teshup's reign had ended only recently (vo. 11ff.). One letter from the Assyrian king seems to have preceded it (to which, in fact, *KBo* I, 14 is in part a reply). This haply preserved fragment of the royal letter-files thus falls at the very beginning of Hattusilis' reign, and although the exact amount of time that had elapsed since his coronation is not indicated by the letter, it can scarcely have been more than two years.

The identification of the Assyrian addressee is of prime importance for the present investigation. Only two Assyrian kings are eligible,[46] viz. Adad-nirari I and Shalmaneser I, and both have from time to time been suggested by scholars.[47] At the risk of going over ground already covered many times by others, I shall outline once again the arguments that bear upon the problem, although, thanks primarily to Rowton,[48] it is now virtually solved in favour of Adad-nirari. Since the available facts prove that *KBo* I, 14 could *not* have been written to Shalmaneser, the argument must take the form of a rebuttal.

Hattusilis, the writer of *KBo* I, 14, chides the Assyrian king for his failure to congratulate him on his accession (vo. 4f.): "did not [my

---

Vorderasien [Leiden, 1957], 136, n. 3). Not long after Weidner's original statement, however, S. Langdon (*JEA* 6 [1920], 202, n. 3) and after him E. Cavaignac (*RHA* [1934], 235) showed that the addressee could not possibly be Ramses. Weidner's subsequent belief (*AfO* 6 [1931], 299f.), shared by A. H. Sayce (*Antiquity*, 2 [1928], 226f.), that Hattusilis was the addressee and not the writer, the latter being the king of Kizzuwatna, is disproved by the passage in which the writer identifies himself with the family to which Urhi-teshup belongs. Nor was there ever any basis for Meyer's supposition (*Geschichte*, II, 1, 529) that *KBo* I, 14 was written by Arnuwandas IV to Merneptah. The case for Assyria as the land to which the letter was destined has been argued conclusively by Goetze (*Kizzuwatna and the Problem of Hittite Geography*, 31) and Rowton (*JCS* 13 [1959], 3 and n. 13).

[46] Tukulti-ninurta I (1244–1207) and his successors are far too late to be earlier contemporaries of Hattusilis: and Arik-dên-ilu is too early (died 1306) even on the highest possibility, viz. 1304, for the accession of Ramses II.

[47] Shalmaneser by Goetze (*Kizzuwatna* . . ., 31), Cavaignac (*RHA* [1934], 237; *Le Problème hittite* [Paris, 1936], 73), Hornung (*Untersuchungen* . . ., 51, n. 7); Adad-nirari by Cavaignac (*RHA* 19 [1935], 122, n. 24; *Les Hittites* [Paris, 1950], 40, n. 1), O. R. Gurney (*Iraq*, 11 [1949], 141), and Rowton (*JCS* 13 [1959], 6).

[48] *Ibid.*, 6f.

father/brother][49] send you the proper presents?" The lost word clearly refers to a predecessor of Hattusilis with whom the addressee had been contemporary; and the lacuna is small enough to allow only a limited number of possible restorations. If the restoration is *a-bi*, the reference must be to Mursilis,[50] a king with whom Shalmaneser could never have been contemporary, regardless of the chronology resorted to. But if the restoration is *a-ḫi*, undoubtedly Muwatallis is meant. In this case, the addressee's accession must have occurred at least eight years before that of Hattusilis. This follows from the fact that Muwatallis's reign ended seven years before Hattusilis came to the throne. If then the addressee be Shalmaneser, who, according to the AKL, acceded to the throne in 1273 B.C., the earliest possible date for the accession of Hattusilis would be 1265. In view of the fact that the twenty-first year of Ramses II follows Hattusilis' accession, this date becomes untenable because of the two possible accession dates for Ramses, viz. 1304 and 1290. Hattusilis must, therefore, have come to the throne before 1265, and consequently Shalmaneser I could never have been a contemporary either of his brother Muwatallis or his father Mursilis. In that case Shalmaneser cannot be the king addressed in *KBo* I, 14.

There is a further argument against identifying the addressee with Shalmaneser, *KBo* I, 14 reflects the reasonably cordial relations that existed between Hattusilis and the contemporary Assyrian king, even though the former seems a little piqued at not receiving the proper coronation gifts. *KUB* 23, 103, a series of rough drafts (in Hittite) of letters to be sent to Assyria, suggests, however, that Hattusilis and

[49] Goetze, *Kizzuwatna* . . ., 28; Rowton, *JCS* 13 (1959), 6; *contra* Cavaignac, *RHA* 18 (1934), 234, and D. D. Luckenbill, *AJSL* 37 (1921), 206.

[50] One might suppose that *a-bi* here is to be rendered "dynastic predecessor," without reference to real familial ties; cf. E. Cavaignac, *Mélanges Maspero* (Cairo, 1934), II, 358; Breasted, *ARE* III, 168, n. *c*. In that case the writer would have Urhi-teshup in mind. The mention of this king, however, in vs. 15 is such as to make it highly unlikely that Hattusilis would have referred to his hated nephew in this way. Moreover, the present question is merely rhetorical, and presupposes an affirmative answer. The relations with Assyria under Urhi-teshup, on the other hand, from all the evidence at our disposal, were consistently strained, perhaps more so than at any other time. A rhetorical question such as this would then have made no sense, since the addressee could have answered with an emphatic "no!"

Shalmaneser were not at all on good terms. The writer of these letters, Tudhaliyas IV,[51] states flatly that his father (i.e. Hattusilis) never wrote to Tukulti-ninurta's father (i.e. Shalmaneser),[52] and goes on to contrast his own good relations with Shalmaneser with those of his father.[53] In the light of this evidence it would be preposterous to make Shalmaneser the friendly addressee of *KBo* I, 14.

There is thus only one possibility, viz. Adad-nirari I,[54] and he fits the description of the addressee of our letter perfectly. The addressee was living at the time of the writer's brother or father: Adad-nirari acceded to the throne in 1305. The addressee is called *miḫru,* "peer," of Hattusilis, who was himself a "great king": Adad-nirari began his reign as a minor king, but because of his triumph over Wasashatta of Hanigalbat, he claimed the formal title *šarru rabû,* "great king".[55] A king of Hanigalbat is mentioned in *KBo* I, 14 (ro. 6ff.) in such a way as to make it plain that he is a vassal of

[51] Rightly identified by Cavaignac (*RHA* 28 [1937], 115ff.) and H. Otten (*AfO* 19 [1959–60], 46) on the basis of *KUB* 23, 103, vs. 20, where the reference is clearly to a projected campaign—known from other sources—of Tukultininurta, the Assyrian contemporary of Tudhaliyas.

[52] *KUB* 23, 103, obv. 16.

[53] *Ibid.,* rev. 1–6.

[54] According to Otten's interpretation of the tiny fragment *KUB* 26, 70:1–3 (*apud* E. Weidner, *AfO Beiheft,* 12 [1959], 67f.), Urhi-teshup's reign partly overlapped that of Shalmaneser I; consequently, Hattusilis's reign would fall wholly within the floruit of the same Assyrian king (Otten, *AfO* 19 [1959–60], 46; Hornung, *Untersuchungen* . . ., 50f., 57). For this there is in fact no evidence. In *KUB* 26, 70, Tudhaliyas IV merely states that Tukulti-ninurta had returned to him the letter Urhu-teshup had written to his (Tukulti-ninurta's) father, Shalmaneser. There is not the slightest indication that Urhi-teshup's letter was written while he was king of Hatte. Indeed, if it had been, why was a preliminary draft in Hittite not available to Tudhaliyas in the Hittite archives? Clearly because the letter had not been written from Hatte, but from some other land in which Urhi-teshup was dwelling; and this immediately suggests the period of his exile. That Urhi-teshup continued to plot against his uncle after his banishment to Nukhashshe is well attested. The letter referred to by Tudhaliyas probably represents one of Urhi-teshup's attempts to get Assyrian support for a renewed attack on Hattusilis. This was Cavaignac's view over twenty-five years ago (see *RHA* 18 [1935], 28f.), and is clearly correct. See now also Rowton, "Chronology: Ancient Western Asia," in *CAH* I (1962), chapter 6, 46, n. 4.

[55] Cf. *KUB* 23, 102:4.

Assyria: two kings of Hanigalbat[56] and perhaps a third[57] were, at different times, vassals of Adad-nirari.

The last observation introduces the question of the exact date in Adad-nirari's reign when *KBo* I, 14 was composed. Adad-nirari reigned in all probability thirty-two years,[58] from 1304 to 1273.[59] From Adad-nirari's own inscriptions we learn that at some unspecified year towards the beginning of his reign he defeated Shattuara I, the king of Hanigalbat, and made him his vassal.[60] At a later date Wasashatta, the son of Shattuara, who had succeeded his father on the throne, rebelled against Assyria, and sought support from the Hittites.[61] The promised support did not materialize, and Adad-nirari was able to devastate Hanigalbat as far as the Euphrates, and carry Wasashatta and family captive to Ashur.[62] That Adad-nirari did not end the vassal status of Hanigalbat by uniting it with Assyria[63] seems to follow from the fact that Shalmaneser I had to fight against Shattuara II of Hanigalbat early in his reign.[64] Most probably Adad-nirari had reinstated a member of the Hanigalbatian royal house (perhaps the son of Wasashatta) late in his reign. The interval between the two defeats of Hanigalbat by Adad-nirari was a long one. This is shown by the fact that two generations of Hanigalbatian kings are involved;[65] Shattuara I continued on the throne until he died, and the statement by Adad-nirari that "each year as long as he lived I received his tribute in my city Ashur"[66] shows that his death did not occur until several years after his defeat had elapsed. How long Wasashatta was on the throne before he rebelled

[56] Viz. Shattuara I and Wasashatta: Weidner, *AfO* 5 (1928), 97f.

[57] Inferred from the fact that Shalmaneser, on his accession, was faced by Shattuara II, now claiming independence, and backed by the Hittites: E. O. Forrer, *RLA* I, 263f.

[58] KKL III, 18; the number is lost in SDAS and the Nassouhi list.

[59] Poebel, *JNES* 2 (1943), 87.

[60] Ashur 10557, vs. 7ff.; Weidner, *AfO* 5 (1928), 97.

[61] *Ibid.*, vs. 18ff. [62] *Ibid.*, vs. 29ff. [63] *Contra* Forrer, *RLA* I, 262.

[64] *AoB* I, 116–19; Weidner, *MVAG* 20 (1915), 4, 70f. It is probably this campaign against Shattuara II that occasioned the muster of troops mentioned in one of the Tell Billa texts: A. Falkenstein, *JCS* 5 (1953), 132 (no. 49).

[65] There can be no lessening of the generation count by supposing that Wasashatta was under age at the time of his defeat; the reference in Adad-nirari's inscription (Weidner, *AfO* 5 [1928], 98, ll.48ff.) to his wives, sons, and daughters shows that he was a grown man. [66] *Ibid.*, 97, vs. 15ff.

we do not know, but it must have taken several years for him to establish himself and persuade the Hittites to help him. These considerations suggest that the second defeat of Hanigalbat accomplished by Adad-nirari comes relatively late in his reign. Rowton[67] has shown that it must have taken place around his twenty-fifth year, though no later than this. The proof consists of the names of six and perhaps seven eponyms who are known from Adad-nirari's own inscriptions to have held office after the defeat of Wasashatta. Rowton claims further to have shown[68] that following the initial defeat of Hanigalbat by Adad-nirari, there were only two periods down to the end of the eleventh century during which Hanigalbat was a political entity under a king of its own, vassal or otherwise. The first period extends from the subjection to vassalage of Shattuara I to the defeat of Washatta; the second occupied an undetermined length of time ending with the overthrow of Shattuara II by Shalmaneser I. Since it was only during these periods that there would have been a "king of Hanigalbat," *KBo* I, 14 must date from one of them. No one doubts the historical fact of these two periods; but Rowton errs when he places *KBo* I, 14 in the first, before the defeat of Wasashatta, a placement which would, in fact, make Wasashatta the king of Hanigalbat mentioned in the letter.[69]

The correct dating of *KBo* I, 14 can be deduced from *KUB* 23, 102, the Hittite draft of a letter destined for Adad-nirari I.[70] The occasion for these heated jottings was the receipt at the Hittite capital of a letter from Adad-nirari announcing that he had defeated Wasashatta, and claiming that this justified his advancement to the status of "great king." The letter also contained an offer of "brotherhood" to the Hittite king, and an enigmatic allusion to the "viewing of Mt. Amanus (in Syria)," which may have been a veiled threat of military action against the Hittite empire.[71] *KUB* 23, 102 is a draft of the Hittite king's reply to Adad-nirari. Grudgingly he admits that the Assyrian has scored a great success in overthrowing Wasashatta, but at the further proposals he bristles with rage. "What's this about brotherhood," he snaps, "and what's this about viewing Mt. Amanus? Wherefore should I write you about brotherhood? Who

[67] *JCS* 13 (1959), 1, n. 6. [68] *Ibid.*, 2f. [69] *Ibid.*, 4f.

[70] *Ibid.*, 10; Weidner, *AfO* 6 (1930), 21f.; Forrer, *RLA* I, 262f.

[71] So Güterbock; see Rowton, *JCS* 13 (1959), 10, n. 46.

should write whom about brotherhood? . . . You and I are perhaps born of the same mother? [Just as my father] and my father's father did not write to the king of Assyria [for brotherhood], so you are not to write to me about [sightsee]ing[72] and about 'great king'-ship!" Since the letter refers to the recent defeat of Wasashatta, it must be dated shortly after the close of the first of Rowton's two periods. Although no clue is given in the text as to the identity of the writer, Rowton unquestioningly attributes it to Hattusilis,[73] and therefore is forced to date it after the writing of *KBo* I, 14. If, then, as Rowton believes, the order of events is: accession of Hattusilis, *KBo* I, 14, defeat of Wasashatta, drafting of *KUB* 23, 102, the reversal of mutual attitudes between writer and addressee in the latter missive becomes utterly unintelligible. For the defeat of Wasashatta was, in Adad-nirari's own eyes, the greatest single accomplishment of his reign, and brought him world renown.[74] If anything, then, we should expect an enhancement of the mutual relationship reflected in *KBo* I, 14, and a marked rise in the status of Adad-nirari I vis-à-vis Hattusilis. In *KBo* I, 14 Hattusilis treats the Assyrian king as an equal, and defers to him on the Turrira affair (ro. 6ff.). But the Hittite king of *KUB* 23, 102 is *talking down* to one whom he considers a "small king," and is enraged at the very idea that this upstart should suggest a treaty of brotherhood. Their fathers had never enjoyed such relations, states the writer. He denies vehemently that Adad-nirari's victory over Hanigalbat has qualified him for the status of great king; on this ground alone brotherhood is unthinkable. The clear inference to be drawn from every statement in the letter is that the writer is, or at least considers himself to be, a "great king," and has never at any time thought of his Assyrian contemporary as a peer.

In the light of these considerations two conclusions are inevitable: (1) *KUB* 23, 102 was not written by Hattusilis, and (2) it does not follow but rather precedes *KBo* I, 14. In other words, the Hittite king who was reigning when Adad-nirari defeated Wasashatta was a

72 The traces suit [*ú-wa-u-wa-*] ⌜*ar*⌝ rather than [ŠEŠ]- ⌜*tar*⌝, as Rowton, *ibid.*

73 So also Schmoekel, *Geschichte* . . ., 136.

74 Adad-nirari is the first king after Shamshi-adad I to employ the title *šar kiššati*, "king of the universe": E. Ebeling, *et al.*, *Die Inschriften der altassyrische Könige* (Leipzig, 1926), 73, n. 13.

predecessor of Hattusilis. Indeed, Weidner long ago proposed Muwatallis as the author,[75] and although the present writer feels that the evidence points to another[76] at least Weidner seems to have sensed that the context of *KUB* 23, 102 demanded a date earlier than the reign of Hattusilis.

Now it has been shown that the defeat of Wasashatta occurred around, but no later than, Adad-nirari's twenty-fifth or twenty-sixth year, i.e. 1280/79. *KUB* 23, 102 was drawn up after this date, but probably not much later; 1277 would appear to be a lower limit. There is no way of telling for certain exactly how long after this date *KBo* I, 14 was composed, but at least one change of reign at Hattusas must have occurred in the interim. Two considerations make a closer dating possible. First, the mention of a king of Hanigalbat who is again active and obstreperous suggests the very end of Adad-nirari's reign. The defeat of Wasashatta, from all accounts, had been so crushing that Hanigalbat did not recover quickly. It could only have been during the last one or two years of Adad-nirari's reign that Hanigalbat regained some of its strength, albeit as a vassal of Assyria.[77] Second, the fact that *KBo* I, 14 is in Akkadian[78] suggests that we have here the version destined for the Assyrian court. But why was it found at Hattusas? Presumably, the reason is that it was never sent. News of Adad-nirari's death must have arrived before the messenger (Bel-qarrad?) had departed, and consequently the letter was filed away and forgotten. *KBo* I, 14 was thus probably written in 1273, the year of Adad-nirari's death, not long after the accession of Hattusilis. To allow sufficient time for the Assyrian letter that preceded *KBo* I, 14—it must be a fairly long period in order to account for the insult Hattusilis felt on not receiving a coronation present—we should place Hattusilis' accession around 1275 or 1276 B.C., but scarcely earlier.[79]

[75] *AfO* 6 (1930), 21f.; cf. also Cavaignac, *RHA* 19 (1935), 120f.; Otten, *apud* Weidner, *AfO Beiheft*, 12 (1959), 67.

[76] In the light of Urhi-teshup's known hostility towards Assyria, is it not likely that he is the author?

[77] So already Cavaignac, *RHA* 19 (1935), 121. The relationship between Adad-nirari and Hanigalbat reflected in *KBo* I, 14 suggests vassal status.

[78] As opposed to the rough drafts in Hittite, which were kept at Hattusas. For examples of such drafts, cf. Otten, *apud* Weidner, *AFO Beiheft*, 12 (1959), 64.

[79] Cf. O. R. Gurney's date, *The Hittites* (Harmondsworth, 1952), 216.

This narrowing of the range of Hattusilis' accession is of great significance for the problem of Ramses II's dates. The upper limit of Hattusilis' accession would have to be placed in the higher 1270's, but in no case before 1280. If, however, Ramses II came to the throne of Egypt in 1304, Hattusilis, who had become king at least three years prior to Ramses' twenty-first year, could not possibly have begun his reign later than 1287. On the evidence of the date and authorship of *KUB* 23, 102 this would be impossible. Thus the accession of Hattusilis, linked as it is to the end of Adad-nirari's reign, constitutes proof that 1304 is too early to be the accession year of Ramses II.[80]

The reign of Urhi-teshup, the nephew of Hattusilis, immediately preceded that of his uncle, and ended with the defeat in battle and banishment of the young man. Nowhere is the length of his reign given explicitly, but it can be inferred from a statement in his uncle's Apology. Hattusilis, who was himself responsible for elevating Urhi-teshup to the throne, claims to have endured his nephew's insults for seven years.[81] Since Hattusilis makes it clear that during Urhi-teshup's entire reign the two were at loggerheads, the seven years corresponds as well to the length of the reign. On the basis of Hattusilis' accession in 1275 Urhi-teshup would have come to the throne in 1282.

It remains to check the possible repercussions to the reign of Urhi-teshup of the date 1304 for the accession of Ramses II. Urhi-teshup's dates would then be *ca.* 1296 to 1289. Now the Apology of Hattusilis tells us that upon his banishment to Nukhashshe after his deposition, Urhi-teshup attempted to stir up hostility against his uncle in Babylonia.[82] He also sent letters to Shalmaneser of Assyria, doubtless to inveigle him too into an anti-Hittite plot.[83] Because of these subversive activities Hattusilis had him removed "across the sea,"[84] by

[80] Professor Albright's adherence to the date 1290 (*BASOR* 163 [1961], 52, n. 72) is thus vindicated, though on different evidence.

[81] Apology 3:63.

[82] *Ibid.*, 4:33.

[83] *KUB* 26, 70; see discussion in n. 54, above. That his correspondence with Shalmaneser must date from his exile in Nukhashshe, i.e. before the treaty with Egypt, is indicated (a) by the fact that the only reference to Urhi-teshup's machinations in the Apology comes during his exile in Nukhashshe, and (b) by the fact that the manifest purpose of removing him "across the sea" was to banish him far enough to prevent the recurrence of such treasonable activity.

[84] Apology 4:35.

which Cyprus is probably meant.[85] With the Egypto-Hittite treaty of Ramses' twenty-first year Urhi-teshup drops out of sight. But if the twenty-first year fell in 1284 (accession 1304), the Assyrian king who was contemporary with Urhi-teshup's exile in Nukhashshe would have been Adad-nirari, not Shalmaneser. Here, then, is further proof that 1304 is too early for the accession of Ramses II.

To sum up the results obtained in the investigation of the Hittite accession dates: the correct order and interpretation of the two letters *KUB* 23, 102 and *KBo* I, 14 show that Adad-nirari's campaign against Wasashatta preceded the accession of Hattusilis, and that the latter event in turn preceded the death of Adad-nirari in 1273 by only a short time. The resultant date for the accession of Hattusilis, *ca.* 1275, renders the highest of the three possible dates for the accession of Ramses II unworkable. The known contemporaneity of Urhi-teshup's exile in Nukhashshe with part of Shalmaneser's reign likewise militates against 1304. With the elimination of 1279 as a possibility on other grounds, 1290 alone remains, and it is herewith accepted as the date of Ramses II's accession. In order to make use of it for our purposes it is necessary only to calculate how long before 1290 the Nineteenth Dynasty had come to power. In terms of reigns this calculation will involve Ramses I and Sety I. Since the length of the former's reign is accurately determined as one and one-half years,[86] only Sety's reign remains to be fixed.

THE LENGTH OF SETY I'S REIGN

Estimates of the length of Sety's reign have varied considerably over the past century. Egyptologists of the nineteenth century were inclined to attribute to this king a relatively long reign approaching three decades;[87] and Maspero's opinion[88] that Sety's mummy was that of a man who had died well past the age of sixty did nothing but confirm their suspicion. When a trend appeared to be developing in

[85] Gurney, *The Hittites*, 37; Otten, *MDOG* 94 (1963), 10; for Urhi-teshup's subsequent flight to Egypt, see now Helck, *JCS* 17 (1963), 87ff.

[86] According to Manetho, one year and four months.

[87] Cf. Wiedemann, *Geschichte*, 416 and 420f.; Petrie, *History, III*, 2f. Wiedemann's twenty-seven years, based on a date in an Abydos stela supposed to come from this reign, was soon shown to be in error: Wiedemann, *Supplement to the Geschichte*, 48.

[88] *Les Momies royales de Déir el-Bahari* (Cairo, 1884), 773.

favour of a lowering of the figure to *ca.* twelve or thirteen years,[89] Breasted provided a rebuttal. It had earlier been assumed that in a Karnak relief dating to Sety's first year, the future Ramses II was shown with his father engaging in a military campaign. In order that Ramses should have been old enough at the beginning of his father's reign to take part in such manly pursuits, and yet still have time to enjoy an independent reign of sixty-seven years, Maspero[90] felt obliged to shorten Sety's reign. Breasted[91] attempted to show, however, that not only does the campaign in which Ramses appears bear no date at all, but also the figure of the young prince and his name are a later insertion in the scene. Thus, he could argue, there is no evidence that Ramses went on a campaign in his father's first year, or, indeed, that he had even been born at that time. On this basis Breasted saw no necessity to confine Sety's reign within a decade or a dozen years, and allotted over twenty to him.[92]

Still the impression has grown that Sety's reign lasted no more than a decade.[93] The reason for the persistence of this impression is the complete lack of dated inscriptions after his eleventh year.[94] In the light of the numerous remains, including many dated texts, from Sety's reign, the silence beyond his eleventh year can scarcely be due to the haphazard of preservation.

Whether Manetho originally gave the correct figure for Sety is a moot point. His lists, as we have them today in Josephus and the epitome, record the Nineteenth Dynasty twice, once in the proper place and once at the end of the Eighteenth Dynasty. Sety appears in both places under the name "Sethos,"[95] but at some point in the

[89] Maspero, *Histoire,* II, 387, n. 5.

[90] *Ibid.*

[91] *ZÄS* 37 (1899), 131ff.; *ARE* III, §§123–31.

[92] *ARE* I, §67; *History,* 418. For a criticism of Breasted's views, see K. Seele, *The Coregency of Ramses II with Seti I* (Chicago, 1940), 23ff.

[93] Bilabel, *Geschichte,* 107; Gauthier, *Livre, III,* 10 and n. 5; M. V. Schmidt, *Recueil Champollion* (Paris, 1922), 154.

[94] G. A. Reisner, *ZÄS* 69 (1933), 73ff. (stela from Gebel Barkal).

[95] W. Struve (*ZÄS* 63 [1928], 47f.) rejects this derivation of *Σέθος,* preferring to derive it from the hypocorism of Ramses II, *Sst.* According to Struve, the name "Sety" does not appear at all in Manetho because of the fact that the god Seth was anathematized in the Late Period. Struve's arguments are ingenious throughout, but on this point he fails to be convincing. There can scarcely be any doubt that *Σέθος,* goes back to **Sĕtᵉḫ* (Akk. *Šuta*); cf. Sethe, *ZÄS* 66 (1931), 1, n. 5.

transmission of the tradition he has been confused with his father Ramses I.[96] The elimination of the duplicate list results in a succession of names remarkably close to historical fact. In Josephus Sety is credited with fifty-nine years, and Africanus and Eusebius have similarly high, though not identical, figures. It is hard to resist the temptation to connect the datum "59" with the fictitious number of years given Haremhab in the inscription of Mes from Sakkarah. This latter figure, as is well known, includes not only the reign of Haremhab (or most of it), but also the reigns of the "heretical kings" back to Akhenaten. The false attribution of this fifty-nine years to Sety in later tradition is by no means implausible. In post-Manethonian tradition Haremhab was more closely linked to the Nineteenth Dynasty than to the Eighteenth. He was, in fact, equated with Danaus, while Sety was identified with Aegyptos.[97] According to the tradition Danaus was a brother of Aegyptos. Both struggled for a time over the rule of the country, but eventually Aegyptos proved victorious. For the Hellenist concerned with chronology, and having a stubborn tradition of a fifty-nine-year reign to dispose of in this general period, the choice between the two legendary heroes was not easy; especially so, if his tradition attached the figure "59" to the first of the pair. For while in one passage Josephus states that Sety (Aegyptos) drove out "Hermaius" (Danaus) and *then* reigned, which indeed implies that the order should be Hermaius–Sety, in another[99] he states that Sety began to reign before Hermaius took the crown and revolted, a strong indication that the order should be Sety and then Hermaius. Although in the original *Aegyptiaca* the fifty-nine years may have been correctly interpreted, the contaminated tradition reflected in Josephus, which made Sety the prime protagonist and relegated Haremhab to the status of a rebellious brother whose end was not long in coming, may well have occasioned the transfer of the fifty-nine-year reign to Sety.

[96] Maspero, *RT* 27 (1905), 19; Helck, *Untersuchungen zu Manetho*, 69; Meyer, *Ägyptische Chronologie*, 90f.; Gauthier, *Livre*, III, 10, n. 1; cf. also Maspero, *JS* (1901), 670.

[97] For the Danaus–Aegyptos legend and its relationship to the late historical tradition in Egypt, see Maspero, *RT* 27 (1905), 25; *idem*, *JS* (1901), 665ff.; M. De Rochemonteix, *RT* 8 (1886), 192f.

[98] *Contra Apionem* I, 26.

[99] *Ibid.*, I, 15.

Only one source gives a figure for the reign of Sety approaching the concensus of the monuments, and that is Theophilus, who gives ten. True, his Sethos comes after Amenophis (Merneptah), which would suggest an identification with Sety II. But not only does the real reign of Sety II (five years) have nothing in common with Theophilus' figure, but also, if this identification were to be accepted, Sety would not appear at all in this source. It is more reasonable to assume that Sety I has been misplaced by Theophilus. Theophilus' witness of a ten-year reign cannot be summarily rejected; it would not be without precedent that a secondary source should have preserved the correct figure where the primary sources have erred. A postulated reign of ten years[100] would be in perfect agreement with the monuments, the Gebel Barkal stela of the eleventh year having then been set up in the year of Sety's death. On the basis of Ramses II's accession in 1290, Sety I would have come to the throne in 1300.

There is an objection that might be raised against a date as late as 1300, and that has to do with the beginning of the Sothic cycle. The meaning and ramifications of the Sothic cycle are known to most scholars, but for the sake of the present discussion a brief description must be inserted here.[101] The Egyptian year of 365 days, because of its deficiency of one-quarter day, is constantly moving forward through the seasonal year. Each year that passes finds the Egyptian calendar starting one-quarter day earlier than the previous year. After four years have elapsed the calendar has lost one whole day, and the heliacal rising of Sirius (Sothis), the phenomenon that should mark the first day in the calendar year, falls one day late on the second of the first month. After eight years it falls on the third day, after twelve on the fourth, and so on. Finally, after 1460 years have passed, if no adjustment has been made in the meantime,[102] the rising of Sirius has passed right through the calendar, and returned to its proper position on New Year's day. This period of 1460 years is called a Sothic cycle. According to Censorinus writing in A.D. 238[103]

[100] Accepted by J. von Beckerath, *Tanis und Theben* (Glückstadt, 1951), 49 and 104. Hornung (*Untersuchungen* . . ., 40f.) allows for a maximum of fifteen years.

[101] For a brief and lucid explanation, see R. A. Parker, *RdE* 9 (1952), 102ff.; also A. Scharff, *Hist. Zeitschr.* 161 (1939), 3ff.; K. Sethe, *Nachr. Gött.* (1919), 308ff.

[102] It is virtually certain that no such adjustment ever took place; cf. Parker, *RdE* 9 (1952), 101ff. and *passim*.

[103] *De die natali*, 21:10.

a new cycle had begun exactly a century before in the second year of Antoninus Pius (139).[104] The rising of Sirius on the first day of the calendar year would have been repeated for four years, from 139 to 142, after which time the calendar would begin one day too early, and the astronomical phenomenon would once again begin its peregrination through the calendar. A period of 1460 years before 139 would take us to 1318 B.C. for the inception of the preceding cycle; New Year's day and the rising of Sirius would have coincided for the four years from 1318 to 1315 B.C. The beginning of this same cycle is apparently reflected in a passing remark of Theon[105] to the effect that "from Menophris"[106] to "the close of the Augustan" period (i.e. A.D. 284), 1605 years had elapsed. Again the starting point for this calculation seems to be 1318 B.C. On the reasonable assumption that Menophris is a personal name, and must belong to a king, scholars have long directed their search for a pharaoh whose name could conceivably have been garbled into this form. "Merenre" *(Mr.n-rʿ)* seemed a likely possibility,[107] but it was known as a royal name only in the Old Kingdom. "Merneptah" *(Mr.n-ptḥ)*, though linguistically less attractive, has received stronger support from scholars; it was pointed out that a common epithet of Sety I was "Merneptah." The only other candidate put forward has been Ramses I, whose praenomen, *Mn-pḥty-rʿ*, would seem an even better *Vorlage* for Menophris.[108] To identify Ramses I with Menophris would have the added advantage of making a new Sothic cycle coincide with a change of dynasty. If then, as many feel, Menophris is either Ramses I or his son Sety I, the beginning of the Sothic cycle must have fallen some time *within* the reigns of these two kings; for the expression "from Menophris"

[104] T. von Oppolzer, *SAWWien* (Math-Naturw. Kl.), 90 (1884), 557f.; E. Mahler, *ZÄS* 28 (1890), 116ff.; Meyer, *Ägyptische Chronologie*, 23ff. This is confirmed by numismatic evidence: Schmidt, *Recueil Champollion*, 155.

[105] See Meyer, *Ägyptische Chronologie*, 29, n. 1 for references.

[106] ἀπὸ Μενόφρεως.

[107] Meyer, *Ägyptische Chronologie*, 29, but rejected by him. R. Weill's attempt (*Bases, méthodes et résultats de la chronologie égyptienne* [Paris, 1926], 10f.) to link Menophris with *Mr-nfr-rʿ* of the Second Intermediate Period was, similarly, never considered seriously by him.

[108] Apparently first suggested by Hincks, and later, independently, by D. Hy Haigh, *ZÄS* 9 (1871), 72f. (who quotes Hincks); cf. also H. R. Hall, *CAH* I (1923), 168; P. Montet, *CRAIBL* (1937), 421; J. Černý, *JEA* 47 (1961), 150ff.

would make sense only if Menophris were upon the throne when the cycle began.

Sethe has attempted to bolster the position of one of these kings further, in his case Sety I.[109] He points to two rare expressions used by Sety in some of his inscriptions, which seem to refer to the commencement of a Sothic cycle. The first is *ḥ3t nḥḥ*, "the beginning of eternity," found in the Nauri decree of year 1[110] and in an inscription of year 4 in the Speos Artemidos.[111] In both texts the expression immediately follows the date. The second peculiar phrase is *wḥm mswt*, "the repetition of births," which also occurs as Sety's *nbty*-name. It is found in the Karnak reliefs, once following the date "year 1"[112] and again as an identification of Sety himself, or better, of his reign.[113] Sethe could not resist connecting these two suggestive epithets with the beginning of the Sothic cycle, especially since the first, "the beginning of eternity," is used during only four years *(sic)*, which is precisely the number of years occupied by the coincidence between the rising of Sothis and the calendrical New Year's day. He concludes: "damit hätten wir eine neues Sothis-datum für das Neue Reich gewonnen. Der Beginn Sethos' I ist jetzt mit einer minimalen Fehlermöglichkeit auf das Jahr 1318 v. Chr. datierbar."[114] But if Sety's reign actually began in 1318, what becomes of our ten-year floruit? He must then have enjoyed a reign of *ca*, twenty eight years.

To Sethe's view there are serious objections. First, there is no real reason other than an apparent similarity in meaning to connect *ḥ3t nḥḥ* and *wḥm mswt* with the beginning of a new Sothic cycle. Two other kings who employ the second expression, Amenemhet I and Ramses XI,[115] do not affix any calendrical significance to it. And as far as *ḥ3t nḥḥ* is concerned, the kingpin of Sethe's interpretation, viz.

[109] See his important article, "Sethos und die Erneuerung der Hundsstern-periode," in *ZÄS* 66 (1931), 1ff.

[110] F. Ll. Griffith, *JEA* 13 (1927), 193ff.; C. E. Sander-Hansen, *Historische Inschriften der* 19. *Dynastie* (Brussels, 1933), 13ff.

[111] *LD Texte* II, 111.

[112] *LD* III, 128a; Sander-Hansen, *Historische Inschriften*, 5.

[113] *Ḥ3t-sp 1 Whm-mswt*, "regnal year 1 of *Wḥm-mswt*"; Sander-Hansen, *ibid.*, 7.

[114] Sethe, *ZÄS* 66 (1931), 4.

[115] For Amenemhet I see the discussion by G. Posener, *Littérature et politique dans l'Egypte de la XIIe dynastie* (Paris, 1956), 58; for Ramses XI, see Drioton-Vandier, *L'Egypte*[4], 389 and the references given there.

that it was employed for only four years at the beginning of the reign, is now known to be wrong: Černý has found an example from as late as year 9.[116] That the recent beginning of a new Sothic cycle may have influenced the choice of locutions is probably true; in 1300 B.C. the rising of Sothis would still be no more than four days late. But there is no need, from the evidence Sethe puts forward, to assume that the reign and the cycle began in exactly the same year. A second objection is that such a coincidence is highly unlikely. Or are we to suppose that Sety actually effected his father's death in order to have his own reign begin with this auspicious event? Until evidence of such skulduggery comes to light, it is better to ignore so wild a hypothesis.

A third and more serious objection is that the name Menophris can only with great difficulty be derived from "Merneptah". The same is true of a derivation from *Mn-pḥty-rʿ*, in Akkadian *Minpaḫitaria*.[117] On the other hand, as many scholars have seen,[118] if one will allow Menophris to be a toponym and not a personal name, there is a perfect *Vorlage* to be found in *Mn-nfr*, "Memphis." Linguistically this is precisely the vocalization that would be expected;[119] and as far as the practice of naming an era after a city is concerned, there is the famous example of the era of the founding of Rome. What historical event is the basis for the expression "from Menophris" is difficult to ascertain; but it may be the transfer of a royal residence to Memphis, a move that would have had the result of transforming that city into the "capital." This event could well have taken place under Haremhab, perhaps in conjunction with his reforms. It may not be without significance that the dated inscriptions of this king from years 1 to 8 have a Theban origin, and some imply the residence of the king in that city. After year 8 the monuments fall silent until

116 Černý, *JEA* 47 (1961), 151. As Hornung has pointed out (*Untersuchungen* . . ., 62, n. 42), its use is not confined to the reign of Sety I; examples come also from the reigns of Amenhotpe II and Haremhab.

117 H. Ranke, *Keilschriftliches Material* (APAW 1910), 13.

118 A. M. Blackman, *JRAS* (1924), 319; Rowton, *Iraq* 8 (1946), 107; J. Vergote, *Bib. Or.* 18 (1961), 212, n. 22.

119 It is, of course, necessary to assume a vocalization of the name different from that which became current as ⲘⲚϤⲈ ; whether the difference between the two is dialectical or temporal (*Men-nofr*[*is*] being an archaic pronunciation that became fossilized) is a moot point; see Vergote, *ibid.*

year 27. Could the silence be explained by the removal of the court around the ninth year to Memphis, the intention being to inaugurate the new Sothic cycle with a new beginning in the political realm?

Whether this speculation has any relevance or not, there is no compelling reason to make Sety's reign begin at the same time as the new Sothic era.[120] Consequently, there is no reason to reject a ten-year reign for him. If he acceded to the throne at the end of 1301 or the beginning of 1300, his father Ramses I will have begun to reign late in 1303 or early in 1302. By whatever figure the length of Sety's reign may in the future be found to exceed ten years, the *terminus ad quem* for the Eighteenth Dynasty will have to be raised.

[120] It seems to have been the feeling that this was somehow necessary that has guided a number of modern scholars in their choice of fifteen to seventeen years for Sety's reign: Wilson, *The Burden of Egypt*, viii; Drioton-Vandier, *L'Egypte*[4], 353f.; A. Scharff, *Ägypten und Vorderasien im Altertum* (Munich. 1950), 154; Helck, *Untersuchungen zu Manetho*, 70; Hayes, " Chronology: Egypt," in *CAH* I (1962), 19. These estimates are guesses; they are supported by neither Manetho nor the monuments.

Appendix

Prolegomena to the History of Syria during the Amarna Period

One of the problems of ancient Near Eastern history that still entices many scholars is the reconstruction of the sequence of events in the Levant during the Amarna period. That yet another attempt should be recorded beside those of the illustrious historians of past and present[1] may seem presumptuous or superfluous, and the writer must beg the reader's forgiveness if this is the impression that the present Appendix conveys. What is herein attempted is, first, to draw together the evidence and conclusions, set forth in Chapter V, which bear on the chronology of Levantine history during the Amarna period and, second, to arrange in sequence a handful of historical events that may prove to be an acceptable framework for more intensive study. Our sources fall into three main groups: (1) the Amarna letters, (2) the Hittite archives, and (3) the Akkadian texts from Ugarit.

1. The date of the "Great Syrian" campaign[2]

It has been argued above that the last of Tushratta's letters to Akhenaten (EA 29) arrive in Egypt in Akhenaten's sixth year, and that this provides us with a *terminus a quo* for the "Great Syrian"

[1] To the names and works cited above (Chapter V, notes 271ff.) may be added the brief, pithy article of Goetze in *Klio*, 19 (1925), 347ff. (a work that may still be consulted with profit); see also K. A. Kitchen, *Suppiluliuma and the Amarna Pharaohs* (Liverpool Monographs in Archaeological and Oriental Studies [Liverpool, 1962]); W. Helck, *Die Beziehungen Ägyptens zu Vorderasien im 3. und 2. Jahrtausend v. Chr.* (Ägyptologische Abhandlungen 5 [Wiesbaden, 1962]), 174ff.; H. Klengel, *MIOF* 10 (1964), 57ff.

[2] I.e. the one described in the preamble to the Mattiwaza treaty: *KBo* I, 1, 17ff. (Weidner, *Politische Dokumente aus Kleinasien* [Leipzig, 1923], I, 6ff.), and probably *KUB* 34, 23 (H. Güterbock, *JCS* 10 [1956], 84ff.).

campaign of Suppiluliumas, wherein Tushratta was utterly defeated.[3] The campaign in question would have to be placed anywhere from years 6 to 8, but scarcely later.

(*a*) Evidence from allusions to Mitanni in the Amarna letters[4]

References to Mitanni in the Amarna letters bifurcate into an earlier group (contemporary with Abdi-Ashirta and the earlier letters of Rib-addi) in which a "king of Mitanni" is active, and a later group in which no "king of Mitanni" is mentioned. In EA 75:35ff. Rib-addi announces to Pharaoh that the Hittite king has taken all the lands belonging to the king of Mitanni. In EA 95:27ff. the king of Mitanni casts admiring glances at Amurru. EA 86:10ff. and 101:7ff, refer to tribute from Syria destined for Mitanni. EA 58 obv. 4ff. refers to a military campaign undertaken by the king of Mitanni. In EA 76:14f. Rib-addi asks indignantly whether Abdi-Ashirta considers himself the king of Mitanni. (For other references to Mitanni from the time of Abdi-Ashirta, see EA 85:51ff. and 90:19ff.) Then the letters fall silent about the king of Mitanni's present doings. When he is mentioned, it is either in an indignant comparison like that of EA 76 (cf. 104:21 and 116:70), or an allusion to *past* relations between Mitanni and Egypt (EA 190:5ff.). From two of Akizzi's letters comes an illuminating passage: "My lord's messenger came to me and spoke thus: 'I have come from Mitanni, and there were three or four kings hostile to the king of Hatte, who sided with me(?)' "[5] (EA 54:38ff. and 56:36ff.). No king of Mitanni is mentioned, but instead several *kings*. Centralized authority had broken down, i.e. Tushratta must have gone. The implication that Akizzi's letters followed the "Great Syrian" campaign will be seen to accord perfectly with the correct date for his correspondence, to be argued below.

The above evidence fits our conclusion that Tushratta disappears (i.e. the "Great Syrian" campaign takes place) *ca.* years 6 to 8 of Akhenaten. In terms of Amurrite rulers, Tushratta is a contemporary of Abdi-Ashirta; the campaign is to be placed around the time Aziru succeeded his father, or very early in his reign.

[3] See above, pp. 162ff.; also *JEA* 45 (1959), 37.

[4] Exclusive of those in Tushratta's letters.

[5] Lit. "stood in my presence" (*ina pâniya šaknū*).

(*b*) Evidence from allusions to Hatte in the Amarna letters

An interesting and most important fact is that nowhere in the long and newsy correspondence of Rib-addi is Etakama, the king of Kadesh, mentioned. Mention of him does occur, however, in letters known to follow Rib-addi's deposition and death, e.g. EA 140 and 151. The conclusion that Etakama ruled as king of Kadesh *after* Rib-addi's long reign came to an end is inevitable. Rib-addi and Etakama, in that order, belong to successive generations. But since, as pointed out above,[6] Etakama belonged to the younger generation at the time of the "Great Syrian" campaign, Rib-addi would have been a contemporary of his father, Sutatarra, whom Suppiluliumas deported to Hatte. Rib-addi, then, must have lived through the "Great Syrian" campaign, and we are justified in searching his letters for some mention of it.

The following is a list of pertinent references to Hatte in the Amarna letters:

1. EA 17:31ff.: Hittite campaign against Tushratta.
2. EA 75:35ff.: successful(?) Hittite campaign, wresting lands that belonged to the king of Mitanni.
3. EA 41 and 44 (*passim*): letters from Suppiluliumas and court(?) shortly after the accession of Akhenaten.
4. EA 35:49f.: imminence of an agreement(?) between Egypt and Hatte and Babylon (perhaps the same treaty referred to by Suppiluliumas when he was before the walls of Carchemish[7]).
5. EA 157: 28ff.: threat that king of Hatte might attack Aziru (Sumur not yet taken).
6. EA 126:51ff.: rumour in Byblos that Hittite soldiers are burning the lands of the king and are coming to conquer Byblos. All Rib-addi's cities are captured. (Cf. also 129:74ff.)
7. EA 161:47ff.: embassy of Hittites to Aziru.
8. EA 51: rev. 3ff.: imminent revolt in Nukhashshe.
9. EA 151:55ff.: Hittite troops absent from Ugarit.
10. EA 53–55, 164–7 *(passim)*: Hittite king in Nukhashshe.
11. EA 140:30ff.: Hittite king and king of Naharin are doing something in concert.
12. EA 196:15ff., 197:24ff.: former Syrian vassals of Egypt are transferring allegiance to Hatte.
13. EA 174–6 *(passim)*: Hittite soldiers are in Amki.
14. EA 170 *(passim)*: Lupakku and the Hittite army enter Amurru.

[6] Above, p. 163.

[7] Güterbock, *JCS* 10 (1956), 98.

Only nos. 1 and 2 are contemporary with Amenhotpe III, the remainder (with the exception of no. 14) falling during the reign of Akhenaten. The chronological order of nos. 1 to 6 is fairly certain. Numbers 7 to 10 come roughly from the same time, and their exact order is in doubt. Numbers 11 to 14, again, are in proper order.

It is difficult to decide which of the above references, if any, is to the Great Syrian campaign. Some of Rib-addi's allusions look suggestive (e.g. nos. 2 and 6), but in view of Rib-addi's well-known bent towards hyperbole, it is wise to take his statements *cum grano salis*. It will be argued below that nos. 7 to 10 refer to a single event, viz. the appearance of Suppiluliumas in North Syria attested by the Ras Shamra texts (see below), which is to be distinguished from the (earlier) Great Syrian campaign. Since nos. 1 and 2 are too early, we are left with 5 (and perhaps 6), and with due caution I take this as an allusion to the incipient Great Syrian campaign. EA 157 is the second letter Aziru sent to Egypt. As yet he had scarcely begun his career. A date *ca.* year 6 to 8 of Akhenaten for this letter would imply an accession a couple of year's earlier, say *ca.* year 4, for Aziru. This would make him a contemporary of Akhenaten, and his father, Abdi-Ashirta, a later contemporary of Amenhotpe III.

2. The historical events in the Amarna period postdating Rib-addi's fall

(*a*) Some individuals whose careers fall in this period (see also above, pp. 162ff.)

(i) Etakama (see above, pp. 163f.)

(ii) Biryawaza.[8] This man was governor of the Damascus region (Ube); ^{LU}*rab* he is called in EA 129:82ff. An attack upon him by Etakama and Aziru (cf. EA 53:28ff., 151:62. 189 *passim*) seems to have brought an end to his career, for he is not heard of thereafter. Presumably he was either killed or replaced. His tenure of office may have begun earlier than Etakama's: he is mentioned in a Babylonian letter to Akhenaten (EA 7:75), which cannot however be dated accurately, and in a letter of Zatatna (EA 234:13), who is known to have been a contemporary of Akhenaten. Biryawaza also occurs in one of the later letters of Rib-addi (EA 129: 81ff.), where the statement that the sons of Abdi-Ashirta had scant respect for

[8] On the reading, see F. Thureau-Dangin, *RA* 37 (1940), 171.

him may indicate that he was newly appointed. His occupancy of the governorship of Damascus can be said to have begun late in Rib-addi's lifetime, and to have terminated before Akhenaten's death. He is thus wholly contemporary with Akhenaten.

(iii) Abi-milki.[9] This king of Tyre is a contemporary of Aziru (mentioned *passim* in his letters), of Etakama (EA 151:59), and of Biryawaza (EA 151:62). He once speaks of the fall of Sumur to Aziru, but this may be some time after the event. It is quite clear from the content of the majority of Abi-milki's letters that his reign at Tyre falls towards the end of the period covered by the Amarna letters. There is no possibility that his rule overlapped with that of Amenhotpe III. Consequently, the *abi šarri* of EA 147:58 cannot be Amenhotpe III, but must be Akhenaten, and the addressee of EA 147 must be one of Akhenaten's immediate successors, either Smenkhkare or Tutankhamun. In view of the reference to ^{SAL}Ma-ya-a-ti (*Mryt-⟨'Itn⟩*) in EA 155, the choice must fall on the former. Out of ten letters, therefore, we can say with some certainty that two (EA 147 and 155) were written to Smenkhkare, either during the corregency during the last three years of Akhenaten's reign, or immediately following his death. Abi-milki's reign thus extends from shortly before(?) Rib-addi's fall to at least the end of Akhenaten's reign.

(iv) Akizzi. Akizzi of Qatna is a contemporary of Etakama (EA 53:8ff.) and of Biryawaza (EA 52:45f., 53:34), and consequently he too, or at least his letters, must be placed in the period following the fall of Rib-addi. He thus belongs to the later generation of Syrian rulers that began to come into its own after the Great Syrian campaign.[10] In that case, however, the Hittite invasion Akizzi is concerned about cannot be the "Great Syrian";[11] rather we must identify it with some later incursion of Suppiluliumas.[12] There is now ample evidence from Ras Shamra to decide on which Hittite incursion Akizzi's letters were written.[13] Some time subsequent to the Great Syrian campaign, Niya, Nukhashshe, and Mukish rebelled against Suppiluliumas and attempted to force Ugarit to join them.

[9] See W. F. Albright, *JEA* 23 (1937), 191ff.

[10] Above, p. 163.

[11] Above, p. 164, n. 318.

[12] So, long ago, E. Cavaignac, *RA* 22 (1925), 130.

[13] See *PRU* IV, 35ff.

Niqmaddu of Ugarit refused, and, apparently despairing of Pharaoh's assistance, appealed to the Hittite king. This was tantamount to offering allegiance to the Hittites, and Suppiluliumas was quick to realize it. The rebels were repulsed by the Hittite troops, and the recalcitrants brought back within the fold; and Suppiluliumas himself descended into Syria to conclude a formal treaty with the king of Ugarit. The king of Nukhashshe at the time is named in the text as one Addu-nirari. He is undoubtedly the same as the Addu-nirari who wrote EA 51, and who is also called king of Nukhashshe. In that letter Addu-nirari informs Pharaoh (undoubtedly Akhenaten) that the king of Hatte has come out against him, and requests that, if the king cannot come himself, he at least send a force of troops to assist the writer. The letter clearly fits the period of the rebellion described in the Ras Shamra texts.

It is to the same rebellion that the Akizzi texts must be dated. Akizzi everywhere refers to the southward advance of Hittite troops, and even to the presence in Syria of the Hittite king (EA 53:8ff.). He assures the king of Egypt that not only he but also the kings of *Nukhashshe*, *Niya*, Zinzar, and Tunanat love Pharaoh and wish to be his servants. In a later letter (EA 55:19ff.) he holds out the hope that if troops are sent at once the whole of the land of Nukhashshe may return to Egypt. Thus the letters of Akizzi come at a time, after the Great Syrian campaign, when the kings of Nukhashshe and Niya, in repudiation of their new Hittite master, have shifted their allegiance back to Egypt and count themselves Pharaoh's vassals. When Akizzi wrote, Tushratta's Mitanni was no more; otherwise the North Syrian kinglets would have turned to her rather than Egypt. The capture of Qatna recounted in the preamble to the Mattiwaza treaty must be either (a) an earlier subversion of the city, or (more likely) (b) an example of "telescoped history," the seizure of the town at the time of the Nukhashshe revolt having been predated to the Great Syrian campaign for greater effect.[14]

[14] The allusion to Qatna in the preamble to the Mattiwaza treaty has always sounded spurious (*KBo* I, 1, vs. 37). It is a terse statement, one sentence in length, which mentions no names or other illuminating details. Moreover, it is sandwiched between the defeat of Arakhti and the invasion of Nukhashshe, when the obvious progress of the campaign from north to south would require the section devoted to Qatna to *follow* the Nukhashshe passage.

(*b*) Activities of Aziru after the fall of Rib-addi

EA 162 is a key letter in reconstructing the course of events during the period with which we are here concerned. It was written to Aziru by Akhenaten after Rib-addi had been ejected from Byblos (cf. 2ff.), and we learn from it that it was in fact Aziru who was responsible for Rib-addi's destruction. The senile ex-king of Byblos had inexplicably placed himself in Aziru's hands, and that worthy had allowed his enemies to do away with him. Akhenaten had previously demanded that Aziru present himself at the Egyptian court, and now reiterates this demand, granting however a delay of one year (42ff.). When the appointed time did arrive, i.e. one year later, Aziru had another excuse for postponing the visit: the king of Hatte had come into Nukhashshe, and was dwelling there in Tunip.[15] It was a real threat, and Aziru dispatched four nearly identical letters to Akhenaten and his highest officials in an effort to impress upon them the validity of his present excuse (EA 164–7). This excursion of Suppiluliumas to North Syria must be linked, not with the Great Syrian campaign as is often done, but with the Nukhashshe revolt, which is the burden of Akizzi's letters and the new texts from Ras Shamra.[16] Another report of the Nukhashshe revolt is supplied by Abi-milki in EA 151:55ff.: "half of the city of the king of Ugarit has been destroyed by fire; his army[17] was not present, nor were the troops of the Hittite forces." Here we have a brief allusion to an episode in the revolt, after Niqmaddu requested aid from the Hittites. Ugarit was partly destroyed by fire (whether accidentally or through the agency of the Nukhashshe rebels is not clear), at a time when its own forces and the auxiliary Hittite troops were not present.

The presence of Suppiluliumas in North Syria, while it provided Aziru with a fine excuse for not coming to Egypt, did not prevent him from carrying on his aggression against his neighbours. He had previously entered into an agreement with Etakama (EA 162:22ff.), and now the two kings made common cause against Biryawaza, the

15 See S. Smith, in *Halil Edhem Hatira Kitabi* (Ankara, 1947), 39.

16 Since they clearly postdate EA 162, which in turn postdates Rib-addi's fall, EA 164–7 cannot possibly describe the Great Syrian campaign, the latter being dated before the close of Rib-addi's career; see above, p. 218.

17 *Mišišu* = Egyptian *mšʿ*+suffix (?); cf. T. Lambdin, *JCS* 7 (1953), 75ff.

pro-Egyptian governor of Damascus. The attack on Biryawaza is reported in the letter of Abi-milki cited above (lines 59–63), in Etakama's own letter (EA 189, *passim*), and in a letter of Akizzi (EA 53:28ff.). All this while, presumably, Suppiluliumas was mopping up in North Syria. Only after the Hittite king retired did Aziru come to Egypt; and only *after* Aziru's visit with Akhenaten was EA 140 written.[18] Consequently the attack launched by Aziru and Etakama on Amki, which is reported as news in EA140 and 174–6, must postdate Aziru's trip to Egypt.

(*c*) Aziru's break with Egypt

It remains to discuss at what point Aziru formally offered his allegiance to Hatte. The pertinent passage in the Hittite–Amurrite treaty reads as follows (*KBo* X, 13; I, 14ff.): "formerly [the k]ing of Egypt, the king of Hurri, the king of [Kadesh, the king of...], the king of Nukhashshe, the king of Niya, the king of [ ], the king of Aleppo, and the king of Carchemish—all these kings at one time—were hostile [towards the Sun]."[19] This statement merely reflects the traditional alignment of powers vis-à-vis Hatte before the conquests of Suppiluliumas; it is not to be understood as reflecting a specific situation sometime during Suppiluliumas' campaigns. Then follows the statement (lines 21ff.): "Aziru the king of the land [of Amurru] revolted against the domination of Egypt, [and] became a vassal of the Sun, the k[ing of the land of H]atte ... he came out of the door of Egypt, and prostrated himself a[t the feet of the Sun, the great king]." It may be that the last sentence is as vague as what precedes; but it is more likely that, as Freydank has seen,[20] it refers to Aziru's return from the Egyptian court. In that case Aziru's formal switch of allegiance from Egypt to Hatte, and naturally the treaty itself, must postdate his correspondence with Egypt and the Nukhashshe revolt. This does not mean, however, that prior to his break with Egypt Aziru had not been friendly (*šalim*) towards Hatte, which relationship a vassal was precisely warned to avoid in the case

[18] Cf. EA 140:22: "Look! Aziru committed a crime when he had an audience with you, a crime against us!"

[19] H. Freydank, *MIOF* 7 (1960), 356ff.

[20] *Ibid.*, 380; *contra* H. Klengel, *MIOF* 10 (1964), 79.

of a foreign king at odds with the vassal's suzerain. EA 161:47ff. informs us that before he repaired to Akhenaten's court, Aziru had already entertained Hittite envoys. The treaty between Mursilis and Duppi-teshup, Aziru's grandson, reviews in brief the vicissitudes of Amurrite–Hittite relations under Suppiluliumas (*KUB* III, 14, vs. 2ff.): "Aziru was your grandfather, Duppi-teshup. He became(?) ⌜hostile⌝ to my father, [but] my father brought him back to his vassal status. When the kings of Nukhashshe and the king of Kadesh became hostile to my father, Aziru your grandfather did not become hostile to my father. He was in a state of friendship, and so he remained *(ki šālmuma šālim)*. When my father fought with his enemies, Aziru your grandfather fought with my father's enemies. . . ." I think the course of events can now be reconstructed as follows: (1) Aziru, at his accession, was a vassal of Egypt (EA 156), albeit one who was already on friendly terms with Hatte (hence the locution of the Duppi-teshup treaty *ana ardūtišu itêršu*, "he brought him *back* to his status of vassal"). (2) At the time of the Great Syrian campaign Aziru, probably in an effort to play both sides against the middle, avoided a confrontation with Suppiluliumas (cf. EA 157:28ff.). Though the latter had conquered as far south as the Lebanons, so that Amurru now lay within his border, Aziru, as a vassal, continued to correspond with Egypt, and even took to raiding farther north (cf. EA 59, anticipating a northward encroachment; and RS 19.68 rct. 5f.; *PRU* IV, 284). This is probably the activity that is construed as Aziru's rebellion in the Duppi-teshup treaty. (3) Aziru came to his senses, sized up the international situation, and decided to side with Hatte. He held talks with the Hittites (EA 161:47ff.), and was brought back to his former friendly relations. Yet he still corresponded with Egypt. (4) When the Nukhashshe revolt broke out, Aziru did not join the insurgents, as both the Amarna letters and the Duppi-teshup treaty attest. (5) Shortly after the revolt Aziru betook himself to Egypt, and when he returned thence to his patrimony renounced for ever his loyalty to Egypt. All pretence was gone; he hastened to do formal obeisance to the Hittite king (probably in Hattusas) and broke off relations with Egypt permanently. When thereafter Aziru wished to know what was going on at Pharaoh's court, he was forced to get his information indirectly through the king of Sidon (EA 147:66ff.).

3. Table of Events

Based upon the above discussion, the following table reflects the course of events in the order in which they probably occurred, beginning with the earlier years of Akhenaten, and ending with the accession of Tutankhamun. The dates given in parentheses are merely rough estimates; the others are based on more or less reliable evidence. All dates are in terms of Akhenaten's regnal years.

Aziru's accession	(*ca.* year 4)
The Great Syrian campaign	*ca.* year 6–8
The Fall of Sumur to Aziru	
Rib-addi driven from Byblos, goes to Beirut	
Rib-addi goes to Aziru and disappears	
Aziru negotiates with the Hittites	
Akhenaten writes to Aziru (EA 162)	(*ca.* year 10)
Nukhashshe revolt; Ugarit appeals to Hittites	
Suppiluliumas comes to crush revolt	
Aziru and Etakama attack Biryawaza	
Suppiluliumas places Tette on throne in Nukhashshe	
Suppiluliumas departs and Aziru goes to Egypt (EA 168)	year 12
Aziru returns, makes a treaty with the Hittites	(*ca.* year 13?)
Aziru attacks Amki (EA 140, 174–6)	
Suppiluliumas and Mattiwaza sign a treaty (EA 140:30ff.)	
Akhenaten attacks Kadesh; Assyrians attack North Syria	*ca.* year 17
Akhenaten dies; Suppiluliumas beats back attacks, invades Amki (EA 170)	
Nefertity requests Hittite prince as her husband	

Special Indexes

Index to Egyptian Words Discussed in the Text

ip ǧt, "count the body," 7 n. 19
imy-r pr ḥǧ, "superintendent of treasury," 150 n. 264
imy-ḫnt (priestly title), 22
ir ḥb-sd, "celebrator of jubilees," 99
iry pʿt, "heir apparent," 126
iry pʿt wrt, "heiress," 55
ʿꜣ, "the great" (epithet), 33
ʿꜣ m ʿḥʿ.f, "long lived," 110 n. 97
ʿnḫ-ḫprw-rʿ (personal name), 170f.
ʿḥʿ, "to arise (of king)," 19f.
wr mꜣꜣw (priestly title), 134
wr mꜣꜣw m ḥwt sr (priestly title), 137
wḥm, "to do again," 130
wḥm mswt (title), 213
wsḫwt, "halls," 123 n. 49
bḫn, "castle," 144
pr, "house, estate," 147f.
pr wr (sacred structure), 137
pr nsr (sacred structure), 137
pr čḥn Itn (name of palace), 146
mꜣʿ-ḫrw, "justified, deceased," 176f.
mꜣʿt, "truth," 140f., 110
mniw, "herdsman," 128
Mn-nfr (place name), 214
Mn-pḥty-rʿ (personal name), 214
Mr-nfr-rʿ (personal name), 212 n. 107
Nb-ḫprw-rʿ (personal name), 159, 165 n. 324
Nfr-ḫprw-rʿ (personal name), 159
nḥb-kꜣw (feast), 124
nḥm, "be poor, orphaned," 31 n. 12
nst, "throne," 119
nčr hqꜣ Wꜣst (title), 142
r-gs, "at the side of," 53
r tnw sp, "whenever the need arose(?)," 61 n. 31
rdi m ḥr, "to charge someone," 139
ḥꜣqt, "plunder," 125
ḥꜣt nḥḥ, "beginning of eternity," 213
ḥꜣt sp, "regnal year," 94
ḥb n ḫʿw, "festival of the accession," 25f.
ḥmt-nčr, "god's-wife," 71, 71 n. 72
ḥqꜣ Iwnw (title), 33
ḥqꜣ Wꜣst (title), 33
ḥqꜣ rsi (title), 33 n. 24
ḥqꜣ ḥqꜣw (title), 99
ḥtp, "to conclude, to set," 5 n. 13
ḫʿy, "festival," 5, 9 n. 20
ḫʿy, "to appear in glory," 4ff., 17f., 20, 21 n. 44, 121 n. 44, 122
ḫʿy-nsw, "king's appearance," 3, 22–25
ḫʿw, "crowns," 18
Ḫʿ-m-ꜣḫt (palace), 144
Ḫpr-ḫprw-rʿ (personal name), 159 n. 299
ḫprw, "forms," 46 n. 96
ẖry-ḥb (priestly title), 22
Sꜣ-Imn (title), 71 n. 73
smn ḫʿw, "to affix the crown," 18
smt šnw, "a *smt*-fabric of net," 46 n. 98
sḫʿy nčr, "to cause the god to appear," 5
sš-nsw nfrw, "king's scribe of recruits," 140 n. 123
šʿty, "(silver)-piece(?)," 132 n. 82
špst, "favourite," 174 n. 28
šndyt, "apron," 114
qn, "the brave" (epithet), 33
qnbt sǧmyw, "council of judges," 129

grg pr, "to found a house," 47 n. 99
Tꜣ-i-sꜣ-ti (place name), 69 n. 65
tꜣ ḥmt nsw, "the king's wife," 162 n. 311
ḏsr ḫprw, "holy of forms," 171

Index to Akkadian Words Occurring in the Text

abu šarri, "father of the king," 220
arki, "afterwards," 193
bêlti bîtika, "mistress of your house," 176 n. 42
ina pâniya šaknū, "stood in my presence," 217 n. 5
SALMa-ya-a-ti (personal name), 220
miḫru, "peer," 202
Minpaḫitaria (personal name), 214
mišišu, "his army(?)," 222 n. 17
LU*rab*, "governor," 219
šadâ emēdu, "to disappear," 187 n. 13
šalim, "friendly," 223
šar kiššāti, "king of the universe," 205 n. 74
šarru rabû, "great king," 202
Šuta (personal name), 209 n. 95
**uklum*, "chief," 188 n. 14

Index to Greek Words Occurring in the Text

ἀβασίλευτα ἔτη (kingless period), 190 n. 14
ἀπὸ Μενόφρεως, "from Menophris," 212
ἐπιτολή "rising, appearance," 5 n. 14
πανήγυρις, "festival," 5 n. 14
Σέθος (personal name), 209 n. 95

Subject Index

www.ingramcontent.com/pod-product-compliance
Ingram Content Group UK Ltd.
Pitfield, Milton Keynes, MK11 3LW, UK
UKHW021917240225
455519UK00005B/16

9 781487 585419